THE PAYNES

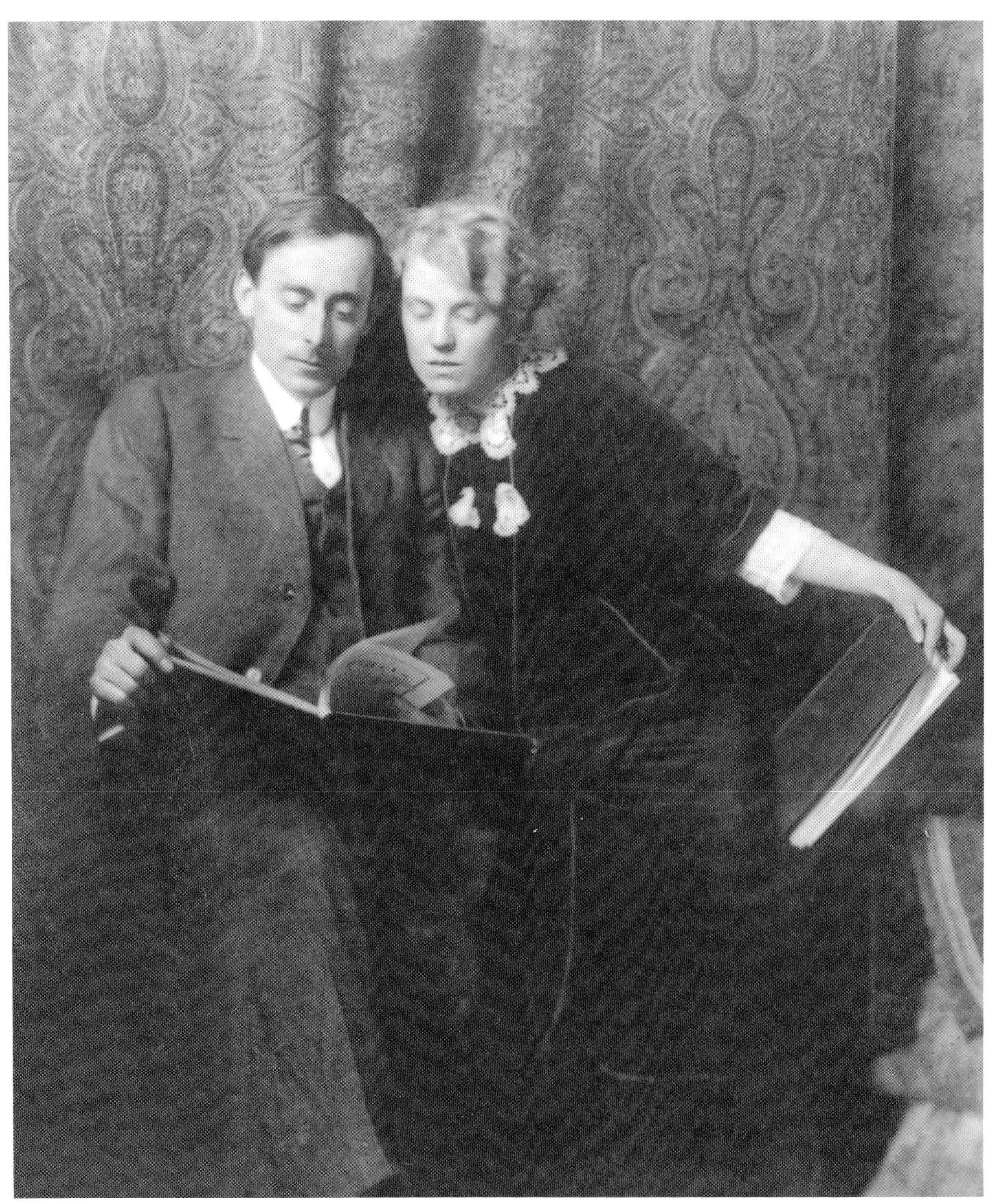

THE PAYNES,
Edgar & Elsie:
American Artists

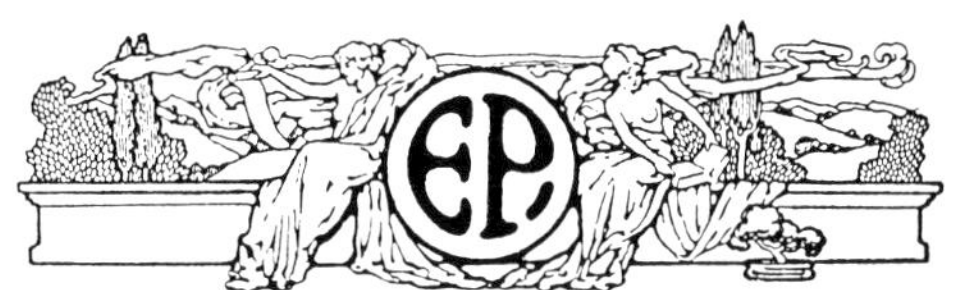

Rena Neumann Coen

Payne Studios Inc.
3104 Silver Lake Road Minneapolis, MN 55418
DISTRIBUTED BY
DERU'S FINE ART BOOKS
213-920-1312
9100 E. ARTESIA BLVD. BELLFLOWER, CALIF. 90706

First Edition

LC 87-63403

ISBN 0-944699-01-4

To the memory of
Joshua H. Neumann,
teacher and scholar.

Acknowledgements

A number of years ago Dr. Evelyn Payne Hatcher, a friend and colleague at St. Cloud State University, first suggested that I write a book about her parents, Edgar and Elsie Payne. At that time I had not heard of either of them and was more interested in art in Minnesota than art in California. As I became familiar with their work, however, the idea of writing a book about the Paynes took root and germinated, resulting eventually in the present volume. Both Evelyn Hatcher and her husband, Dr. John B. Hatcher, are, in effect, the creators of this work, having researched and organized much of the Payne material before I ever got to it. I am more than indebted to them since they are, in no small way, co-authors of this book.

Others to whom I am grateful for timely and generous help in the preparation of this volume are Judge J.V. Boles of Danville, Indiana and Ms. Ellen Lee and Mr. Martin J. Radecki of the Indianapolis Museum of Art. In Los Angeles Mrs. Ruth Westphal, Ms. Nancy Moure, Mr. George Stern, Mr. Jean Stern, Mr. Dewitt McCall and Mr. Tom Enman went out of their way to be helpful. Dr. William Otten of the Laguna Beach Art Gallery, Mr. Andrew Voth of the Carnegie Cultural Arts Center, Oxnard, California (where the Elsie Palmer Payne exhibition will open in February, 1988), and Dr. Lyndel King of the University of Minnesota Art Museum were encouraging and cooperative, as was Dr. C. Lance Brockman, University of Minnesota, who found information and the cartoon from the scene painting period. The interest and kindness of all those, identified in the List of Illustrations, who so kindly supplied transparencies and permitted reproduction of their paintings is gratefully acknowledged. I am grateful also for the help of the librarians at the Archives of American Art at the Huntington Library, San Marino, California and at the Special Collections, UCLA Libraries, Los Angeles. St. Cloud State University, through its Office of Sponsored Programs, awarded me a grant to pursue research in Los Angeles. Last but certainly not least, I owe a debt of gratitude to Mrs. Betty Kane of Minneapolis who, at short notice and with great dispatch, carefully read and edited the manuscript, making good suggestions for its improvement. To all of them I offer sincere thanks and beg forgiveness for any sins of omission, commission or false interpretation that might be contained herein.

Rena Neumann Coen
Minneapolis, 1987

Table of Contents

List of Illustrations

Unless otherwise noted, all of the art works are by Edgar Alwin Payne or Elsie Palmer Payne, and their names are abbreviated by the initials, EAP or EPP. The source, unless otherwise noted, is Payne Studios Inc. In the measurements, which are in inches, height precedes width. The following abbreviations are utilized for the more common media and supports: G, gouache, opaque watercolor on paper; W, watercolor on paper; OC, oil on canvas on stretcher; OCB, oil on canvas board; OB, oil on board; P, photograph.

Chapter 1: Introduction

Among California artists, Edgar Alwin Payne and his wife, Elsie Palmer Payne, have been accorded unequal recognition. Each created a body of work that is distinct, original, and thoroughly professional, yet Edgar earned for himself an established place as a leader of the California landscape painters while his wife's work has been largely ignored. The reason for this may be that Elsie, throughout her life, was far more active in promoting her husband's work than her own. But even more important is the fact that while Edgar's paintings fitted right into the mainstream of the Southern California plein air landscape tradition, rising indeed to the very height of that genre, Elsie's work, by contrast, was not focused primarily on nature, but rather on the people around her, and thus lay outside the dominant style of the region. While her husband was celebrating California's sunny groves and rugged mountains, Elsie was turning out drawings and paintings that had less to do with dramatic landscapes than with local neighborhood or genre themes. This difference prevailed even when the Paynes travelled together in Europe, where Edgar concentrated on the snowy peaks of the Alps or the colorful fishing boats in the harbors of Italy and France, while Elsie directed her attention to the human element in the Old World towns they visited. And even when Elsie did paint landscapes, they were drawn in a flat, decorative style that was quite different from Edgar's, and in fact typical of northern California rather than the south. For, unlike Edgar, who came from the central states and was largely self-taught, Elsie grew up and went to school in the San Francisco Bay area where, though there were Impressionist painters there too, the decorative, linear style of Arthur and Lucia Mathews was more pervasive.

Moreover, Elsie had worked successfully as a commercial artist in the years prior to her marriage, and she retained throughout her life a feeling for strong pattern and expressive line that set her apart from the Impressionist landscapists with whom she and Edgar associated. And though both of them had reservations about the modernist art of the twentieth century and its denial of the visual experience as a basis for the artist's work, Elsie nevertheless was closer to them than to the Impressionists with her insistence that pictorial reality was a function of the artists personal vision which need not strive to capture on canvas the visual truth of nature even in all its vibrant and light-filled moods.

Indeed, while Edgar was using the broken color technique and broad brushwork of the Impressionists to achieve his vivid suggestions of nature's transient moments, it is to the Post-Impressionist painters that we must look for a parallel to Elsie's intuitive imagination. Closer to home some of the painters of the Taos, New Mexico school, especially Ernest L. Blumenschein (whom the Paynes knew) provide a similar correspondence to her work. Like them, Elsie gently, but insistently, reminds us that the picture is a flat, two-dimensional surface upon which an arrangement of color and form, developed through an expressive line, shapes the patterns of the composition and defines its subject.

Though references to Edgar Payne's paintings are found in numerous reviews, newspaper articles and exhibition catalogues, reports of Elsie's work are scattered and meager. This is so in spite of the fact that she was active as a California artist for six decades, and lived for many years in Beverly Hills where, during her separation from Edgar Payne, she taught art and maintained a studio and gallery. Both before that separation and after it, notices of Elsie's work, if found at all, appear as off-hand references in the many articles devoted to Edgar's career. "His wife was also an artist," we read, with no further elaboration. Or more fulsomely, in another account, "Elsie exhibited her tempera drawings winning warm praise from the critics."[1] Just what attracted that praise is not disclosed, nor are there many mentions, much less listings, of Elsie's paintings in specific identified exhibitions and catalogues. Nevertheless, one perceptive observer, Arthur Millier, art critic of the *Los Angeles Times,* noted of Elsie's work that "although she has painted side by side with her artist husband, no trace of his style invades hers — she shows a very definite viewpoint of her own."[2]

The close relationship between creative talents who are married to each other has never been adequately studied, though such an examination offers a unique opportunity for investigating the influences of proximity of the most intimate kind on the style of two separate artists. Though a psychological analysis of the Paynes relationship would undoubtedly reveal much that is paradigmatic of creative individuals working together yet essentially competing with each other, such an inquiry is outside the scope of this book. From an art historical point of view, however, by contrasting their artistic output, particularly in the same or very similar subject, it is possible to discover and illuminate that which is special to each artist. It is for that purpose, therefore, that this examination of Edgar and Elsie Payne's work is undertaken in an attempt to remove Elsie's achievements from the powerful shadow of her husband's and to accord to both Edgar and Elsie their due in the history of art in California.

Chapter 2: Origins

According to a driver's license application signed in France in 1922, Edgar Payne was born near Washburn, Missouri on March 1, 1883, the second child and first son of John Hill Payne and Nancy Ellen Reed. He was a descendant of the Paynes and Herefords of Virginia to whom family legend ascribed some aristocratic pretensions. It is known that in the years following the Civil War John Hill Payne wandered westward from Virginia, joining the great migration from the eastern seaboard to the western frontier. Eventually he found himself in the Ozarks, where he met and married Nancy Ellen Reed, the daughter of a Scotch-Irish family of mountaineers who could neither read nor write, though apparently the girl herself had had whatever schooling the district had to offer. The young couple settled on a farm near Washburn and in the ensuing years added two daughters and six sons to the Payne family.[3]

Edgar's childhood was that of a youngster whose family eked out a meager living on a hardscrabble farm. From a very early age he had to work long hours on the farm, and his opportunities for education were thus severely limited. He chopped wood, did farmyard chores, and helped his father in the painting or building jobs that occasionally came his way. For such outside work he earned twenty-five cents a week with which he bought bacon and flour to help supply the family table. But though the farm was poor, and living difficult, the mountainous area was beautiful and it may well have inspired Edgar's lifelong devotion to nature and passionate love of the outdoor scene.

When Edgar was about eleven years old the family moved to Prairie Grove, Arkansas, his mother having inherited some property there. It was here that Edgar made his first attempts at painting. He had always been fascinated by whatever pictures he had seen, but his father, a tyrannical man, punished the youngster for wasting his time making pictures. Nevertheless, Edgar persisted, experimenting with his mother's bluing, his father's white lead housepaint and a red color he managed to make out of pokeberry juice.[3] He later said that the first painting he remembered seeing was a small oval scene painted on the back of a farm wagon, a scene he tried to copy at night on paper, boards, or anything else he could lay his hands on. On one occasion he recalled, he had walked ten miles to the town of Fayetteville to look at the paintings on other farm wagons lined up for sale.

The drudgery of farm labor was something the boy Edgar decided early to escape and at about the age of ten or eleven he ran away from home. After a few days, however, he had to creep ignominiously back home again, starving, filthy, and with a case of measles that the other children quickly caught. Planning his next escape more carefully, he obtained a job janitoring and painting at a boys school in exchange for board and tuition. He was quite happy there until his father discovered his whereabouts and forced him to return home and resume his farm and household chores.

At the end of the summer of 1900 the Payne family moved to Lovelady, Texas. Edgar was allowed to help drive the team of one of the covered wagons,[4] an experience that for the first and perhaps only time in his life, made him feel close to his father. But his father still disapproved of his son's attempts to spend his time painting, even though Edgar was beginning to do so more and more successfully. By 1902 he had painted the scenery in the Lovelady Town Hall and the battleship Maine in the Conroe, Texas High School. There was even a New England winter coast scene (undoubtedly copied from a postcard or advertisement) mounted over his uncle's fireplace, an honor that undoubtedly meant much to the aspiring artist.[5]

At some time during this period, Edgar left home again, this time for good. He tramped through the countryside painting fences and barns, teaching himself to letter, and occasionally getting a job painting signs. For a time he also travelled with a barnstorming theatrical troupe, painting and rigging up scenery, sometimes stepping in to act, and generally doing anything needed as handyman and roustabout. The stint as a scene painter was an experience that Edgar shared with many other contemporary American artists who often found their first professional employment in this aspect of their craft. In Edgar's case it undoubtedly taught him the broad brushwork and rapid technique that he later used, in a more sophisticated manner, in his landscape paintings.

Around 1905 or 1906 Edgar moved to Houston and set up housekeeping there with his two sisters, Fleda and Nora. He was then earning his living by housepainting and paperhanging, and at the same time, spending every spare moment hanging around a scene-painting shop learning whatever he could of the tricks of that trade. Eventually he and a partner set up their own scene-painting shop, the Payne-Morris Studio, at 142 Pearl St., Dallas (Fig. 2.01). Here he continued to improve his technique and began to attract commissions in his favorite line of work. Some years later, in Chicago, he even painted scenery for Maude Adams and for Sarah Bernhardt, who complimented the young artist on his work.[6,7]

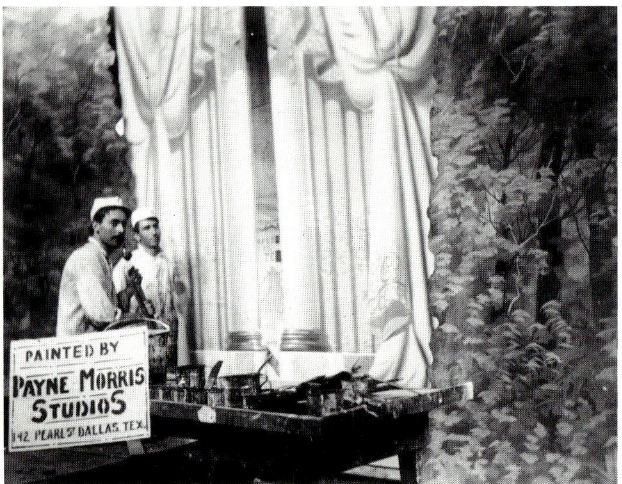

Fig. 2.01. Edgar Payne and Morris, scene painting, early 1900's.

By 1907 Edgar was in Chicago and on April 1st of that year he enrolled in a portrait painting class at the Art Institute of Chicago, dropping out of the class after only two weeks.[8]

Though he continued scenery painting, he began to devote more time to his real passion, landscape painting, doing decorative wall murals as well as small easel pictures such as *Early Landscape, Illinois* (Fig. 2.02). His education did not end, however, with the short-lived class at the Art Institute of Chicago. For a short time he received some criticism and direction from two Chicago artists, Ralph Clarkson and Charles Francis Browne.[9] And though his formal schooling had not lasted beyond the fifth grade, his quick native intelligence led him to make up for his lack of education by reading extensively in the public library. If he had to paint the scenery for a play

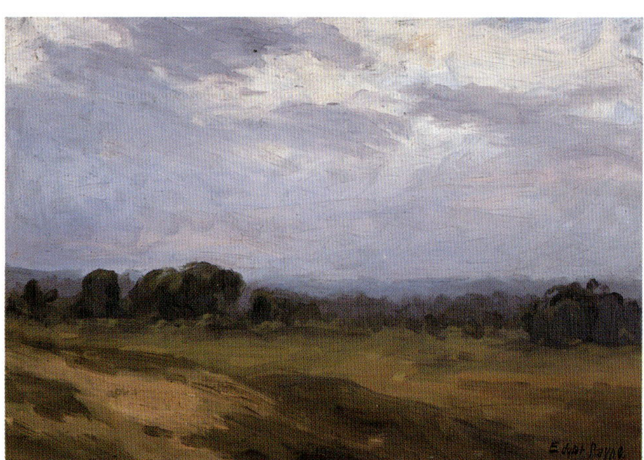

Fig. 2.02. Early Landscape, Illinois, by EAP.

set in Napoleonic times, for example, he would read everything he could about the period, including not only the architectural styles and furniture design, but also biographical material about Napoleon and the history of his battles and political conquests.[6]

While he was earning a living painting scenery for theatrical productions and backdrops for stores and other commercial enterprises, Edgar was also beginning to sell small easel paintings from exhibitions of the Palette and Chisel Club in Chicago. Few of these early works survive, but *Spring in Lincoln Park* (Fig. 2.03) a sketch of about 1910, was probably typical of this period. Its muted tones and soft, atmospheric light were to give way later to bolder use of color and brushwork, but it tentatively suggests the balanced composition,

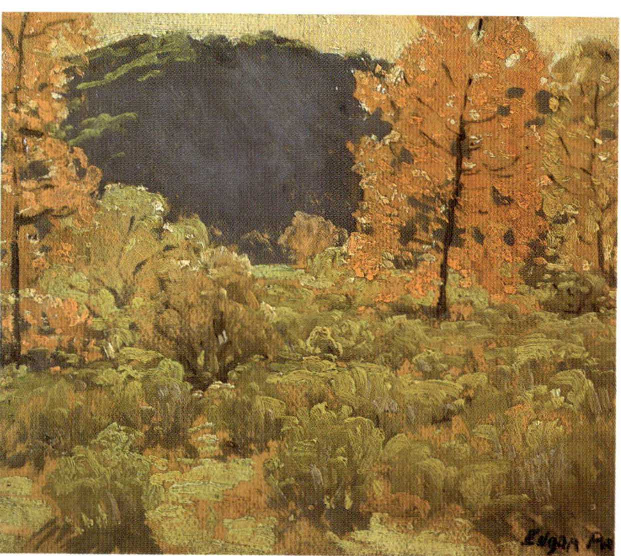

Fig. 2.04. Early Fall Trees, California, by EAP.

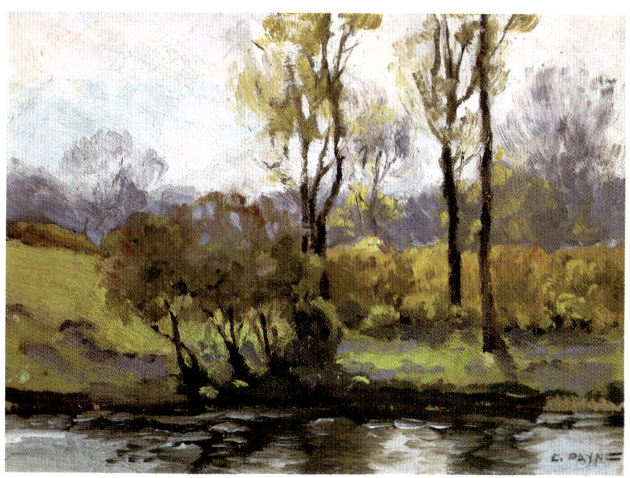

Fig. 2.03. Spring in Lincoln Park, Chicago, by EAP.

clear sense of design, and above all, the keen observation of nature that was to distinguish Payne's mature work.

In 1909 Edgar Payne made his first trip to California, where he would eventually fall under the spell of its spectacular scenery and golden light. *Early Fall Trees* (Fig. 2.04) is a sketch of this early period. It is similar in both subject and style to that of Hanson Puthoff, an artist friend from the Chicago Palette and Chisel Club, who had moved to Southern California and become part of a group of landscape painters, working in an Impressionist style. Edgar's painting still retains the softer tones of his Chicago landscapes, but with a greater vigor that speaks of a new direction in his art.

During this first visit to California, Edgar spent some time in Laguna Beach, south of Los Angeles, then a quiet little seaside village whose spectacular scenery and mild climate had begun to attract a number of artists. It was soon to become an artists' mecca, especially favored by a group of plein air painters who found perfect subjects in the rocky coastline and distant views of hills and offshore island. Some years later Edgar Payne returned to Laguna Beach to make his home there, and to become, in time, the chief organizer of the Laguna Beach Art Association.

His discovery of Laguna Beach was not the only significant event in this early 1909 trip to California, for he took time for a brief three-day visit to San Francisco, to meet an attractive young artist named Elsie Palmer, to whom he had been given a letter of introduction by Gordon St. Clair.[10]

This Elsie Palmer whom Edgar met first in San Francisco came from a much more privileged background than Edgar's, and a great deal more is known about it. She was born in San Antonio, Texas, on September 9, 1884, the eighth and last child of William and Amelia Lake Palmer. Elsie later recalled that when she was about ten years old and beginning to ask questions, she was told that the doctor, in delivering the newborn infant to her mother, had remarked, "Well, Mrs. Palmer, here is a little artist for you." "A boy?" asked Elsie's mother, showing the first sign of interest. "No, a girl," was the reply, and all interest was gone.[11]

The incident is probably apocryphal, but the attitude it reveals is not. All her life Elsie was dogged by the prevailing opinion that significant achievement was a male prerogative, and though she never subscribed to that notion herself, she was undoubtedly aware of it and struggled purposefully to overcome it. Of course Amelia Palmer quickly reconciled herself to the fact that the youngest child was female, later telling her daughter that though she had been an unwelcome addition to the struggling family when she was born, she became the most loved one after she arrived. Nevertheless one cannot help wondering what effect the rejection implied in the story of her birth might have had on the young and impressionable child, and on her perception of her self worth.

Elsie's family was of English stock, her father coming from the landed gentry, breeders of a strain of fine blooded horses, and her mother from a family of jewelers and clockmakers with an establishment on London's Regent Street and a coveted Royal Warrant as "Jewelers and Clockmakers to her Majesty the Queen."

Because Amelia's family, the Lakes, were "in trade" as the expression went, William Palmer may have been considered as marrying beneath him. When her husband's stock was destroyed by an epidemic of hoof and mouth disease, Amelia, who had suffered from the real or imagined snobbery of her in-laws, was not unhappy to move with him to America. Around 1880 or 1881, therefore, the family emigrated to America — to Texas — where William's experience with blooded stock would, they were convinced, make them a fortune in no time at all.[12]

Life, however, has a frequent habit of disappointing expectations. Soon after their arrival in Texas, Amelia and William suffered the tragedy of the death of three of their children from diphtheria and whooping cough. (One other child had died in England.) William's experience in breeding horses did not bring the hoped for prosperity in Texas, and his chronic ill health added to the family's burden. They were supported mainly by Amelia, who taught drawing in a girls' school, and, in addition to caring for her family, gave painting, singing and piano lessons. She also took advantage of the tourist trade, already evident in frontier San Antonio, by painting for sale small pictures on parchment of the Alamo and other Texas missions or watercolor scenes of European landmarks, undoubtedly copied from postcards or engravings.

In early 1886, when Elsie was about eighteen months old, the Palmers decided that Texas was not, after all, the place where the family fortune was to be made. Perhaps, they thought, California would be better, both for William's health and their economic prosperity. But train fare to California for a family of six was not cheap, and their finances were at a low ebb. Never at a loss for ideas, Amelia wrote to Collis Huntington, owner of the Southern Pacific Railroad, asking for free tickets to California for the entire family because "this was a free country, wasn't it." Incredibly, something in her letter must have touched a responsive chord, or perhaps to catch Huntington's attention she had included some drawings or sketches. For whatever reason, the return mail brought railroad passages for the entire family. Amelia even managed to persuade the station manager demanding payment for the baggage that Mr. Huntington undoubtedly intended that it should also go to California without charge.

Having travelled in style but quite broke, the Palmers arrived in Los Angeles, hoping to get ahead in the building, contracting, and land speculation of the booming city. The family first rented half a house in the suburbs at 7th and Spring Streets. With his oldest son Charles, William then built a little four-room house in a walnut grove far out beyond Figueroa and bought and sold some land. But fame and fortune continued to elude the family even in Los Angeles, and after three years they moved to Oakland in the San Francisco Bay area, where Elsie grew up.

They prospered well enough here, William engaging again in contracting and real estate as well as making an unsuccessful attempt from 1891 to 1895 to establish a coffee plantation in Guatemala. Amelia continued to help support the family by teaching china-painting classes and giving singing lessons. Though frequently strapped for funds, the household was seldom a penurious one, for Elsie later remembered a large house with her father expertly cutting the "joint" at the Sunday table, spread with the damask, heavy silver and good china the family had brought from England. She also remembered her mother seated at the piano in the parlor singing and making long runs and trills while her father made mulled wine. Her parents knew "the arts of living so well," she later observed, "but oh earning the living was different."[13] Nevertheless, it was a comfortable environment which nurtured the child Elsie, one that was nourished by an appreciation of good literature, music, and art, presided over by her father's quiet gentle manners and her mother's indomitable spirit and many talents. Elsie told in later years how her mother would read aloud to the children while making intricate pieces of Irish crochet, and how she, Elsie, crawled under the table to hide her tears because *Alice in Wonderland* was so sad. Indeed from her early childhood, Elsie developed a lifelong habit of hiding her sensitive feelings and showing only a cheerful face.

Around 1899, upon her father's death, Amelia came into some money and the family moved across the Bay to a new house in San Francisco.[14] Elsie was in high school at the time, and she did not like the new school in San Francisco. However, in her senior year, having a spare period, she took her first formal lessons in drawing to fill the time.[15] She had always drawn well, even in grammar school, and her mother had promised that after she reached a certain point in her piano lessons she could study art. As she had never reached that point in her music, however, the art lessons had been continually postponed. The high school lessons were enough, however, to convince Elsie that if she couldn't be an actress, her childhood ambition, she would make the practice of art her lifetime goal.

The first step in achieving that goal was, of course, an art school education, and around 1902 Elsie enrolled in the Best Art School at 1625 California Street in San Francisco. The school had been established by Arthur William Best (1859-1935) who, with his brother, Harry Cassie Best (1863-1936) had wandered west as a member of a musical band that had been formed near their home in Peterborough, Ontario. Arthur played the clarinet and Harry the violin; but when the band broke up in Portland, Oregon Harry devoted himself to landscape painting. Around 1895, he sold a painting of Mt. Hood for $100, and the unexpected windfall enabled the brothers to move to San Francisco where Harry worked as a cartoonist for the *San Francisco Post.* Two years later they organized a sketch club that led to the establishment of Arthur's "Best Art School" which he conducted for many years at the California Street address. Arthur's wife, Alice M. Leveque Best was a teacher at the school from 1897 to 1920, a woman Elsie later remembered most vividly and the only one she credited with influencing her career. But since Alice Best's style was in the tradition of the 19th Century Barbizon and Impressionist painters of France, it was probably not her style but her other activities which made Elsie remember and admire her. For, when not painting or teaching, Alice Best lectured widely on art, philosophy, and political issues, and was known as a champion of women's suffrage,[16] all activities that would have interested and attracted Elsie. One of the stories about Mrs. Best reveals something of their relationship as well as Elsie's ideas about art. In Elsie's words:

> "When I was going to Art School in San Francisco, one of the students brought an old fashioned civil war vintage costume . . . so Mrs. Best . . . asked me to pose in it as I was very slender and very blonde, so I did . . . [A]nd Mrs. Best made the most delightful black crayon drawing with a few color watercolor washes on it. The whole paper was only about 12 × 16 inches, so that the head was about an inch long, with no attempt to get a likeness. It turned out to be a most charming sketch . . .
>
> "[Y]ears later I received a letter from [a friend in] Seattle [who] said that he had attended an Art exhibition there and seen a little sketch signed by one Alice Best of a little girl in an old-fashioned dress that

so reminded him of me that he had to write me. Under all those folds and bonnet and all, Mrs. Best has so caught my personality that he, not knowing anything about her or the picture had recognized me. That's Art.

"Well, many, many more years after that I had just returned from Europe and was engaged to speak before an Art Club in Berkeley, California and while being introduced several prominent artists in the audience were introduced to me, one of them being Alice Best. I said, 'Oh, Alice Best was my first instructor and taught me almost everything I know.' She said, 'I was thinking of you just the other day, I was looking through an old portfolio and came upon that little sketch I made of you in that Old Fashioned Dress.' So I told the story of my friend seeing the sketch in Seattle . . . Someone in the audience asked if it could be shown, as Mrs. Best had a studio in that building, so she produced it and the lady was so intrigued with the delightful little picture and the story that she bought it then and there."[17]

Elsie spent about two years in what she later described as "intensive art school training"[18] at Best's Art School, drawing first from plaster casts, as was the established practice, before progressing to oils. At that time she was hoping eventually to become a portrait painter. But after leaving school she found that advertising art was a more immediate source of income, and from 1904 to 1907 she worked for Rimes Illustrating Co. for $5 a week, designing catalogs and drawing advertisements for clothing. But such fashion work was seasonal, and when Elsie was told she could get more steady work if she could letter, she quickly taught herself to do so. The new skill raised her pay to $35 a week and Elsie was particularly proud of the fact that she was earning a man's wages. It was enough to support herself and her mother, who had written from England where she was visiting (she had gotten free passage around the Horn on a sailing vessel as a companion to the captain's wife) to say that she was coming back to San Francisco to live with her.[19]

Around 1907, Elsie got a better job at Barney and Green, outdoor advertising, designing and drawing the billboards for such national accounts as Kellogg's Corn Flakes, Pabst Beer, and Old Dutch Cleanser. She even made the design drawings for a theater curtain — which had to be completed in a single day — advertising a furrier's business and including in the design not only stylishly fur-wrapped women, but icebergs and a dog-sled team. She worked all morning and used her lunch hour to rush home and consult, for authenticity, a photograph of her mother, wrapped in furs, on a dog-sled, as she traveled from Dawson to Whitehorse, Alaska, in −92° weather. The indomitable Amelia had spent some time in the Yukon writing for newspapers during the gold rush of 1898.[20]

Thus when Elsie first met Edgar in 1909, she was already established in the Bay area as a commercial artist, designing advertisements. On a Sunday morning the two went sketching together, after which Elsie invited him home to dinner. At the Palmer table, Edgar, who had been saving his money to stay as long as possible in California, filled himself with biscuits as inconspicuously as possible, a bit embarrassed by his hunger at the well appointed Palmer table.[21] Elsie remembered that dinner long afterward, possibly because the young Chicago artist had already stirred her interest as a person as well as a painter.

Apparently, however, Elsie did not think very much of Edgar's work at the first encounter. His colors were too dull, she wrote to Gordon St. Clair, another artist and mutual friend who had introduced them, and who advised her that Edgar was the best painter of the younger set in Chicago. St. Clair, then in Chicago, wrote back. "To your California bred eyes, I guess his colors *are* dull. He's used to these silvery tones around Chicago. But don't worry," he added, "he'll get it." And "get it" he soon did.

It was while still working at Barney and Green that Elsie had been encouraged by coworkers to consider travel and she thought of Europe and New York. Since she had won a prize for designing an insignia for the Outdoor Advertising Companies United (the Outdoor Advertising Trust that was later dissolved as a result of the trust busting initiated by President Theodore Roosevelt) she felt confident of being able to find jobs elsewhere.[10]

Her first trip was to Chicago, partly to see Gordon St. Clair, with whom there had been an informal engagement. Soon after her arrival she went to Cusack Outdoor Advertising who said, "We've heard of you" and gave her a job right away — at more money than she had made in San Francisco.[21] The next year Clague Advertising in Chicago offered her an even better deal, and she worked for them from 1911 to 1912.[22]

Edgar's 1911 California trip included a four months stint of scene painting in the Edwin Flagg Studio in Los Angeles (Fig. 2.05) but he also brought back to Chicago many sketches. And when Elsie met Edgar again after his return, a real romance developed. She visited his studio where he showed her his most recent California sketches, and there began a period of regular Saturday night dates; Edgar took her to a chop suey dinner and then to a movie for two westerns.[10] Actually Edgar was very interested in western scenery, and when he did the scenery for a western play, the audience applauded every evening when the curtain went up on the set. He also was commissioned around that time to transform a run down theater into a beer garden, with a huge rose arbor effect. But Edgar had continued his landscape painting too and, utilizing his small sketches from California, he sold some paintings, through exhibitions at the Palette and Chisel Club and at the Art Institute of Chicago.

Fig. 2.05. Postcard, from EAP, Los Angeles, to Thomas Moses, Chicago, September, 1911.

Meanwhile, Elsie's informal engagement to St. Clair had been broken, apparently to the relief of both parties, and the romance with Edgar grew. On November 9, 1912, Elsie Palmer and Edgar Payne were married in Chicago, taking up residence immediately after in the Tree Studio Building at 4 East Ohio Street. By then Elsie had completely revised her original assessment of Edgar's talent, and, as she repeated the marriage vows, she promised herself that "Come hell or high water, I would never stand in the way of this very talented man's art."[23]

STUDIO of
EDGAR PAYNE - ELSIE PAYNE

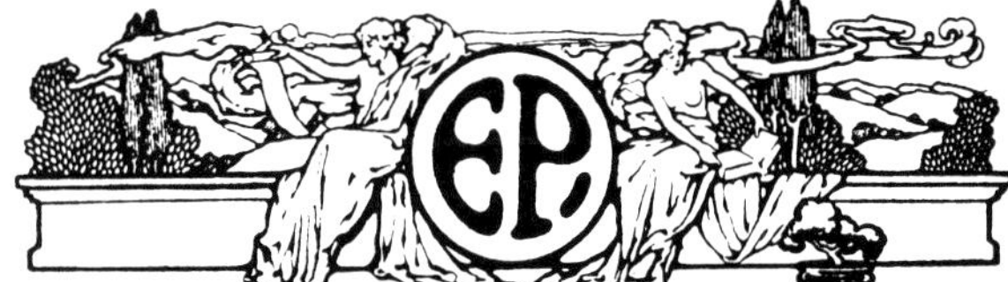

No. 11 STUDIO BUILDING
4 EAST OHIO ST. CHICAGO
TELEPHONE NORTH 3383

Just what that commitment meant became quite clear that very day. At the time of their marriage, Edgar was under pressure to finish a scenic backdrop he was painting for Mandel's Department Store. The marriage had been scheduled for the morning, but Edgar, already busy at work on the mural, wanted to postpone the ceremony until the evening as the light was particularly good for painting that day. And Elsie, though she realized, she later said, that she would always have to take a second place to Edgar's art, "was quite in love with art" herself and considered the postponement of her marriage a matter of course.[23] She later wrote: "We went to work the next morning, Sunday, all alone in that big department store and both painted on the back drop. I don't suppose I was much help, as I was not used to standing to work nor to painting such large things. In the afternoon I found a nice comfortable bed on display so took a nap while poor Edgar toiled steadily on. I felt like a heel but just could not keep awake." It was thus that they started their new life together (Fig. 2.06).

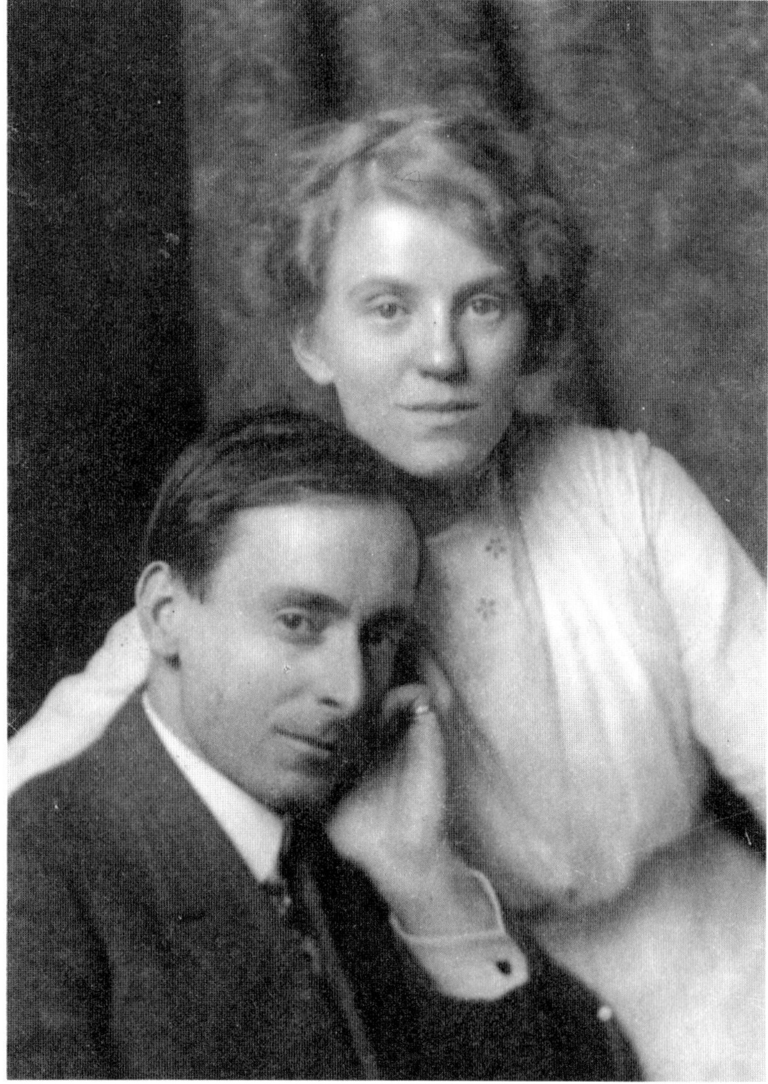

Fig. 2.06. The Paynes, 1913.

Chapter 3: Chicago

At the time of his marriage, Edgar was already beginning to make a name for himself, not only in Chicago, but well beyond it. In the summer of 1912 he was invited to become a member of the Paris based Union des Beaux Arts et des Lettres, an invitation which he accepted.[24] Of much more practical value, however, was the attention his work was beginning to attract in Chicago, especially in exhibitions of his easel pictures at the Art Institute of Chicago and at the Palette and Chisel Club. Indeed, his exhibition record at the Art Institute begins as early as 1910 when *A Sunny Hillside* was shown from January 4th to 30th at the Fourteenth Annual Exhibition of Works by Chicago Artists. Later the same year, an Edgar Payne picture of the *Sierra del Burro Mountains, Mexico,* was included in the Art Institute's Twenty Second Annual Exhibition of Water Colors, Pastels and Miniatures from May 10th to June 8th. The existence of this painting provides tenuous confirmation of Edgar's later offhand references to a trip to Mexico in his youth. It may have been just a brief excursion across the border while he was living in Texas and working as a stage scenery painter, and it probably lasted only as long as it took to paint the Serranias del Burro Mountains. Located near the Texas-Mexico border in Coahuila Province, these mountains were, especially at that time, a wild and untravelled place. They may well have stimulated Edgar's appetite for remote mountain vistas, a subject he later developed in his many paintings of California's high Sierras, upon which, to a large extent, his reputation depends.

By 1912 Edgar had exhibited in several Palette and Chisel Club showings, and was represented by no less than four paintings at the Sixteenth Annual Exhibition of Works by Chicago Artists at the Art Institute of Chicago from February 1st to 28th. Three of the paintings bear such characteristic Edgar Payne titles as *The Patriarch of the Canyon* (#204), *The Shadow of the Canyon* (#205), and *The Bay of Avalon* (#206). But the fourth painting, listed as #207, has the unusual title, *The Day of Aviation.* As Edgar never otherwise painted subjects having to do with modern technology, one can only guess at what this picture may have been about. But Edgar's 1911 summer trip to California included both Catalina Island and Laguna Beach[25], and it is easy to conclude that at least three of these paintings originated in sketches of the area of Laguna Canyon, and Avalon on Catalina Island, just off the coast. It was in fact this same trip that was the basis for his earliest marine of the Laguna coast (Fig. 4.01) which is discussed below in Chapter 4. Still another of Edgar's paintings of Laguna Canyon, entitled *Western Hills,* won the $100 prize at the Tingel Tangel of the Palette and Chisel Club in January 1913 and was raffled off among the members.[26]

When, about six months after Edgar and Elsie's marriage, 65 of Edgar's small landscapes were exhibited at the Palette and Chisel Club from May 3rd to 17th, they were described as "vivid and glowing studies of the hills and canyons of California."[27] To the delight of the young Paynes, before the exhibition was over every one of them had been sold. Characteristically the couple immediately took off on a sketching trip to California.[28,29]

Though no listing exists of this show, one of the paintings may well have been *Balm* (Fig. 3.01),

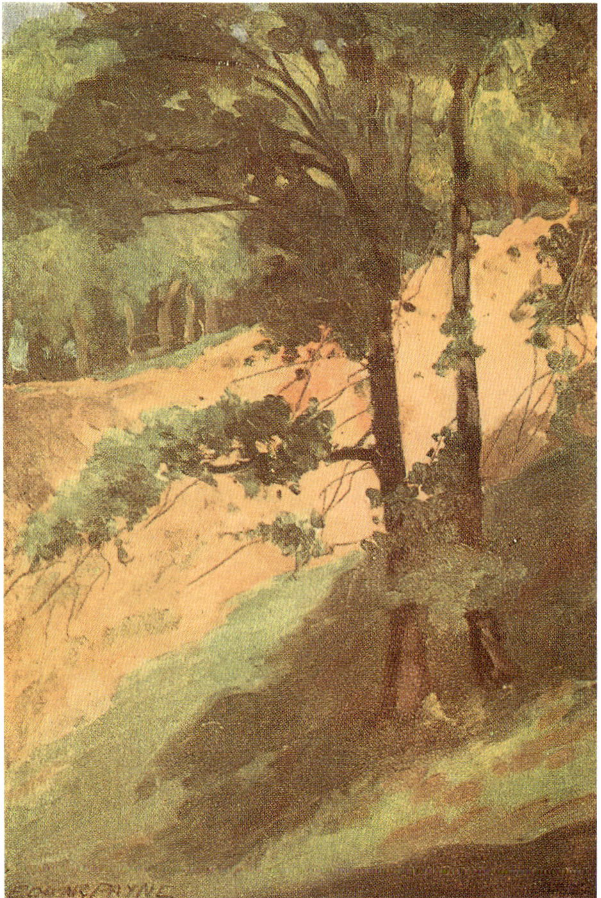

Fig. 3.01. Balm, by EAP. Reproduced from a 1914 color reproduction of the original.

now lost, that revealed Edgar's increasingly sophisticated sense of design and sensitivity to nature. Printed by the Henry O. Shepard Company of Chicago to advertise their expertise at color reproduction, it was one of several such prints inserted in the Club's journal, *The Cowbell,* during 1914. It was chosen, among seven other paintings, to be presented to the Henry O. Shepard School in Chicago by its namesake, the head of the company.

A correspondent for the *Chicago Evening Post,* describing this Palette and Chisel Club exhibition, took note of the fact that "Mrs. Elsie Payne is represented by a delightful 'Marsh at Sundown' and it may be other pictures in her husband's collection."[27] But landscape was not really Elsie's chief interest and though she occasionally did turn to it, because she accompanied Edgar on his many landscape sketching trips, she much preferred figure studies. In an exhibit at the Art Institute of Chicago held from March 25th to April 27th, 1913, for example, her painting, *Children at Play* was shown alongside a decorative panel and *An Idyll* by Edgar.

Indeed, the Payne's separate talents were beginning to attract not only attention but commissions to do murals for theaters and courthouses in the Middle West. Typically, after Edgar did the preliminary design, Elsie would draw the figures and make the large outline "cartoons" which were transferred to the canvas. Edgar did the actual painting and the landscape background. Like many so-called murals of the period, these were actually pictures painted in oil on canvas or muslin that was fitted and attached to the wall, rather than a true mural or fresco painted into the wet plaster. Elsie later observed that it was only after she joined him in such enterprises that Edgar began to receive the mural commissions. He was never as good as she at drawing figures so "I used to draw them and he'd paint them and we had all the work that we could do . . . It wasn't such a bad idea."[30]

Late in 1913, when Elsie was pregnant with their only child, Evelyn, born on January 12, 1914, Edgar received an important commission from Mitchell and Hallbeck Decorating Company of Chicago to create a mural for the Hendricks County courthouse in Danville, Indiana.[8] It is unknown who originally proposed the subject, the Liberation of Vincennes (Fig. 3.02), an important episode in Indiana's history, for there is no documentation on the choice of theme. But Edgar probably proceeded typically by doing his own research, reading everything he could about the subject from whatever source he could find in the public library.

The Danville mural is important for a number of reasons. For one thing, its very survival makes it unique. For another, though it was a collaborative effort, it is the earliest extant work by Elsie and an early example of Edgar's. It was, moreover, the most ambitious joint enterprise of the two artists up to that time and may well have led

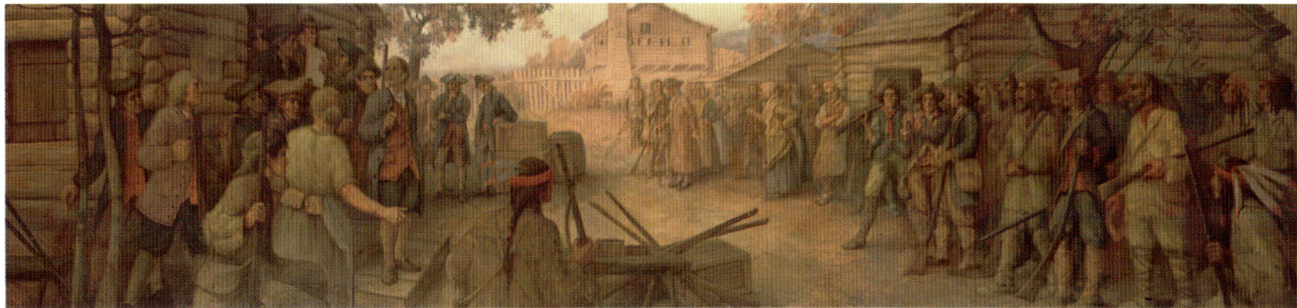

Fig. 3.02. Danville Courthouse Mural, by EAP and EPP.

to other commissions that they received later on. Of course, since Edgar alone negotiated and signed the contracts for such mural commissions, it was not generally known that Elsie worked on them too, especially since she never insisted on being recognized in this way.

Though the Paynes painted the usual allegorical subjects for other county courthouses (e.g. the Clay County Courthouse in Brazil, Indiana), the Danville mural is unusual for the time in that it illustrates an episode in the pioneer history of the state. It thus avoids the mannered themes of civic virtue or quasi-religious exhortation that were generally preferred. Indeed, the last decades of the nineteenth century and the early years of the twentieth witnessed a flowering of mural painting in government buildings and public institutions throughout the United States. Though some artists, such as John Singer Sargent in his richly decorated Boston Public Library murals of 1893-95, displayed an originality of design and diversity of color, most mural painting of the period was academic, dry, and frequently bombastic. The Payne Danville mural, however, avoids the usual moral allegories typically clothed in classical garments and focuses instead on local legend and Indiana history.

The liberation of Vincennes from the British on February 25, 1779, is an Indiana story commemorating local heroism and familiar at that time to every Indiana schoolchild. The heroes are the historical figures of George Rogers Clark and the citizens of Vincennes. The town had just been recaptured by Clark from the British after a difficult 160 mile march from Kaskaskia with 53 stalwart men who sank into freezing marshes on their way, the misery of their cold and bedraggled condition compounded by the fact that there was little food to sustain them. Wet and starving, they nevertheless reached their destination and, catching the British by surprise, forced the surrender of the garrison, thus encouraging the citizens of Vincennes to swear allegiance to the United States and to the state of Virginia to which the Indiana Territory then belonged. Clark is undoubtedly the youthful figure at the left beside a priest, probably Father Gibault, shown reading a proclamation to the citizens gathered round. Gibault, of French background and sympathetic to the American cause, had been dispatched by Clark to Vincennes the previous June to win over the French settlers to the American side. This accomplished, he joined up again with Clark at Kaskaskia and accompanied him on the historic march to Vincennes, thus winning a place as one of Indiana's pioneer heroes.

Edgar, as was common, took liberties with historical fact in such murals if it suited his pictorial purpose. The scene, therefore, takes place not on a cold February day but in late autumn when the sun would glow with a brighter light and Elsie's figure drawing could be seen to better advantage. The mural was planned as an integral part of the interior architecture of the courthouse, and besides providing an appropriate pictorial background to the court's proceedings, produces an atmosphere of color and richness as well. It also creates an illusion of a larger interior space through Edgar's expert representation of linear and atmospheric perspective.

These years found the Paynes working on a number of other painted murals for theaters and hotels. Among them were the American, Empress and new Apollo Theaters in Chicago, the Queens Theater in Houston and the Northern Hotel in Billings, Montana. Of these, the commission for the American Theater in Chicago won the most attention at the time. Writing in 1914 in the *Chicago Evening Post,* Lena M. McCauley described the ensemble of 21 decorations for the theater which stood on the west side of Chicago at Ashland Avenue and Madison Street. She noted approvingly ". . . the superb California landscape on the curtain [and]. . . the subject panels on the walls." And she said ". . . it is only right that the American Theater decorators should have paintings illustrating American history both to adorn their building and entertain their audiences."[31] The largest subject was the painting over the proscenium arch, an allegorial "Progress" that measured 6 by 60 feet. There were 14 smaller panels that constituted a veritable survey of American history from the early days of discovery and adventure in the New World, to wagon trains marching westward in which the long lines of covered wagons fitted admirably into a long, narrow space. The decorations on the walls of the lobby were seven lunettes, or half circles, of explorers in America, Christopher Columbus appearing in one panel and the Fathers Marquette and Joliet in another. Others of the larger wall panels depicted frontier life in the colonial period, Paul Revere on his midnight ride, and the battles of Lexington and Concord. In addition, the Civil War battle of Gettysburg was shown; and one panel repeated the Danville mural theme of George Rogers Clark in the Vincennes territory.

In painting these large theater pictures, the Paynes were following a well established tradition in the history of American art. Stage scenery painting was, in fact, so much a part of the common experience of young American artists in the 19th and early 20th century as to be considered almost a necessary training ground. Such work offered an opportunity to earn a living with the brush while establishing a reputation as a "fine artist". Elsie, with her background in commercial art, had already had considerable experience in painting the broadly patterned illustrations that both advertising art and mural painting demanded. Edgar, for his part, had an innate feeling for landscape design and a brush that was facile enough to capture its characteristic qualities in an easy and fluid manner. Thus, though they came from different artistic directions, Elsie retaining her flat illustrative style and Edgar adopting the broad, loose brush strokes that later characterized his Impressionistic landscapes, the collaboration between the two artists worked, as Elsie had remarked, very well.

Though none of these theater paintings survive, preliminary studies for four of them, commemorations of the history of France and Spain in the New World, have recently come to light. They

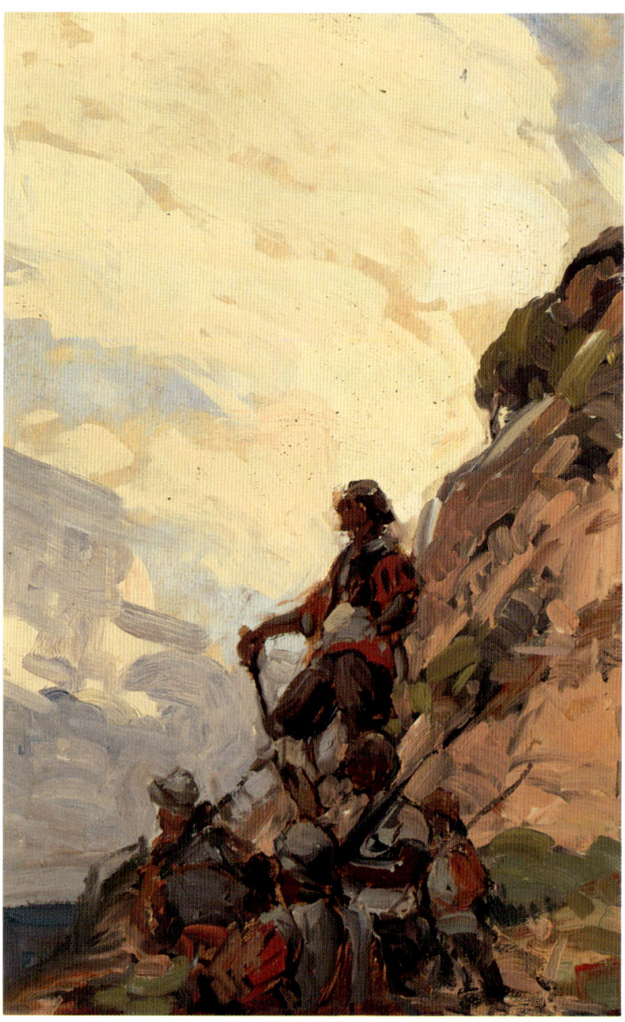

Fig. 3.03. Sketch for American Theater mural: La Salle, by EAP.

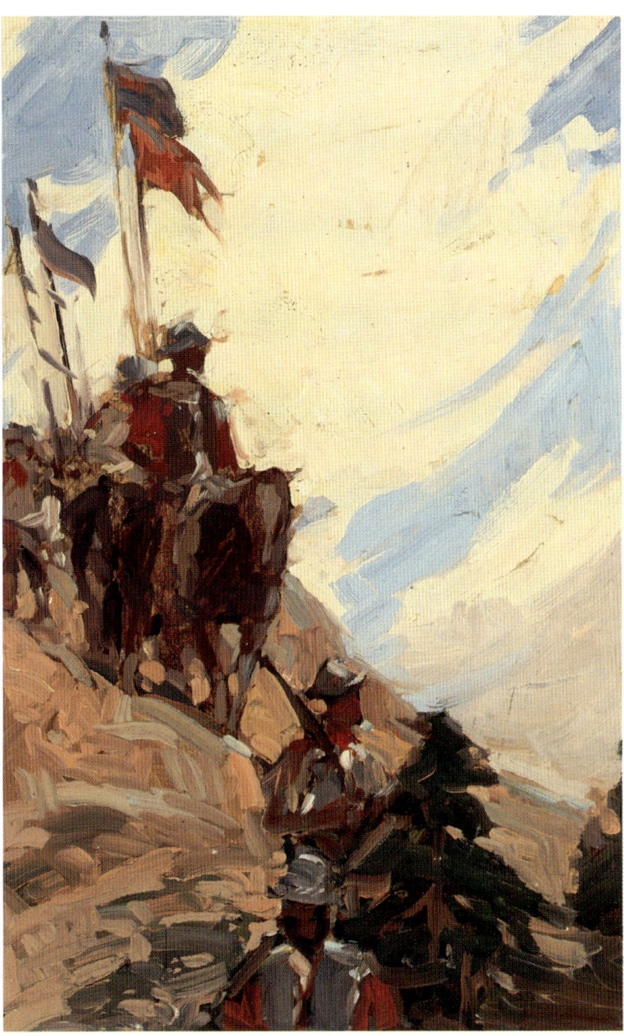

Fig. 3.04. Sketch for American Theater mural: Spanish Exploration, by EAP.

are all small sketches, masterfully composed. One of them shows LaSalle proudly claiming the country for France (Fig. 3.03) while another depicts the Spanish exploration of the South (Fig. 3.04). In this picture the drama is heightened by the strong diagonal formed by the sharply sloping line of conquistadores, balanced by the oblique thrust of the cloud banks at the right. With banners bravely flying and military bearing intact, the procession conveys, with just a few rapid strokes of the brush, the taut wariness of the band of explorers in unknown territory. Like the work of Newell Conyer Wyeth (1882-1945) and other contemporary illustrators, these pictures have a swashbuckling vitality entirely appropriate to the subject.

The *Design for a Triptych* (Fig. 3.05) with its castle and men at arms may well have been painted with a hotel or theater decoration in mind. The knights in armor, sketchily laid in

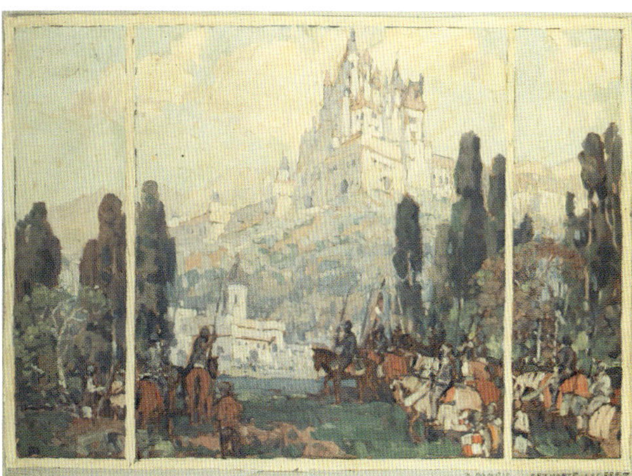

Fig. 3.05. Sketch for a Triptych, by EAP.

beneath a castle towering above them in the mist, are depicted in a subdued palette, tending toward pale pinks and greens, that is more characteristic of Edgar's early decorative work than his later landscapes. Here too the sense of story book adventure, of high romance, is typical of the stage scenery painting that occupied him at this time.

During these Chicago years, as noted previously, the Paynes were living in the Tree Studio Building, a structure that had been erected on property originally owned by a Judge Tree. Mrs. Tree, a lover of the arts, persuaded her husband to build a complex of artists' studios on the site since there was no place in Chicago, aside from dingy boardinghouses, where struggling artists could live and work. The Tree studios were rented to artists at a very reasonable rate, made even more reasonable by the promise of a month's free rent if that for the other eleven months was paid by the tenth day of each month.[32] Edgar and Elsie would sublet their studio during summer sketching trips. Once, on their return from California in the fall of 1913, when Elsie was pregnant and they were flat broke, Edgar had to pawn a treasured revolver in order to come up with the rent in time to qualify for the special rent concession.[23]

The regular summer trips were mostly to California, but they included the Southwest too (see Chapter 7). They all furnished the basis for the easel paintings completed during the winters in the studio. Occasionally, however a more decorative picture still appears, as in *Fantasy* (Fig. 3.06) which again uses a palette that has more to do with theater drops than the real world. The painting, said to be an idealized conception of California,[33] is an unusual combination of stage painting and easel picture in a period which was still a transitional one for the artist.

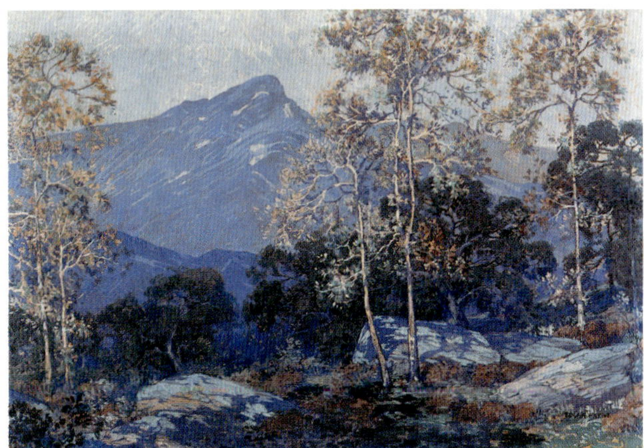

Fig. 3.06. Fantasy, by EAP.

Though the Paynes eventually became known as primarily California artists, during the five years they were Chicago residents in the Tree Studio Building, Edgar's work was almost exclusively exhibited and sold in the Chicago area. Though there is one incomplete record of an exhibition elsewhere—in Santa Barbara with O. Irwin Myers, probably in 1915—he could, at this time be called a Chicago artist and he exhibited as such at the Art Institute there. In February 1914, for example, the Art Institute of Chicago exhibited one of three versions of *Hills of Marin*, painted in the Chicago studio. It was purchased by the Peoria Society of Allied Arts in 1914 and was one of the first large studio pictures Edgar sold. Peoria loved the painting and described it enthusiastically in the local press[34], but it disappeared without a trace in Peoria in the 1930's.

In late June 1914 a number of Edgar's small canvases were sold from a joint exhibition with the sculptor, Nancy Cox McCormack, at the Palette and Chisel Club.[35,36,37] (There was to be another joint exhibition by the two in Paris in 1924.) And from March 17th to 27th, 1915, there was yet another exhibition of Edgar's work at the Club, [38,39] this one including "several small sculptural bookrocks by Elsie Payne."[40] At the same time more of Edgar's paintings were exhibited at the Art Institute.

In 1915 the Paynes' summer trip took them first to San Francisco to visit Elsie's family and see the Panama-Pacific International Exposition, where some of Edgar's works were being shown and from which his *Infinitude* was sold. The exhibition, which had opened in February, 1915, was seminal in the development of California art. Indeed, it can be considered a West Coast equivalent of the International Exhibition of Modern Art which had opened in New York's Sixty Ninth Regiment Armory in February, 1913, thereafter known as the New York Armory Show.

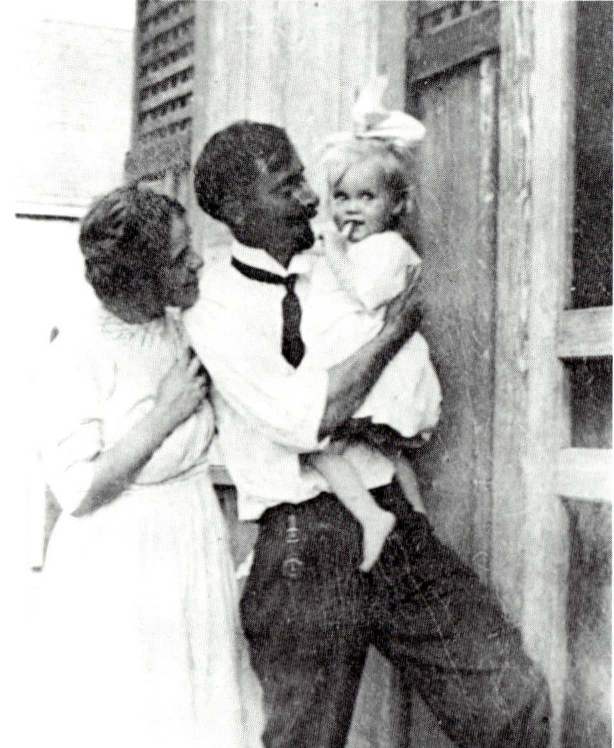

Fig. 3.07. The Paynes in Santa Barbara, 1915.

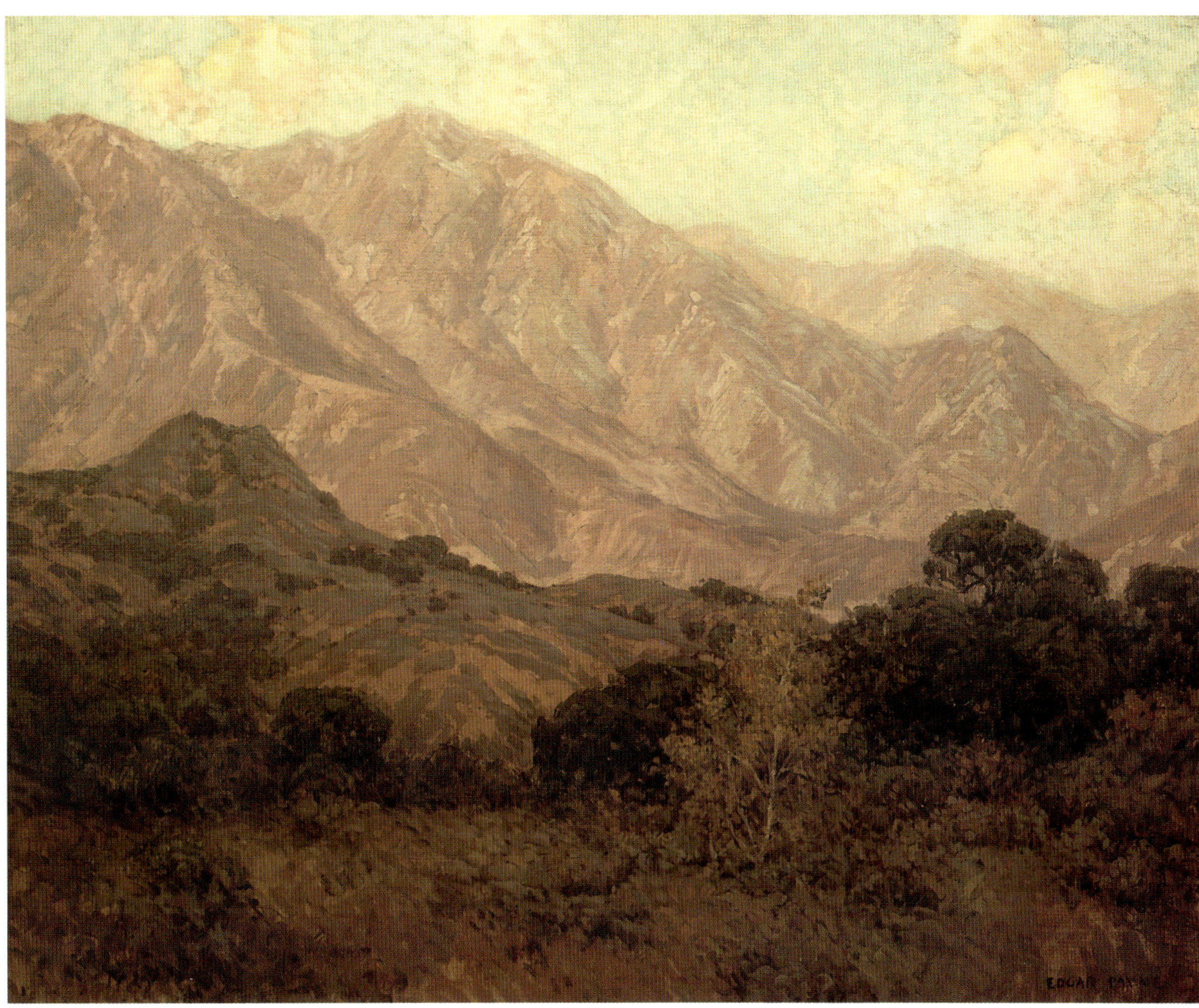

Fig. 3.08. Santa Barbara, 1915, by EAP.

Both exhibitions, in New York and San Francisco, displayed the vanguard of European and American styles, though the one in San Francisco was less radical in its approach and proved immensely popular. It provided an opportunity to show as a group the work of French and American Impressionist masters and won general approval, on the part of public and artists alike, for the light-filled, colorful, seemingly spontaneous canvases of that style. It undoubtedly encouraged the development of Impressionism in California and fostered the talents, as well as strengthening the patronage, of artists already active in the plein air tradition. For Edgar, particularly, the Impressionist pictures hanging in the exhibition must have been a revelatory experience for they confirmed his own response to nature and encouraged his self-taught attempts at revealing its changeable moods on canvas.

After visiting the Panama-Pacific Exposition, Edgar and Elsie went south, to Santa Barbara, where they rented a small house and spent the summer sketching and painting (Fig. 3.07).[41] Edgar's *Santa Barbara* (Fig. 3.08) of 1915 reveals the firm hand of the maturing landscape painter, now fully attuned to nature's moods. Studying light as a compositional element, he painted the distant peaks as a glowing backdrop to the foreground hills, all in a flowing rhythm that beats with the living pulse of the outdoor scene. By

1917, in another rare dated canvas, entitled *Blue California Hills* (Fig. 3.09), Edgar had moved even closer to the Impressionists in his confident manipulation of a broader brush stroke that captures, in a seemingly spontaneous manner, the essence of the California scene.

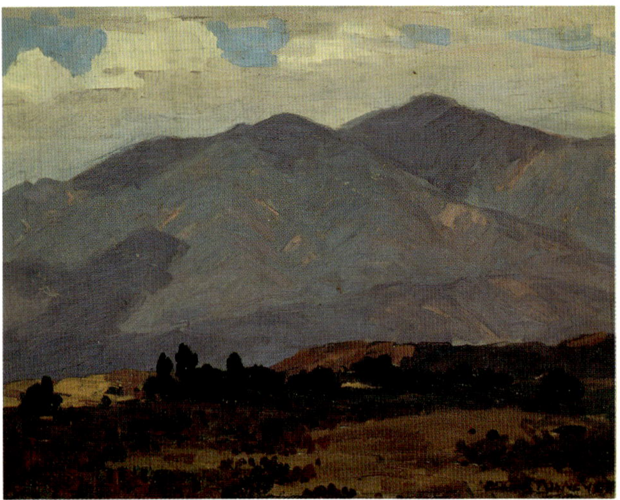

Fig. 3.09. Blue California Hills, by EAP.

The 1915 trip to California also included a number of excursions to the wilderness of Santa Cruz Island (just off the coast of Santa Barbara)[42] where Edgar made many sketches (Fig. 3.10) and photographs, and Elsie was busy with the camp cooking, looking after 18-month-old Evelyn, and admiring the curvilinear patterns in the island's cliffs and caves. There was a second week-long trip, with several companions, including a Mexican cook who taught Elsie to make Spanish rice, and an artist friend, O. Irwin Myers of Chicago, on whose behalf Elsie tried some (unsuccessful) matchmaking. Edgar took along a rented pirate costume in which they took turns posing, for Edgar had become fascinated with the buccaneers of old. On this trip a storm and high waters made it impossible for the mainland boat to get to the island and take them off, so they were stranded with their infant daughter for a week more, with a leaky tent and nothing left to eat but beans.

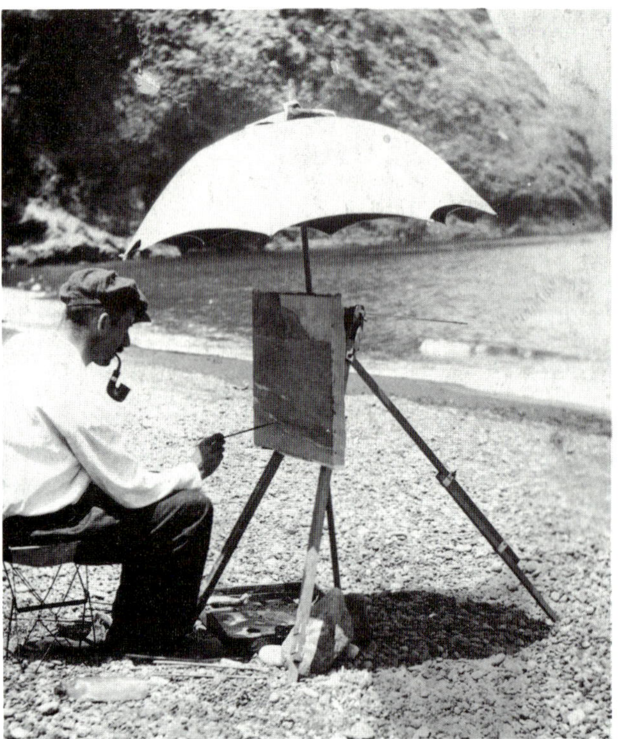

Fig. 3.10. Sketching on Santa Cruz Island, 1915.

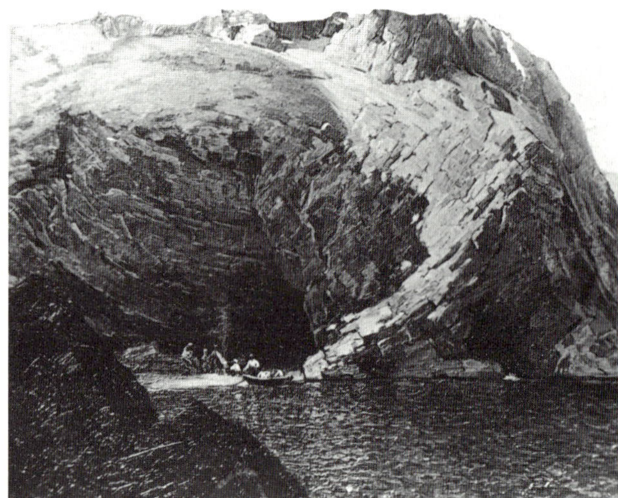

Fig. 3.11. The Rendezvous, by EAP.

Of the several paintings Edgar did on the subject of pirates, *The Rendezvous* (Fig. 3.11) was exhibited at the Art Institute of Chicago in February 1916 as #226 and at the Palette and Chisel Club a month later. *The Buccaneers* (Fig. 3.12) of the same period is more revealing of Edgar's rapid artistic growth, for the painting demonstrates his now mature mastery of the human figure. He had, since his short lived class at the Art Institute, taught himself, undoubtedly with Elsie's guidance, to paint figures and he does

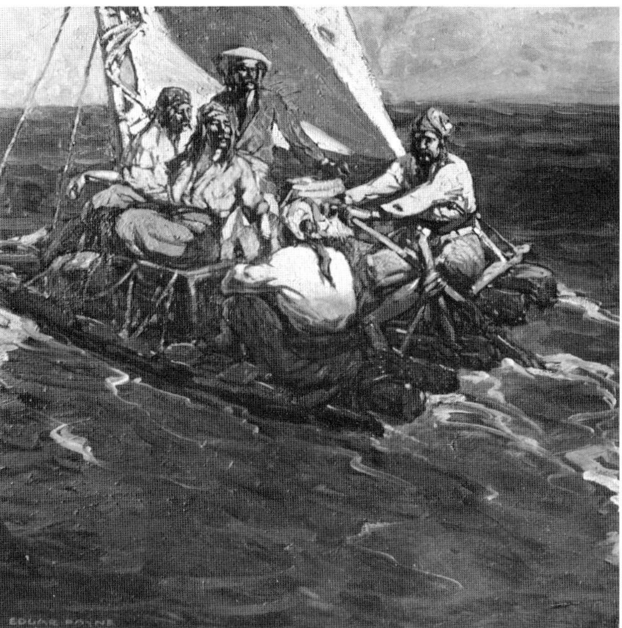

Fig. 3.12. The Buccaneers, by EAP.

so here with a sure and fluent brush.

When the painting was displayed at Stendahl's Gallery in Los Angeles in February 1921, it was described as "a picturesque group of men on a raft, sailing a dark and fateful dark-blue ocean, a subject full of dramatic suggestion."[43] That dramatic suggestion is heightened by the strong diagonal of the composition, which suggests in turn that most famous picture of shipwrecked victims clinging to a raft, Theodore Géricault's *The Raft of the Medusa* of 1819, which Edgar may well have known through engraved reproductions. When he later saw Géricault's original in the Louvre Museum in Paris, it may well have struck him as a déjà vu experience. Both *The Buccaneers* and *The Rendezvous* are unlocated today.

Edgar was involved in two more 1916 exhibitions, both based at the Palette and Chisel Club. The first of these was a traveling exhibition, which opened in Peoria on March 15, in St. Louis on April 3, and sometime after that in Lexington, Kentucky. It was arranged by a trio of Carl Krafft, Walter Ufer, and Edgar Payne, and included paintings by members of the Club as well as their own.[44] The second was an exhibition in April with two other members at the Club, Martin Hennings and Maxmilian Hoffman; Edgar's exhibited paintings deriving from the California trip of the previous spring.[45]

Of the California scenes of this period, marine paintings were becoming an increasingly frequent subject in Edgar's artistic vocabulary, and a commercially successful one as well. In a large marine entitled *The Restless Sea* (Fig. 3.13) that Edgar painted late in 1916 in his Chicago studio from sketches made earlier in Laguna Beach, he was able to capture the energetic flow of the moving waters as they eddy close to the shore, then wash out to sea again. The intense chromatic combination of vermillion and ultramarine that the artist was later to use to describe the California hills in characteristically strong evocations of their light and shadow, he adapted equally successfully in his paintings of the sea. At the same time, his handling of the pigment coincided with the massiveness and weight of the water and produced a soft, vibrating quality that echoes the movement of the ever-changing sea.

The Restless Sea was exhibited in February 1917 at the Art Institute of Chicago and was quickly purchased. The purchase was made part of a family morality tale; Evelyn was taught very early the basics of proper behavior with guests to the studio, and she was later told how she "sold" this painting. Visiting, with her mother, the John and Anna Lee Stacey studio upstairs from the Paynes in the Tree Studio Building, Evelyn was offered a hassock to sit on and a little cracker to eat. She politely, without prompting, thanked Mrs. Stacey, and this politeness impressed another of Mrs. Stacey's visitors very much. The visitor was Mrs. Emma Hawter Sweetser of Indianapolis, who was planning to buy a John Stacey painting for the John Herron Art Institute of Indianapolis. Evelyn was always told that it was as a result of her good behavior that Mrs. Sweetser also bought Edgar's *The Restless Sea* for the Herron.[32] The painting arrived in Indianapolis in May and became part of the permanent collection.[46]

The previous summer, in June 1916, following arrangements Edgar made with the Santa Fe Railroad, the family had travelled to the Southwest, where Edgar first painted the famous Canyon de Chelly. The unique scenery and colorful

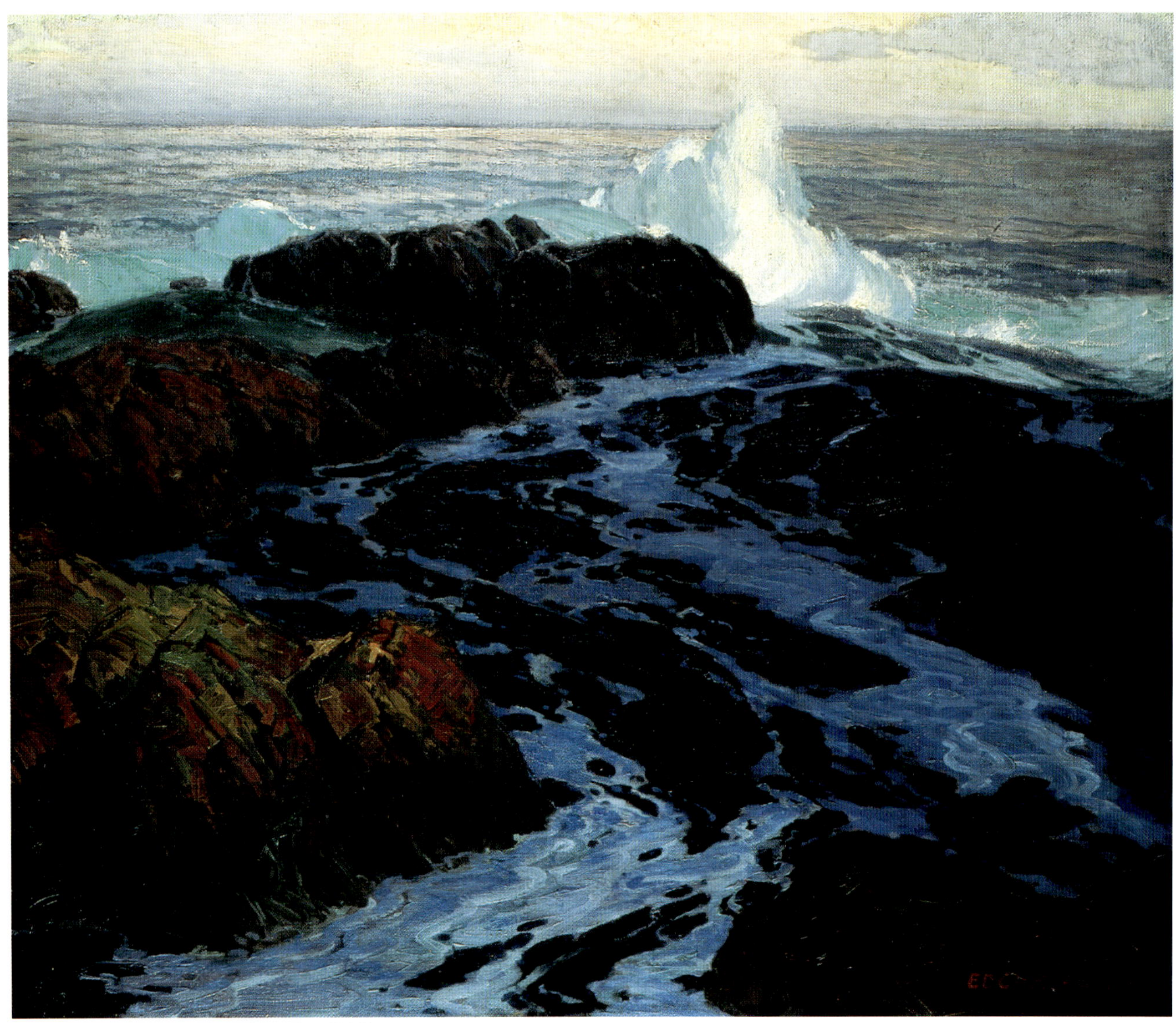

Fig. 3.13. The Restless Sea, by EAP.

inhabitants of the area so attracted the artist that following this first visit of four months, Edgar was to return to the area throughout his life, as discussed in Chapter 7 below.

As Edgar was beginning to earn enough through the sale of easel pictures, which he preferred, he was turning down offers of mural commissions. His last mural, which he could not turn down because of the attractive fee, was the largest he ever did. On July 2, 1917, Edgar signed a contract with Holsag and Company of Chicago to paint a continuous set of decorative murals for the corridors of all eleven floors of the new Congress Hotel on Chicago's Michigan Avenue. Immediately after signing the agreement, the Paynes gave up their Chicago studio and moved to Tropico (now Glendale) California where Edgar enlisted the help of his friends, Peter Neilson, Jack Wilkinson Smith, and F. Grayson Sayre. Of these, Jack Smith had, like Edgar, come from a background of commercial scene painting, having worked for Gardner Symons on the window settings for several of Chicago's large department stores.[47]

Conrad Buff, a Swiss-born California artist, heard that Edgar was looking for a helper to work on a big mural project, and he applied for the job. He recalled, many years later, that he was hired at the very fair wage of three and a half dollars a day, but before the project was finished, Edgar had raised him to five dollars a day.

According to Buff's memoirs, "Payne rented a piano factory in Tropico with two floors. We built racks there to stretch canvas . . . I stretched canvases on long stretchers and Payne would come and make out the dimensions for each picture . . . I painted the sky and the clouds. He outlined the mountains . . . Jack Wilkinson Smith, who was the landscape painter and Payne himself painted the foreground, the flowers and everything and Peter Nielson who was the decorator on flowers painted garlands of flowers all over the place. Then Sayre who had been an illustrator was trained to help on the foreground.

"The five of us worked all summer there," Buff's account continues. "We painted yards and yards and yards of scenery. Every time a rack was finished we rolled it up and sent it to Chicago . . . We got along fine."[48]

Apparently Elsie did none of the painting, but she kept track of the dimensions from the blue prints, and was very proud that when it was all delivered, there were only a few feet left over. The mammoth project took four concentrated months, with the artists covering nearly eleven thousand square yards of the muslin and using up ten thousand pounds of white lead.

There is now no known photograph of these murals, and no complete original sketch; one may have been submitted, but the closest item that remains is a *Decorative Landscape Panel,* admittedly incomplete, that Elsie exhibited as the sketch for the project at the Laguna Beach Art Association, in August 1947, and at the Bowers Museum in February 1948. Since Edgar exhibited five various "Decorative Panels" at the Art Institute of Chicago from 1913 through 1917, these had pretty well advertised his capabilities and interest in such work. In any event Edgar added to the mural some elements that were uncharacteristic of his work but fashionable at the time, such as stone urns and balustrades. His experience in painting stage scenery and commercial backdrops stood him in good stead again, for the purpose of the picture was to provide background decoration rather than to focus on a single pictorial idea. Such background art was not uncommon at the time, for it was used by artists and decorators to lend a note of stylish elegance to interior architecture. And Edgar was expert at adapting his flair for capturing nature in a vivid and seemingly spontaneous moment to a more subdued and frankly ornamental interpretation of the out-of-door scene.

When the Congress Hotel project was finished, the artists all took off for Laguna Beach to paint and sketch there. Edgar first rented a small rustic cottage named "Indiana" (the Sayre's nearby cottage was named "Illinois"), and also a store on Glenneyre Street to serve as a studio. Before they left Glendale, Edgar and Conrad Buff had become good friends and Edgar offered Buff a different kind of job. " 'I am going to build a house in Laguna Beach,' " he told Buff. " 'If you want to come down and cook for us I can give you a little house and you can live with us.' I thought that was wonderful," Buff recalled. The Paynes first rented house "had a garden house that he [Edgar] fixed up for me to sleep in. So I had a house . . . and all I had to do was cook breakfast and dinner for them and then I could paint for the rest of the day. Peter Nielson came down too . . . We sketched all day long and in the evening I cooked. Then he [Edgar] built his new house and he asked me to paint the house on the outside."[48]

What Buff did not know about the sleeping and cooking arrangements was the Edgar had not consulted Elsie at all. She had wanted to have the small studio for herself, and would have been quite willing to do the cooking in return for it. But she said nothing, because as she says in her biographical notes, "I was not consulted until the arrangements were all made, then I was Told. But I said nothing as Edgar thought he was doing something great in relieving me of the cooking."[49]

Regardless of Elsie's hidden feelings about the small studio, the Laguna period which begins at this time was to be a very happy one for them all.

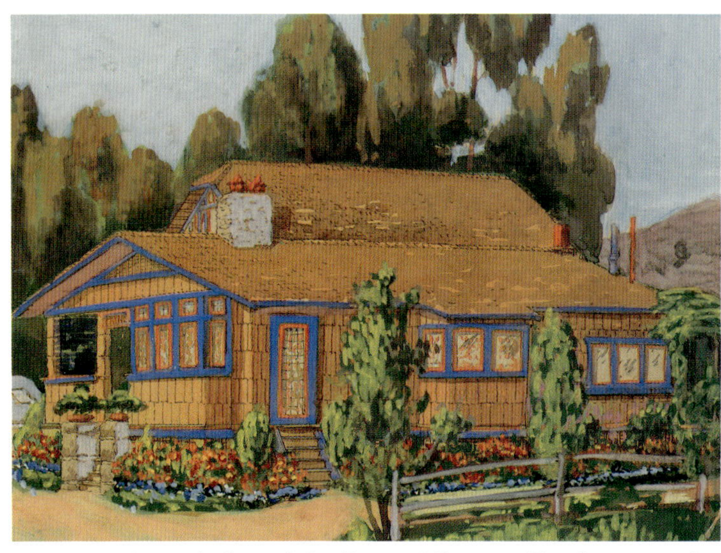

Fig. 3.14. A rendering of the Paynes' Laguna Beach cottage by an unknown artist.

Chapter 4: Laguna Beach

The Laguna Beach to which the Paynes moved from Glendale after the Congress Hotel murals were finished was an ideal spot for their home. Its climate was mild almost the year round and perfect for out-of-door sketching. The surrounding area was well known for its scenic beauty; and its vast sweep of beach, its rocky headlands and quiet coves, its nearby groves of sycamore and eucalyptus, and its deep, shadowy canyon that cut through the hills to reach the sea, all seemed to have been created for the artist's brush. Edgar and Elsie were among a number of painters who were attracted to the rather isolated little beach town. Already living in Laguna were Anna Althea Hills and William Wendt and his wife, the sculptor Julia Bracken Wendt. Evelyn remembered finding the latter fixing the roof, and William cooking the dinner to which they were invited. From Elsie's notes:

> "There was an interesting group down there that winter. The very serious Conrad Buff, the debonair Jack Wilkinson Smith — Elmer Wachtell of the sardonic wit who a few years later died of indigestion while on a sketching trip in Mexico. The genial William Griffith [and] Cuprien the self-sufficient and picturesque. In the mainstreet was a rough wood moving picture house, an ice cream parlor, and a bowling alley under a tent. We used to all come there of evenings to bowl. Elmer Wachtell christened it 'The Gilded Palace of Vice'. On Friday evenings a picture was shown and the whole town turned out."[50]

And it was here in 1918 that Edgar and Elsie bought and then extensively remodelled a studio home at 506 Glenneyre with some of the proceeds of the Congress hotel murals. When finished, the cottage was a modest brown shingle structure with a blue and yellow-orange trim, a color scheme that Elsie repeated in the calendulas and bachelor buttons she planted around the house. She also planted a chayote vine to grow over the pergola. The vine not only pleased the eye but the palate as well, since the fruit could be added to the dinner table, especially when Edgar brought unexpected guests home to dinner.

The large studio was the most important room in the house. It was usually a clutter of paintings, painting gear, and art objects. Some of the furniture was made by Edgar — some rough, some finely carved. Santa Clara and Nampeyo bowls held spiky bouquets of paint brushes. A handsome paisley shawl and India prints could be thrown over stacks of sketches and art magazines. A snakeskin hung on the wall, one of the largest of the many rattlesnakes Edgar had killed on sketching trips. He long told a story on himself — of how he had once looked and looked for a rattlesnake in the yard, when it was the snakeskin near the door doing the rattling.

The living room was decorated by Elsie, and included a large rug that she had finger woven in "basket weave" or plain twill, using some of the two miles of eight-inch-wide strips of muslin left over from the Congress murals. These she dyed in batches obtaining a number of shades of lavender and "old gold" (chartreuse). The bentwood furniture of the room was painted to match, and the walls stippled in the same colors. The rustic look, so much a part of the esthetic of art colonies of the time, was enhanced by a fieldstone fireplace with a bearskin rug in front of it. The house was much admired by fellow artists, and all three Paynes were fond of it.

Before the house was finished, Edgar had rented a small store that he used as a studio, and which later became a frame shop. From the earliest times Edgar had made many of his own frames, and he later taught the business to others. In Laguna the first was Harold Weaver, who preferred to be called Buck. He was a young Englishman who had been a jockey and had made his way to America to become a cowboy and see the world. About 1917 he drifted into Laguna, where Edgar Payne taught him framing. Buck turned out to be a fine craftsman, and took over the frame business, making carved and gold leaf frames that were highly esteemed.

Edgar had known Laguna Beach since his first visit in 1909,[51] and his painting *Laguna Beach Coast, 1911* (Fig. 4.01) expresses his love of its expansive sweep of shore, its golden sand and deep blue waters. Laguna was still a rather remote and isolated place in 1911 and in Edgar's picture there are only a few scattered houses on top of the cliff that descends majestically to the water's edge. It is a loving portrait by a young artist of a young place just on the edge of discovery, before its natural beauty drew so many others to the site that it lost its frontier freshness.

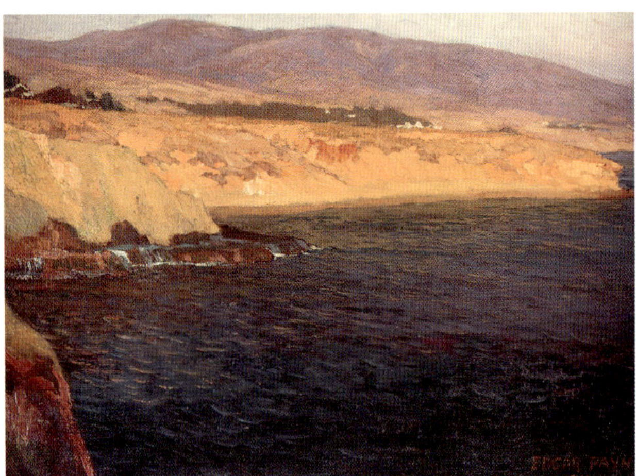

Fig. 4.01. Laguna Beach Coast, 1911, by EAP.

When the Paynes moved to Laguna Beach in 1917, they joined, as already noted, a community of artists who had either established residence there or were frequent visitors to the place both for its scenic beauties as well as social attraction of fellow artists. The community interests did not ignore the entry of the United States into World War I, and there was a great deal of patriotic fervor and anxiety. Edgar's younger brother Alonzo and their artist friend Irwin Myers were at the front, so there was personal concern. Elsie was very active in Red Cross work with other women and conscientiously saved in all the recommended ways. The Paynes were the prime movers in the stimulation of community artistic cooperation, resulting in the establishment of the Art Gallery and then the Laguna Beach Art Association. These projects provided some escape from the tension of the war.

It was Edgar who conceived the idea of using the old community house, or pavilion, for a meeting place and gallery, and he secured permission for the artists to use it.[52] Set in the midst of what was to become an eucalyptus grove, across from the general store and post office, the place had originally served as a dance hall on Saturday nights, and a Sunday School the next morning. It had deteriorated, though, into a storage area for the old frame Laguna Beach Hotel next door.[53] A collection was taken up among the artists in the town, and the old pavilion was cleared and cleaned, electric lights installed, the walls covered with grey building paper and the furniture painted to match. The windows were taken out and set into the roof to make a skylight and window openings closed up. When they finished the renovation, the space, though spare in the interior, was clean and neat and the grey walls served as a perfect counterfoil to the bright pictures of the Laguna Beach artists.[54] It opened with the artists' first exhibition on July 17,1918, and a sign with Elsie's lettering stood in front. (Fig. 4.02)

The Laguna Beach Art Gallery immediately proved a highly successful enterprise, with 300 visitors signing the guest book at the first exhibition, and 2,000 the first month.[56] Clearly an organization was needed, and on August 15th the organizational meeting of the Laguna Beach Art Association was held at the Payne home. Its purpose was the advancing of public knowledge and interest in art, fostering cooperation between artist and public, and perhaps most importantly, maintaining a permanent gallery for the exhibition

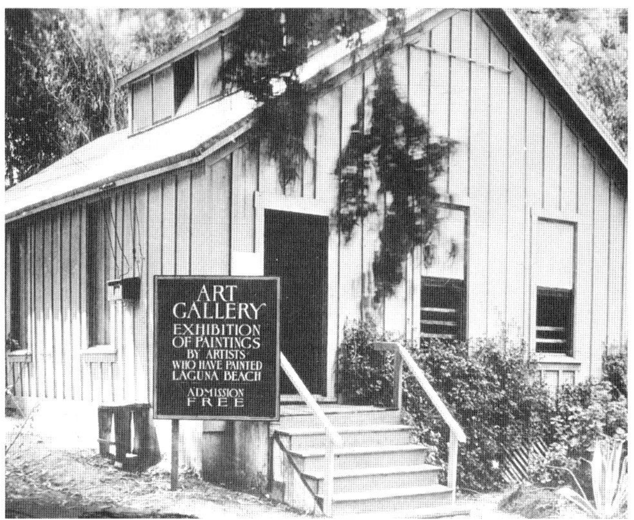

Fig. 4.02. The Early Laguna Gallery with Elsie's sign.

and sale of the artists' work. Anyone interested, artist or layman, could join the Association for a dollar a year. Edgar Payne was elected first president of the association, and Anna Hills the first vice-president. Also present that evening at the Payne home were Alice Fullerton, Anne Mason, Frank Cuprien, Conway Griffith, Roy Coleman, and Nevada Lindsay. The artists themselves and their wives took turns acting as curator of the gallery, which was open from one to five every afternoon, but as some were more conscientious than others at this duty, it was decided to charge admission and pay a regular curator. On Saturday evenings there would be a reception and the whole town and their guests (as Elsie said, when you live at the beach you have plenty of guests) would turn out to see the latest work displayed in the gallery and be entertained by visiting musicians and others who donated their talents to the association.

Of the 150 founding members, 35 were artists — a roster of Southern California plein air painters.[55] The Association was incorporated as a non-profit corporation in 1920, and prospered and continued to attract new members. In little more than a decade the community possessed one of the largest artist colonies in the United States, and the Laguna Beach Art Association had some 700 members, of whom 180 were professional artists.[56] Indeed the association and its Gallery became so well known that they began to run out of space. Edgar had traded a painting to the architect Myron Hunt for a sketch plan of a new multipurpose center, but this early idea was not implemented.[57] Eventually a committee was elected to find a new site for a gallery. Local property owners sold them the land where the present Museum is located for $2,000 — a half price for those days — and construction of a new gallery began in August 1928. Designed by the prominent architectural firm of Myron Hunt and H.C. Chambers of Los Angeles, it was opened to the public on February 16, 1929.[56]

Busy as she was, Elsie still found time to devote to creative work. In Chicago she had started modeling small figurines, and she continued this work in Laguna Beach. She said later that modeling with plasticene was more easily left and taken up again than painting, a distinct advantage when Evelyn was small. There is very little record of these works, and her daughter believes that some of them were sold with reproduction rights to manufacturers of bookends and the like. Some done in Europe were cast in bronze. The only ones still known are plaster casts in poor condition, believed to have been done in the Laguna period. Fig. 4.03 is a drawing of one of these, an incense burner in the form of the Fisherman and the Jinni.

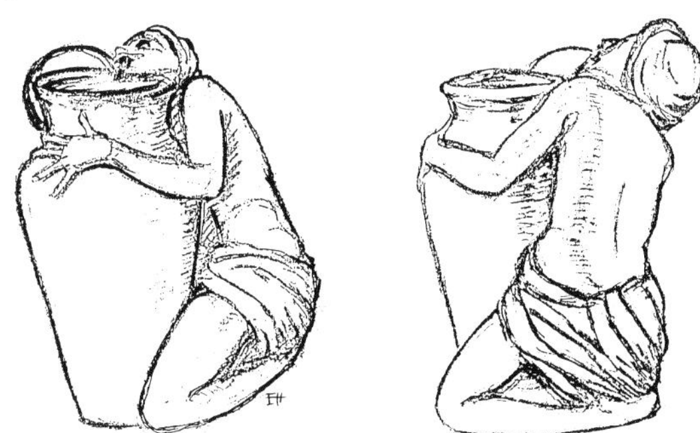

Fig. 4.03. The Fisherman and the Jinni, by EPP.

During the period they lived in Laguna Beach, the Paynes began their many High Sierra summer sketching trips to the higher peaks and remote areas of the Sierra Nevada range that can be reached from the east. Where there were roads, usually narrow and unpaved, the trip would be entirely by car, to places like Tioga Pass and

Mammoth Lakes, but in many cases the car would have to be left at one of the little towns in Owens Valley, and a pack train hired to get to places such as up Big Pine or Bishop Creek. Later, as the roads extended farther into the mountains, with lodges and the pack stations near the end of the road, the all-day pack trips became shorter, and it was easier to reach the highest elevations in the remote regions that Edgar loved.

The family became known to many of the packers working out of places near Big Pine, Independence, or Bishop. Two of the men who often took Edgar in and up Bishop Creek, George Wilson and John Schober, were also lovers of the High Sierra country. They had even lugged heavy five-gallon cans of hatchling trout long distances to stock the higher lakes, all on their own.[58] Later in the 30's they built a stone cairn and named one such lake "Payne Lake" because Edgar had painted it, or in the area, so often (Fig. 4.04).

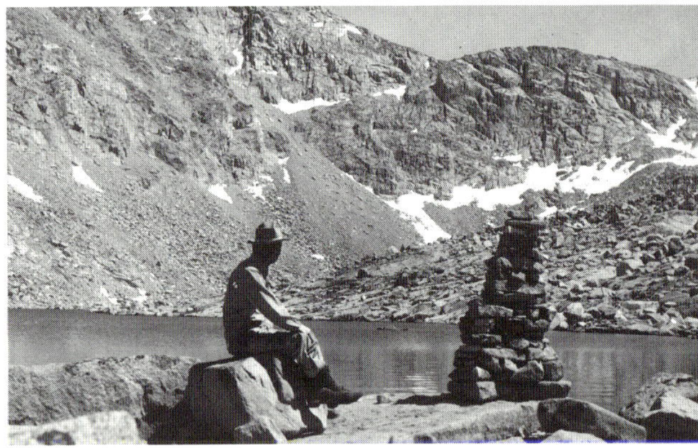

Fig. 4.04. Payne Lake and cairn with name.

Situated at 11,216 feet on the south side of Piute Canyon its name was misspelled "Paine" on some maps — a mistake officially corrected in 1986.

All the early sketching trips were family affairs, but as Elsie was camp cook and companion for Evelyn, she did not have much time for painting. She did, however, sometimes paint the mountain peaks that were Edgar's specialty, as well as scenes of nature on a smaller scale. As she rarely — almost never — dated a painting, it is difficult to establish a chronology of her work that would follow the development of her style. Nevertheless a Laguna Beach period can probably be assigned to two paintings that offer significant contrasts with Edgar's style. *California Canyon* (Fig. 4.05) and *The Minarets* (Fig. 4.06) are gouache paintings, typically flat and decorative in their depiction of the California landscape. The expressive, sinuous line that traces the contours of the mountains

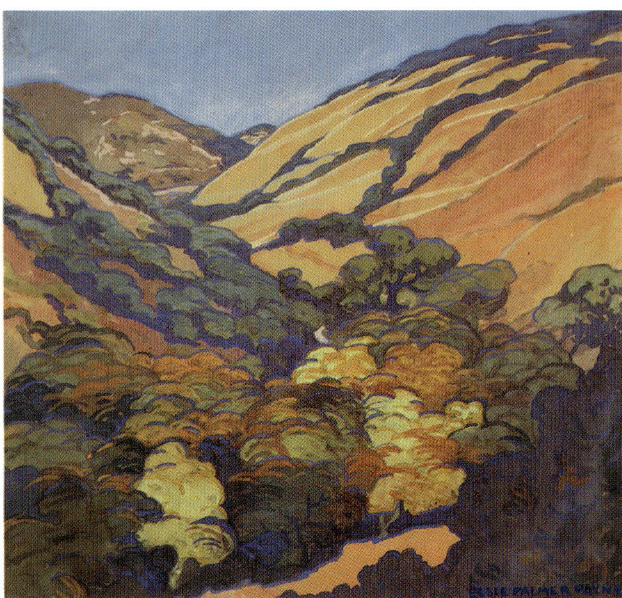

Fig. 4.05. California Canyon, by EPP.

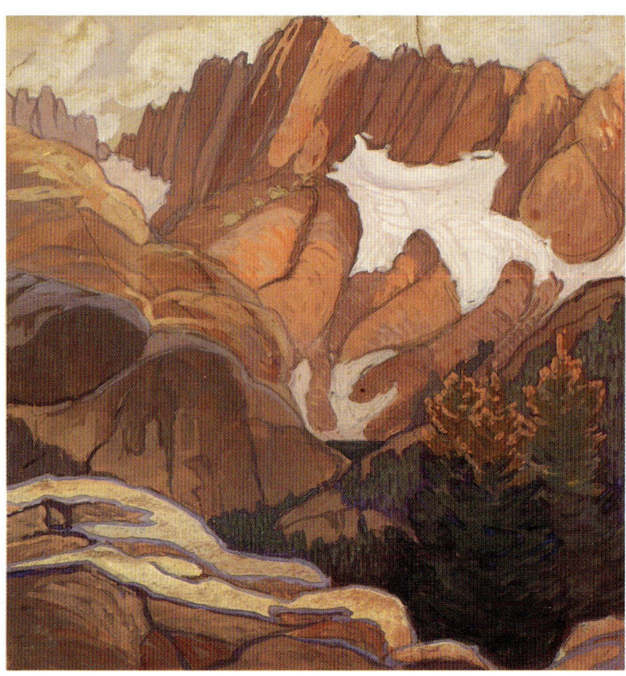

Fig. 4.06. The Minarets, by EPP.

in *The Minarets* and the hills and trees in *California Canyon* are characteristic of her style at this time. So is the patterned effect created by the broad, contrasting color areas. The undulating rhythm of orange golds and dark blue-greens set against a turquoise sky in *California Canyon* captures the hot intensity of the state's lowlands just as a similar design of flat curves and elegant shapes in *The Minarets* describes the cold and rocky peaks of its highlands. Neither painting has anything to do with the use of a broad brush stroke and broken color to suggest the transient effects of light and shadow that was the style of the impressionist artists around her, including Edgar. Elsie's meticulous drawing and flat designs created pictures that, in a sense, summarized the landscape while Edgar's work evoked it. Thus *his* painting of the Sierras near the Minarets (Fig. 4.07) with its sun-tipped crags towering above a cold, blue lake suggests with its quicker brushwork a passing moment in the California mountains. The strong play of light and shadow is heightened by the same combination of vermillion and ultramarine blue to emphasize shadows against the light that he was already using to good effect in other landscapes as well as in some of his marines.

Edgar's paintings of the High Sierras will be treated more fully in Chapter 6, but it was during this period of the early Sierra trips that his fame as a mountain painter was first established, by paintings such as *Fifth Lake, Big Pine Creek* (Fig. 6.06) which is now in the National Academy, and his *Rugged Slopes and Tamaracks.* The latter was exhibited at the 33rd Annual Exhibition of American Oil Paintings and Sculpture at the Art Institute of Chicago, and was awarded the Martin B. Cahn prize on November 3, 1920.[59] Following the Chicago showing, the picture was exhibited on both the east and west coasts, first at the Pennsylvania Academy of Fine Arts[60] and then by the California Art Club in its Western Painters Selected Works traveling exhibition.[61]

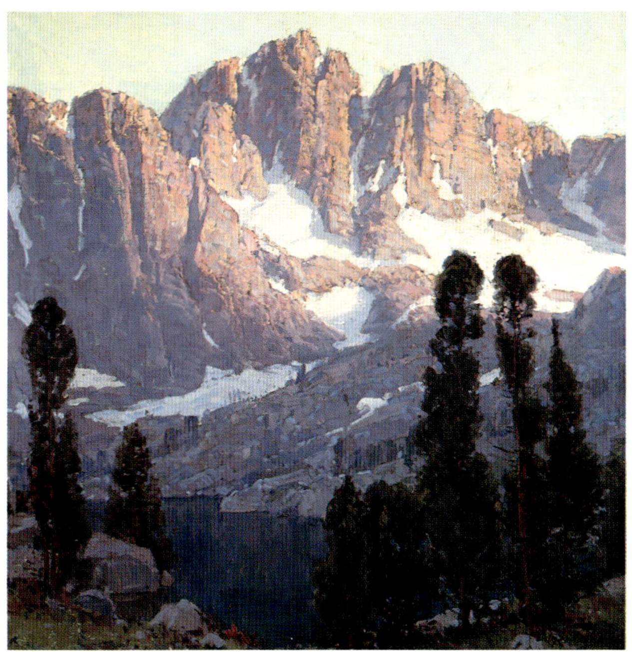

Fig. 4.07. The Minarets, by EAP.

But during this Laguna Beach period marine pictures were almost as important a subject for him as the California mountains. He followed up his success with *The Restless Sea* which he had sold in Chicago, with many more paintings of the

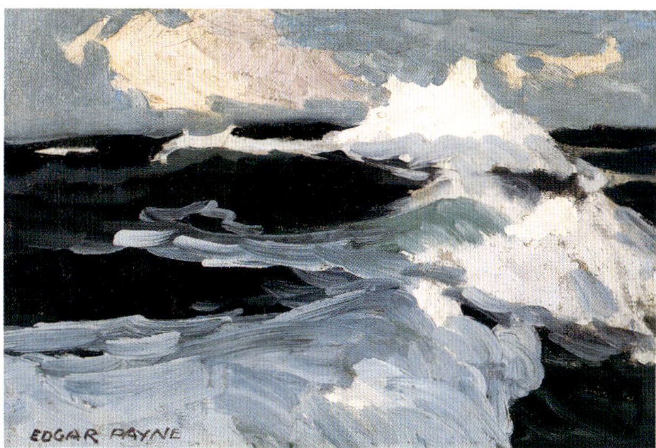

Fig. 4.08. Rhythmic Sea, by EAP.

Pacific coast off Laguna. One of them is the small but delightful *Rhythmic Sea* (Fig. 4.08) in which the churning whitecaps spill over each other with a gay — but controlled — abandon as the moving surf pounds toward the shore. Edgar limited his palette here to tones of creamy white and greenish blues and, in a rather uncharacteristic way, he allowed the seemingly random splash of bursting spray and churning foam to dictate an essentially linear and decorative composition. Perhaps this painting is a rare attempt on Edgar's part to assimilate something of Elsie's flair for decorative line. For Edgar was primarily a "painterly" painter, taking pleasure in the quality of the paint itself as it was applied to the canvas, and frequently using it in a thick impasto for its own textural effect. Nevertheless, he was not oblivious to the importance of line in composition, indeed stressing, in a book he later wrote as a guide to younger artists, *The Composition of Outdoor Painting,* the proper use of linear design. He was aware that one could manipulate "the curve [to] indicate . . . movement or activity and rhythm" and that though the glance will follow the unbroken line, the artist must "create balance and . . . cause the eye to wander slowly over the canvas, pausing temporarily on the main interest and less on the smaller points."[62] Furthermore, he observed that since, in marine subject, shape and position change so rapidly, "occur[ing] even between the glance and the mark on the surface," that "depicting them is practically a memory proposition" and one must therefore learn typical aspects of marine views before selecting the main point of interest. This main interest can, in fact, be "slowly moving foam on the top of boiling water . . . [or] a bit of spray lightened by sunlight" or even the vibrant pattern of the foam itself as it contrasts with the heavy mass of the sea water from which it erupts.[63]

A similar contrast, this time between the light areas of the breaking sea and the rocks in the foreground, forming opposing areas of dark, is to be seen in his small *Marine* (Fig. 4.09). Perhaps less playful than *Rhythmic Sea*, it is more typical of Edgar's marines and exploits his perception that "since the eye sees the quickest motion first" it is best to select, as the main point of interest, breaking waves and spray set against darker rocks, thus offering the greatest contrast and more interest to the movement.

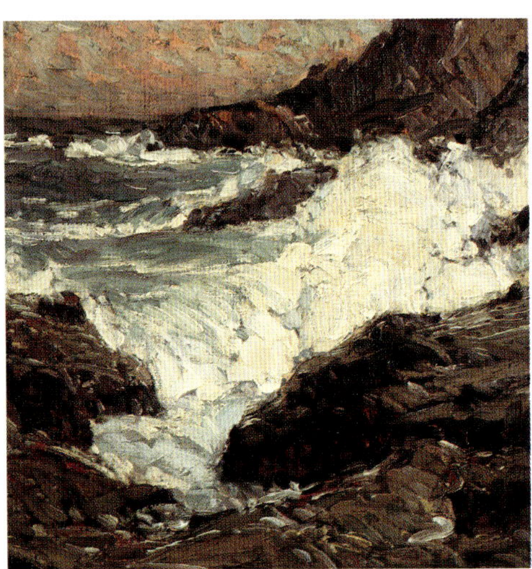

Fig. 4.09. Marine, by EAP.

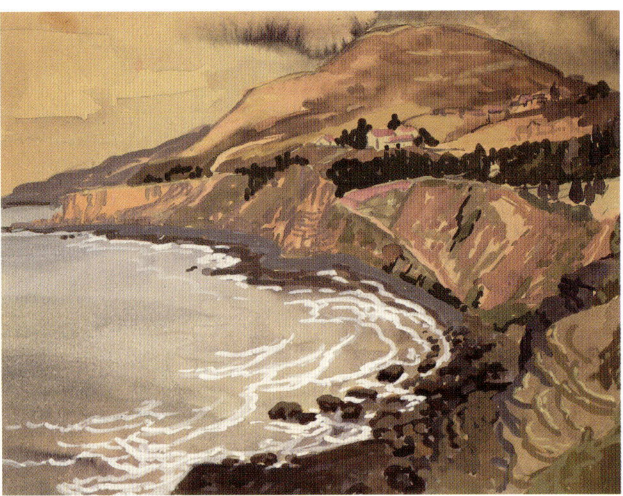

Fig. 4.10. Laguna Coast, by EPP.

Elsie's version, on the other hand, in *Laguna Coast* (Fig. 4.10) uses an unusual palette of greens, yellows, and a pinkish lavender and concentrates frankly and unequivocably on the ornamental patterns created by the repeating curves of hills, rocks, surf, and bay. Her vision, as ever, was more abstract than Edgar's and in her hands pictoral reality was described through decorative qualities that conveyed the *feeling* of the scene. Thus her paintings are frequently enjoyable more for their abstract arrangement of line and pattern than for their literal truth to nature.

The groves of sycamore and eucalyptus in Southern California also attracted the attention of the two artists and was again reflected in their individual pictorial styles. Edgar observed that in painting trees, the variety of species and even variations within the same species, gave the artist an unlimited field in which to study their growth. He felt that trees "are living, growing and expanding things that give beauty and rhythm to pictures." Furthermore, their texture adds a unique quality of contrast in their substance since, he commented, the trunks and large limbs are

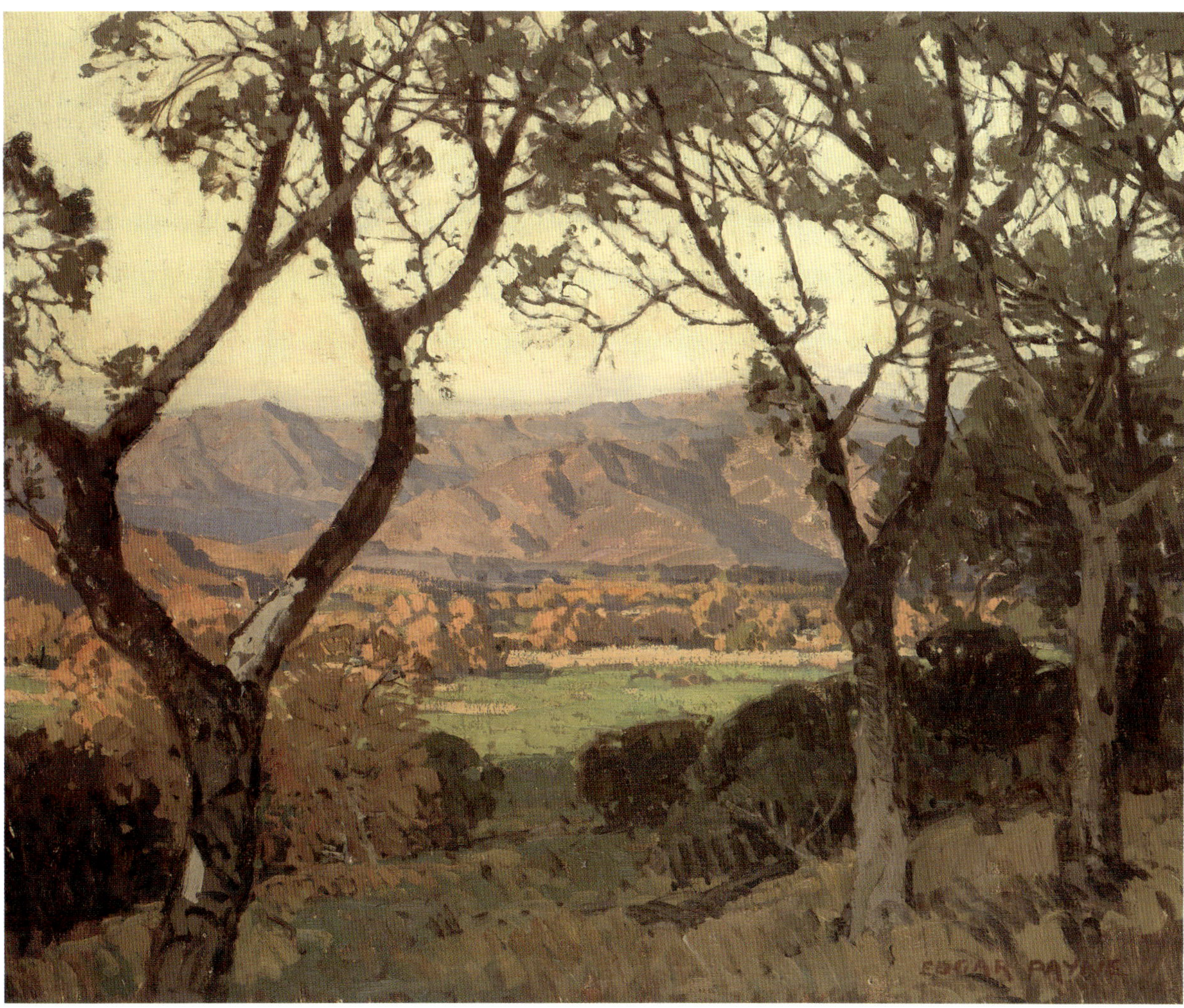

Fig. 4.11. Vista through Sycamores, Ojai Valley, by EAP.

rigid and solid while the fluffy leaves and twigs provide movement.[64]

Vista Through Sycamores, Ojai Valley, (Fig. 4.11) a painting of about 1918, describes the characteristic twisting trunks and patchy foliage of sycamores as they frame the sunny vista of Ojai Valley. Stability and balance are given the composition through the vertical direction of the roughly textured trees in the foreground against the smooth, horizontal planes of the distant valley and background hills. Edgar followed in this painting his own advice that the placement of trees must seem casual but that their essential characteristics must always be maintained. If that is done, then they "may be enlarged, reduced, or their appearance changed without creating disrespect for nature's truths."[64] Indeed, the contrast between the shadowy foreground and bright sunlight beyond illustrates the "glare esthetic" of American Impressionist painting, described as strong tonal contrasts in which intense daylight achieves the effect of glare from surfaces that seem to reflect it. The darker shadows of clearly defined objects are cast against this brightness, thus intensifying color and light without dissolving form.[65]

In contrast to this approach, Elsie's painting, *Eucalyptus Trees* (Fig. 4.12) is, again, a characteristically flat and decorative design, conceived in terms of the curvilinear forms of the massed foliage that is repeated in various permutations of green, and contrasting with the vertical white

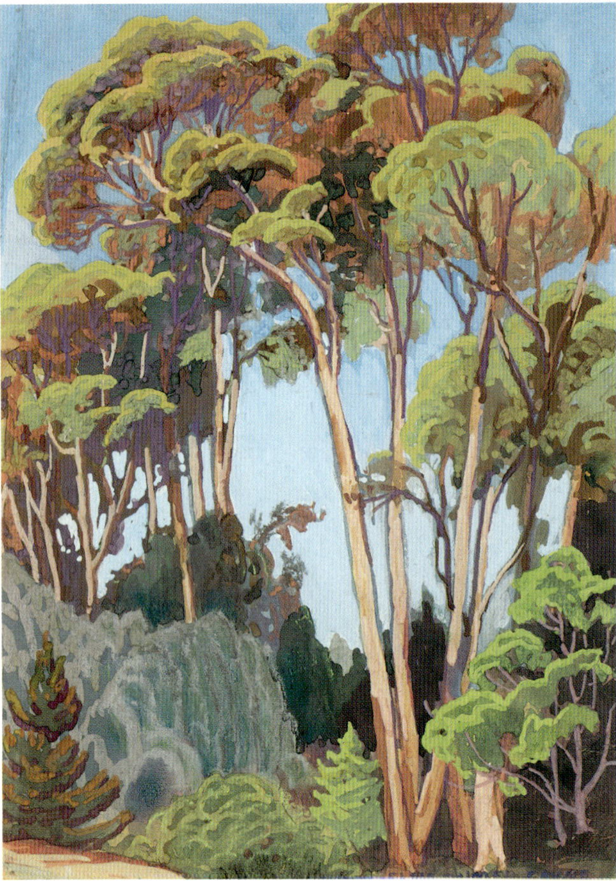

Fig. 4.12. Eucalyptus Trees, by EPP.

trunks of the trees. In this period particularly she saw the out of door scene as a continuous pattern of interesting shapes while her husband saw it as a vast space in which form described perspective and provided the illusion of three dimensional reality.

By late 1920 Edgar's term as President of the Laguna Beach Art Association was over. Laguna was at that time still a rather remote place so the family, following their more usual pattern, moved to Los Angeles. The pattern of summer field work and winter studio work was not haphazard, but a rational life-style. Summer was the time of field work and vacation fun; winter was the time of converting sketches to salable merchandise and of business activities. The business part of being an artist was focussed on the galleries in the cities, and the Paynes' winter quarters were typically in the larger cities. This probably was an important reason for abandoning Laguna as a base. Earl Stendahl, one of Edgar's major dealers, may have encouraged this move, for he was steadily showing Edgar's work. As manager of the Cannell and Chaffin Gallery in Los Angeles, Stendahl had already been promoting Edgar's work, and when he opened his own gallery in the Ambassador in 1921, he continued to handle Edgar's paintings and give him major exhibitions. Later on, he opened branches, or "salons" of the Stendahl Galleries in the Hotel del Coronado, the Vista del Arroyo, the Maryland and the Huntington Hotels, where he continued to show and sell Edgar's pictures. As the galleries major clients in the twenties were winter visitors from the East and Midwest, Edgar's work continued to spread beyond the Los Angeles area through this outlet as well as other exhibitions throughout the country.

Edgar's paintings were selling well at this time. The Southwest Museum in Huntington Park, California, though it was a museum devoted mainly to the art and culture of the American Indian, also had for many years a number of Payne paintings of the High Sierras in its library. In 1921 it awarded Edgar its first prize for *Topmost Crags,* a Sierra mountain scene of exceptional power and majesty.

Edgar was also gaining attention through the California Art Club which in 1926, was to elect him to a term as president. Meanwhile, of course, he was continuing to exhibit and sell his pictures through the Laguna Beach Art Gallery.

By the spring of 1922 he and Elsie were planning the realization of a dream they both had long cherished, that of travelling to Europe to paint its varied scenery and study the art treasures in its many museums. With careful limitations on spending, and the proceeds of the recent successful exhibitions, they decided that the time had come to exchange, at least temporarily, the New World for the Old.

At the end of May, 1922, there was a big send-off banquet at the Stendahl Galleries.[66] It was supposed to be a surprise for Edgar, but he found out about it, and quickly painted, and framed in gilt frames, forty miniature land and seascapes as party favors for each of the invited guests. These were the cream of Los Angeles art patronage as well as a number of Edgar's artist friends. The party was a stag affair, but Edgar painted two more of the tiny but complete paintings for Evelyn and Elsie, which still exist.

Two features of the affair are noteworthy: first, it included a speech, broadcast over radio KHJ by Fred Hogue, of lavish praise and good wishes for Edgar, likening his paintings to the poetry of the ancient Greek bard Homer. And second, the sale of one of Edgar's paintings was announced, bought as a gift for the Southwest Museum by James Slauson. This patron was so intrigued by the miniature favors that when he found that there were three extra, he promptly wrote a check for them and gave it to Edgar, who in turn gave it to Stendahl to pay for the whole banquet.[67]

The next morning the family set off for a two year trip to Europe, to paint, as Edgar remarked, "all the paintable things there." "If anybody can cover the ground in that period, Edgar can," wrote the art critic Vandyck Brown.[66]

A brief stopover in Chicago was extended when Evelyn came down with whooping cough. So there was time for a brief exhibition from July 2nd to 10th, in their friend Grace Hickox's studio in the Fine Arts Building on Michigan Avenue. Finally, all three Paynes embarked from New York in mid-July for what was to be the most significant adventure of their lives. Though they later visited Europe again briefly in the summer of 1928, the two-year trip of 1922-24 provided the experiences and fondly remembered scenes that nourished the artists' imaginations for years to come.

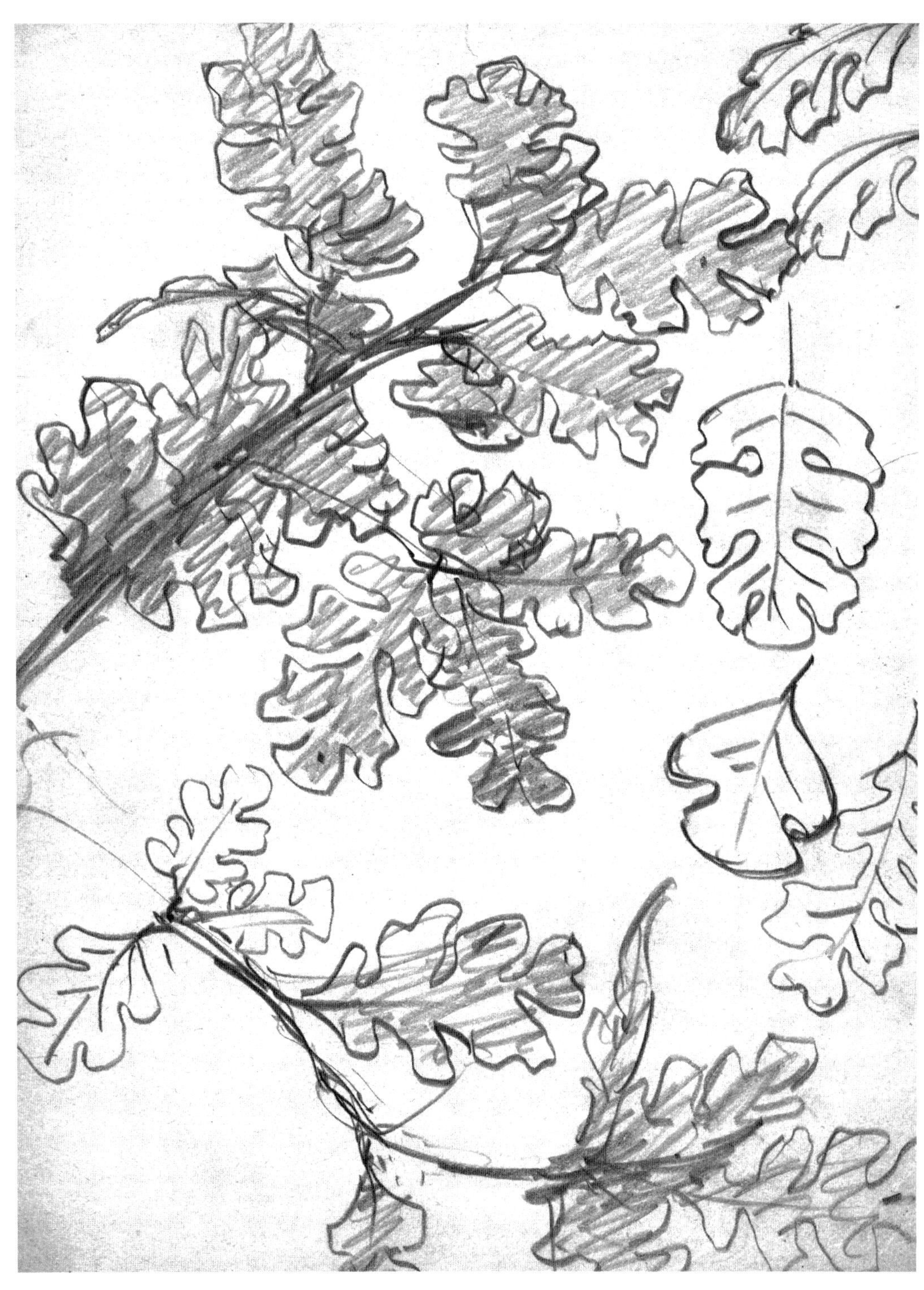

Chapter 5: Europe

The Paynes' first stop in Europe when they arrived in 1922 was Paris, a mecca for the several generations of American artists who had preceded them on such a pilgrimage. It was not only the many museums with their vast collections of the old master paintings that attracted them but the presence of many like minded artists from all over the world, especially those who, like Edgar, admired the French Impressionist masters of the late nineteenth century. Edgar, though generally rather shy, must nevertheless have enjoyed the stimulation of contact with other artists, as well as that provided by concentrated study of the art of the past. And Elsie too, less retiring and equally devoted to the study of art, was just as enthusiastic as her husband at her first exposure to all that Paris had to offer. The museum and gallery visits were very much a family affair, for the Paynes took their eight-year-old daughter with them, where she too learned about the great art of the past and was encouraged to think for herself about their styles and meaning. Elsie was a born teacher and the child could have had no better mentor in her early introduction to art, which eventually emerged in her professional focus on the anthropology of art.

The picturesque towns nearby also drew the two artists, especially after Edgar bought an unused U.S. Army surplus model T and began to drive the family on a number of trips outside of Paris. On one such excursion they went to Chartres, where Elsie painted the famous Gothic cathedral (Fig. 5.01), not as the main subject of the painting but as a decorative backdrop to a pastoral scene with a shepherd and his flock. She was far more concerned here with developing the smooth pattern of receding planes provided by the white sheep in the foreground and the more distant red roofs of the town than she was with paying pictorial tribute to one of the major monuments of medieval France.

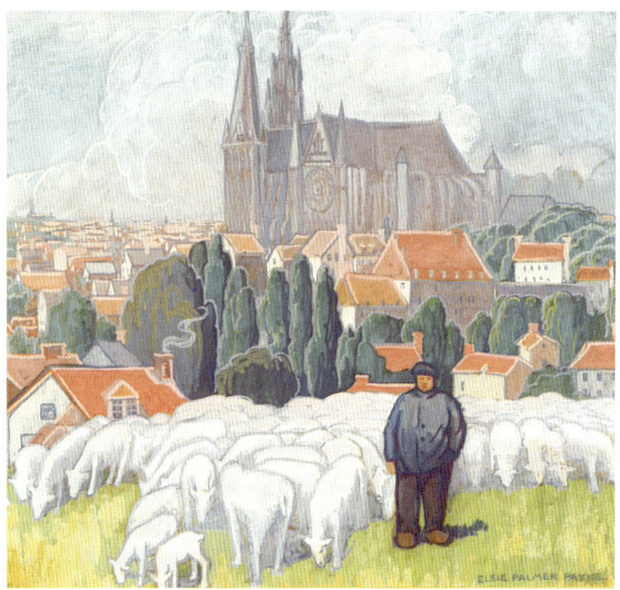

Fig. 5.01. Chartres, by EPP.

In September 1922 the Paynes left Paris, on a trip south that was to last nearly a year. They visited the battlefields of World War I and then drove, with frequent stops and detours for sketching, down the Chamonix Valley through the Haute Savoie and French Alps towards Marseilles. Eventually they reached Mentone on the French Riviera where they stayed for a month, sketching the lowland Riviera and admiring the warm glow of the yellow and orange houses against the blue-green of the Mediterranean Sea.[68] Finally in November the Paynes crossed into

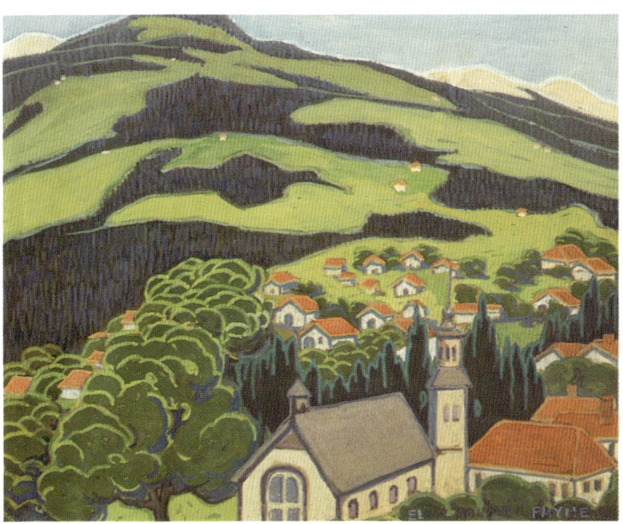

Fig. 5.02. Alpine Pattern, by EPP.

Italy, and settled in Rome for the winter months.

Both Edgar's sketches of the French Alps, and the final paintings based on such sketches give a far more dramatic view of the mountains than Elsie's. Her *Alpine Pattern* (Fig. 5.02) from this period reveals a fresh, almost naive vision of a small town whose cottages nestle comfortably around the church situated in a green and gentle valley. As in *Chartres*, the red roofs create a patchwork effect set against the deep blues and greens of nature. Similarly, her picture of the *French Alps* (Fig. 5.03) traces the curves of hills and glaciers which offer tonal and textural contrast

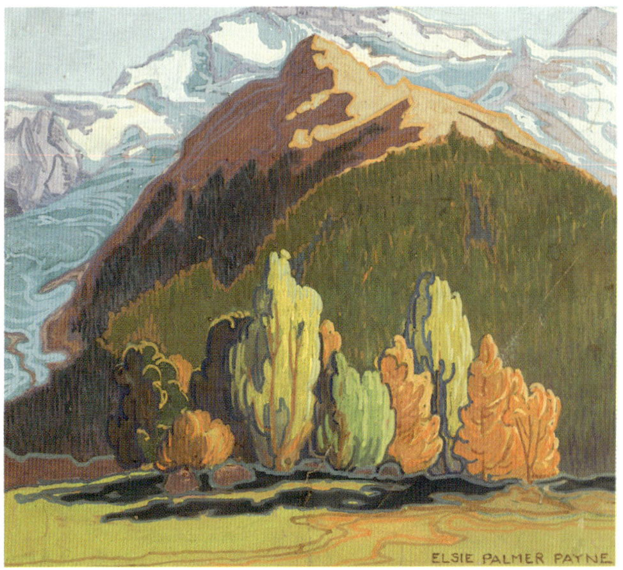

Fig. 5.03. French Alps, by EPP.

with the warm colors of the autumn trees in the foreground, silhouetted against the mountain peaks beyond.

In *Alpine Village* (Fig. 5.04), Edgar's view of the French Alps, we feel the powerful surge of the mountain as it dwarfs the scattered human habitation at its foot. Characteristically, it was painted with a far looser brush than Elsie's and comes much closer to the Impressionist esthetic. Even

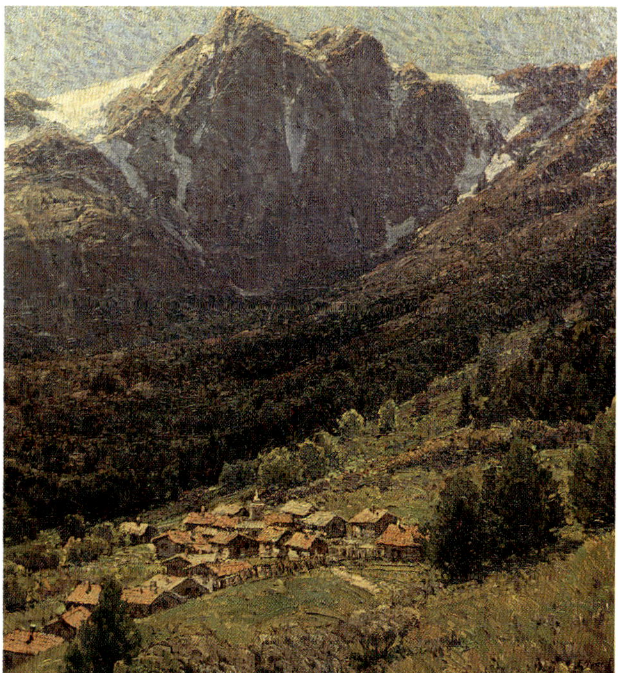

Fig. 5.04. Alpine Village, by EAP.

more so is the second *The Great White Peak* (Fig. 5.05), a painting that clearly demonstrates Edgar's complete mastery of the fluid brush stroke and broken color of Impressionist painting. In this representation of Mt. Blanc, the artist presents a shimmering view of one of the most impressive peaks of the Swiss Alps. In contrast with Elsie's concentration on flat pattern and a controlled design well contained within its frame, Edgar's view is far more expansive, even to the point of creating tension in the pressure of the mountain against the picture's limits. It portrays nature's overwhelming power not through decorative detail but through the artist's fluid brush work, suggesting not only the enormous weight and volume of the mountain mass but also the flow of light and shadow across its transient scene.

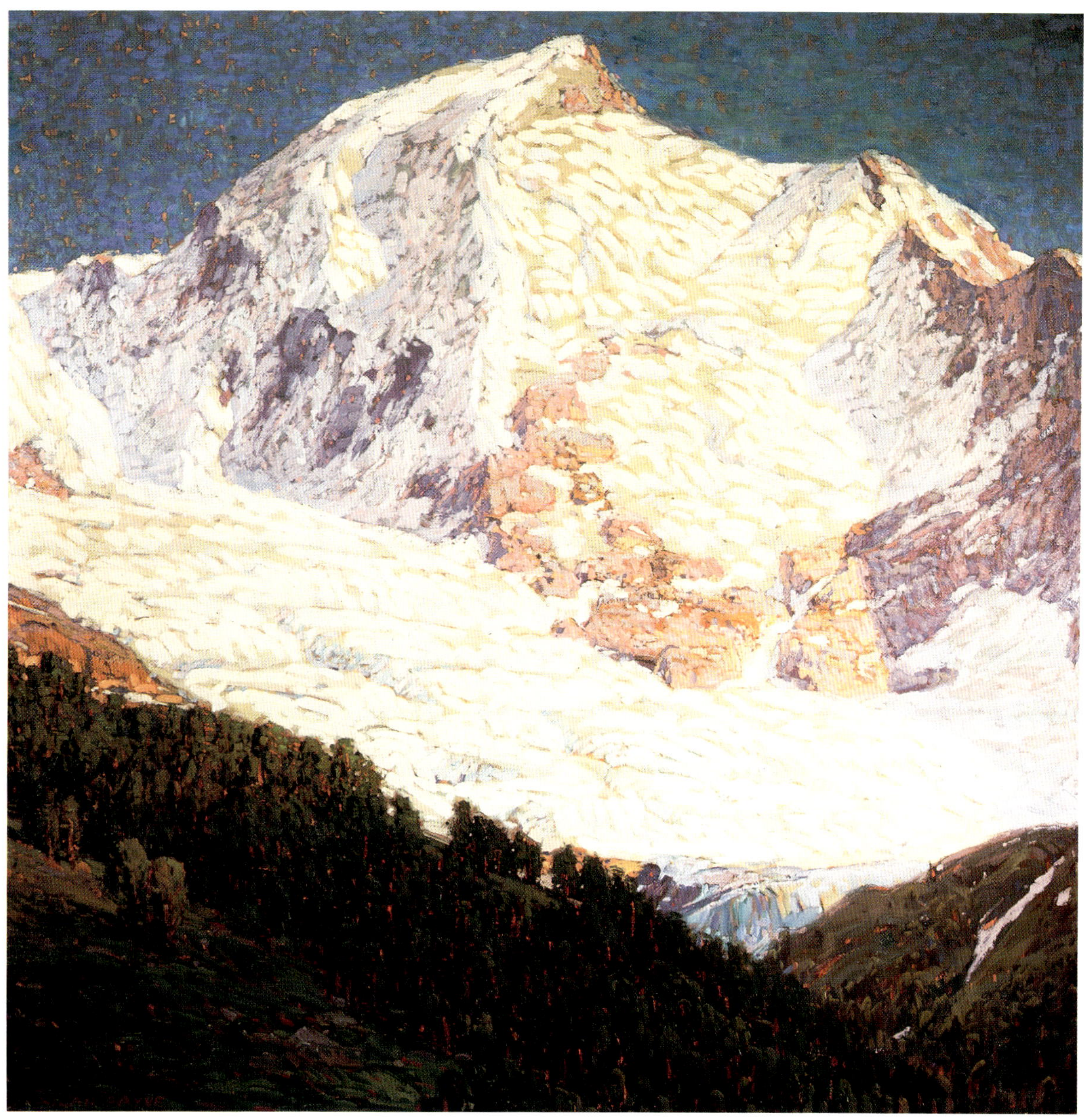

Fig. 5.05. The Great White Peak (#2), by EAP.

As usual Edgar painted these easel paintings in his studio in Rome or Paris during the winter, utilizing the summer field sketches. Elsie's, however, are the actual field sketches. Living in Rome had its advantages for the Payne family, but keeping warm there proved to be something of a challenge. Many years later Elsie said of their winter in the Eternal City that she agreed with Nathaniel Hawthorne who, in the introduction to his book, *The Marble Faun,* wrote that after spending a winter in Rome he determined to spend his winters where winter was a "recognized fact." Elsie described it as "Sunny Italy, with icicles hanging on the fountains and huge marble palaces 'heated' by one little charcoal brazier."[69]

Edgar had rented a studio with a two-bedroom apartment in the Piazza Dante in a large building that had housed the Belgian Academy before World War I. The studio was an immense space, measuring about 45 by 60 feet with only a small pot-bellied stove in one corner to warm it. The owner of the studio was an Italian miniature painter who proved most helpful to the Paynes since he had been to America and spoke English. He assisted them in getting settled and even accompanied Elsie on her first shopping expeditions for groceries and provisions to familiarize her with the idosyncracies of Italian shops. On visiting the studio one day, he was amazed to find that Edgar had purchased wood for the stove, enough to last through the winter, and as there was no storage space, had stacked the wood against the walls the whole length of the studio and even under the furniture. Elsie recounted that, as Europeans only buy wood for one fire at a time, the miniature painter couldn't resist asking what all the wood was for. "We are going to try to keep warm" was Edgar's simple reply. He built a sort of inglenook around the pot-bellied stove and the family more or less lived in it during the winter months.

Edgar and Elsie were proud of the "bargain" they had in their rent since they were paying only $75.00 a month for the studio and apartment. But when Elsie met two Italian journalists and invited them to tea in the hope that they would admire Edgar's paintings and give them a good write up in their journal, she was surprised that they seemed more interested in the apartment, and especially the wood, than they were in Edgar's paintings. When the article about the Paynes and their work did appear, they were even more astonished to read a tirade against "these rich American artists who come over here and pay such exorbitant rents that the Italian artists are tempted to rent their studios, then have no place to paint." Elsie said that "that was a new one on us — we were used to be being patronized in America as 'poor artists' . . . I think artists are a very level headed group," she added, "for they get such adulation one minute and ill bred patronage the next."[70]

Edgar worked through the winter of 1922/23 in the Rome studio. He finished painting the first *The Great White Peak* and shipped it to Paris, where it competed with 7000 other paintings, many by the best-known artists of the day, for inclusion in the 1923 Spring Salon. It not only won the honor of inclusion in the Salon, but was awarded Honorable Mention as well. Later, in 1926, it was exhibited at the Stendahl Gallery in Los Angeles, and was properly described and identified as No. 23 on page 40 of the Stendahl Catalogue.[71] This prize painting, measuring 43 × 43 inches is now in the Ruth Stover Fleming collection of the Newport Harbor High School in Southern California, and has frequently been reproduced.

Edgar occasionally painted more than one version of a scene, the case here. The second painting of *The Great White Peak* (Fig. 5.05) is even larger than the Salon piece, measuring 62 × 62 inches. Though it was also based on the 1922 sketches it was actually painted in Edgar's studio in Paris in 1924. The Stendahl Catalogue misidentifies a photograph on p. 17 as "Edward [sic] . . . working in his Paris studio on the canvas that won for him 'Honorable Mention' at the Salon of 1923," but the laid-in charcoal sketch on the easel is the actual beginning of this second painting. The photograph can be shown to be one of a series taken in 1924, at the time of the Seligmann exhibition, since the other photos of the series all show identical background details, especially in the edges cropped for reproduction. Moreover one of these includes the sculptor Nancy Cox McCormack, who was in and at the 1924 exhibition, but not in Paris much before then. This second, and some say better, painting is in a private collection in Southern California.

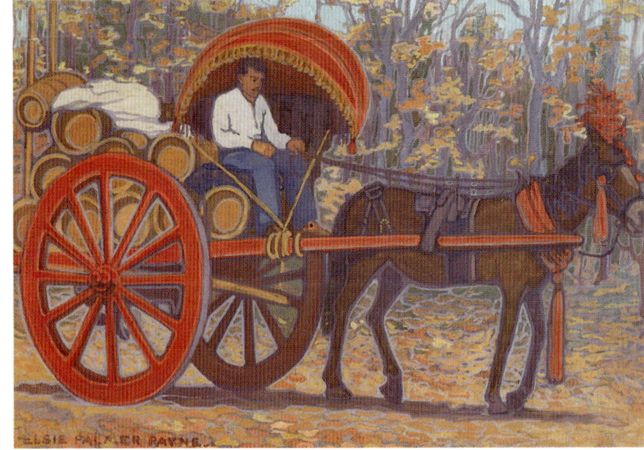

Fig. 5.06. Italian Wine Cart, by EPP.

During the winter Elsie modelled small figurines in clay, as she had done earlier in Laguna Beach. They were vivid miniature sculptures on various themes. The only one from this period whose subject is known is of the woman later painted in her watercolor *A Decent Burial* (Fig. 8.06). Elsie also painted a number of pictures in tempera, one of which is a cheerful description of an *Italian Wine Cart* (Fig. 5.06). The driver's tasselled canopy, the large red wheels of his cart, the wine barrels piled on it, create a pattern of curves and circles which, with the horse's decorative trappings add to a gay and festive mood. Elsie, however, got considerably less exposure of her finished work than Edgar was receiving for his. Indeed five of Edgar's canvases were exhibited at the Rome Biennale that year, and 26 of his paintings were shipped to the Stendahl Galleries in Los Angeles where they were shown and admired in April, 1923.[72]

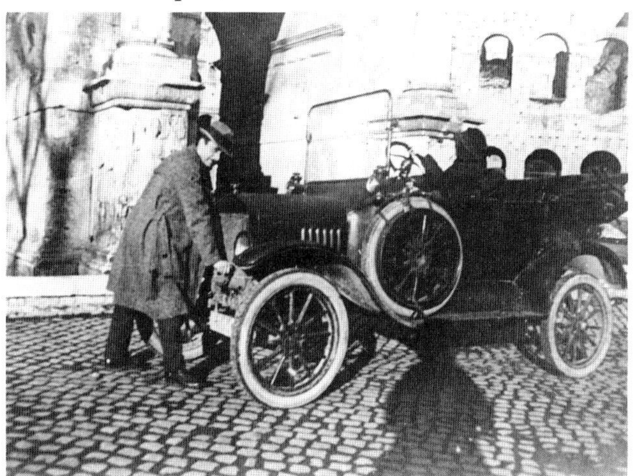

Fig. 5.07. The Payne "flivver" in Rome.

On March 24th the family left Rome for Switzerland, visiting on the way Tivoli, Perugia, Florence, Genoa, and many smaller places, where, as Edgar noted in a letter dated April 15th, "Spaghetti was served, more or less . . . and someone spoke English." Of Florence's Pitti and Uffizi Galleries he was of the opinion that "in spite of the religious subjects, some of these men could *paint,* although, as elsewhere in Europe, most of the paintings are more or less mediocre; about 15 or 20 percent are real works of art."[73]

After finding the mountain passes closed, Edgar loaded the family "flivver" on a train from Domodossola through the Simplon tunnel, the Paynes arriving "in the country of the Swiss . . . among the Alps at last. There is no appeal like the mountains," he wrote, in his element again in Europe's equivalent of the High Sierras. "Up here, among these peaks it is almost unspeakably sublime . . . The interesting peaks," he continued, "are within a radius of fifty miles, which makes it very convenient. I find the Swiss very efficient in everything, and particularly in the arrangement of the mountains."

Swiss efficiency in arranging their landscape for the benefit of the artists resulted again in a number of sketches and studies of their most famous peaks, but not right away. It was still early in the year, and the high altitude too cold for outdoor sketching. The Paynes thought it might be better at a lower altitude, so they drove down the Rhone to Lake Geneva. They found this a pleasant place, but not much warmer, and so, finally, after deciding not to leave Evelyn in school in Geneva, the whole family took the train back to the warmer climate of Italy.

They headed for Venice, that magnet for American artists since the years following the Civil War. Attracted by the city's Mediterranean light and color, the architectural splendor of its Byzantine and Gothic past, and the changing luminescence of its lagoons and canals, these artists would have agreed with William Dean Howells who in *Italian Journeys* of 1867, had declared that "Venice is, and remains, the most beautiful city in the world."

By the end of the nineteenth century, Venice had supplanted even Rome and Florence in drawing the American traveler. And, indeed, the Paynes found that a large group of American artists had already established residence there of varying degrees of permanence. But it was not so much the glory of Venice's many palaces and churches shining golden in the sun, nor the deep, transparent blue of its southern sea and sky that attracted Edgar's brush, as did all of the colorful fishing boats decked out in their ancient rigging tied up at the quays or sailing majestically out to sea.

Nevertheless, one small picture Edgar painted of the City on the Lagoons is evidence of his sensitivity to its special beauty. In contrast to the large and boldly Impressionistic picture of the Matterhorn, this intimate view of Venice (Fig. 5.08) is almost tonalist in its muted color scheme. In subdued tones of purple and blue, the church of Santa Maria della Salute is silhouetted against the light of late afternoon. But the expanse of turquoise water looking across the Guidecca from the Doge's palace, and the dark red sails of the boats dimly seen against the city, provide enough color to avoid true tonalism and bring the picture back to Edgar's more typical Impressionistic style.

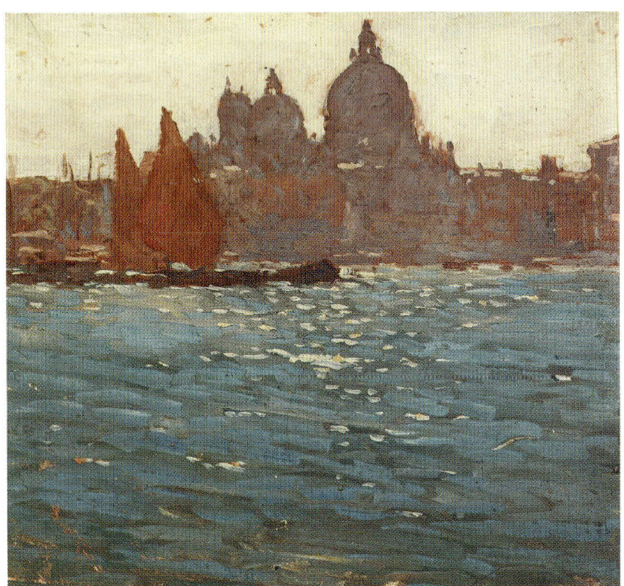

Fig. 5.08. Venice, Santa Maria Salute, by EAP.

Indeed, *Adriatic Cargo Boats Near Venice* (Fig. 5.09), a larger picture painted from sketches made on this trip presents a bolder more dramatic composition, and one that is much more Impressionist in its technique. Here, a bright, slanting light, conveyed through broad strokes of the brush, illuminates the colorful hulls and sun-washed sails strung in time-honored fashion from the diagonal spars of the Venetian lateen rigging. As in many of Edgar's California scenes, there is something here of the "glare esthetic" mentioned above in which intense daylight, portrayed in strong tonal contrasts, achieves the effect of glare from reflecting surfaces. In this case it is the

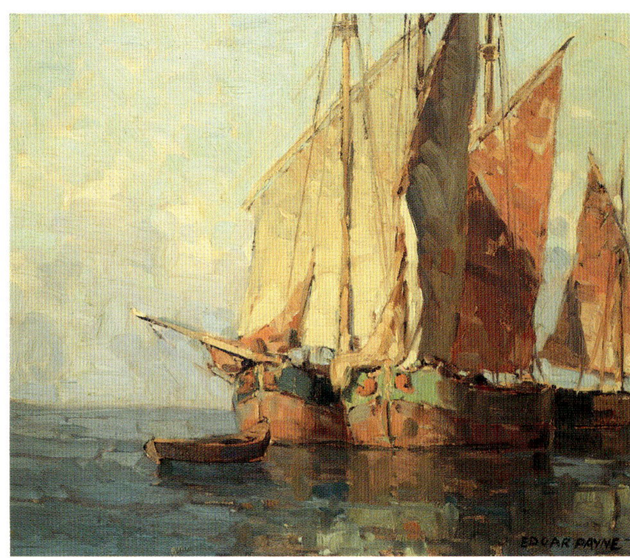

Fig. 5.09. Adriatic Cargo Boats, by EAP.

planes of the multi-hued sails that function as mirrors reflecting the bright sunlight against which other sails cast their shadow thus emphasizing color and light but without dissolving form.[65] Moreover, within the Impressionist vocabulary of a fleeting moment in time, a delicate but firm balance in this off center composition creates a monumental image of the ancient vessels still plying the waters of the Mediterranean Sea.

The Paynes did not, however, stay very long in Venice. After exploring the sights there they took a boat a little farther down the Adriatic to Chioggia, which still retained the look of previous

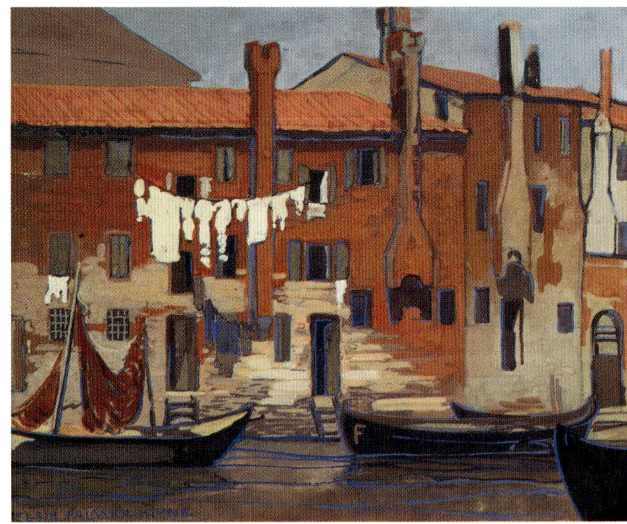

Fig. 5.11. Laundry, Chioggia, by EPP.

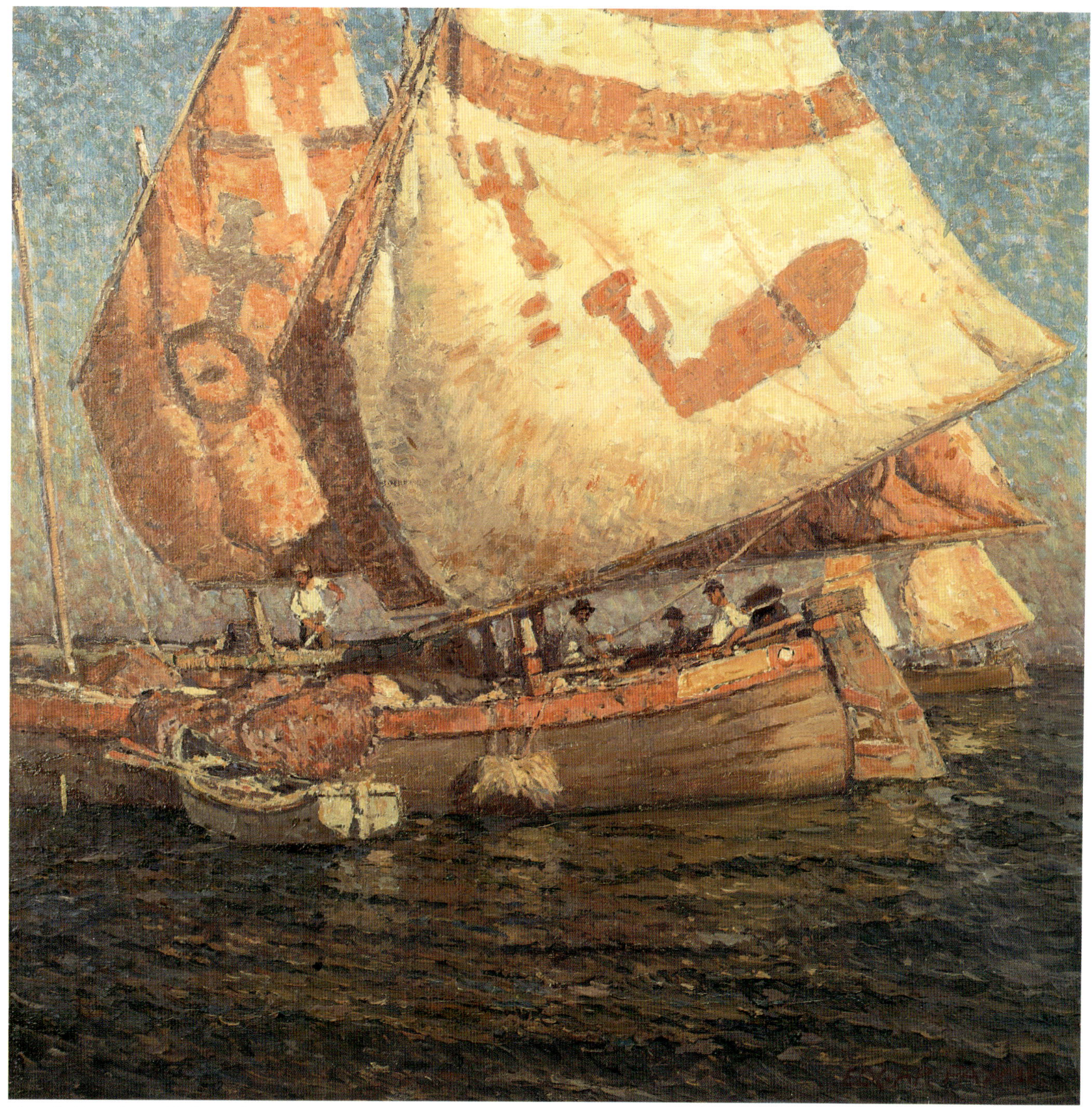

Fig. 5.10. Marco Polo Relic, Adriatic (Thus Did We Sail for the Doge) by EAP.

centuries. There Edgar took an even closer look at the Adriatic fishing boats with their brightly decorated sails and painted hulls. In *Thus Did We Sail for the Doge* (Fig. 5.10), the patterned sails themselves are the subject of the painting as they billow gently above the busy life on the deck. Meanwhile, Elsie typically focused on the genre subjects of the city life around her,[74] observing especially the life of the streets and marketplaces, the often vehement quarrels of the women, and the activity of their children at play. "I like to paint the women's side of life," she later said.[75] *Laundry at Chioggia* (Fig. 5.11) does just that, treating the ordinary household wash like decorative white banners strung across the brick colored facades on the Chioggia quayside. This gouache painting, with its mood of cheerful domesticity reflects the pleasure Elsie took in her new surroundings.

From Chioggia the Paynes returned, via Venice and the trains, to Switzerland, where they travelled and sketched for more than two months in the mountains so efficiently arranged for the artists' convenience. Elsie painted Lake Brienz and other scenes, including all the wildflowers Evelyn found as she roamed over the meadows. Edgar sketched Lake Lucerne, but mainly focused on sketching the higher peaks of Grindelwald, the Jungfrau, and of course the Matterhorn, mostly from a base in the Krebs Hotel in Interlaken.[76] The sketches were later translated into the larger easel pictures painted the following fall and winter in his Paris studio. One of these, *The Matterhorn from Zermatt* (Fig. 5.12), was undoubtedly intended as an exhibition piece. In it, under a bright summer sky, the mountain, powerful and still, like an eternal sentinel, dominates the shadowy valley below. At the lower right, a grove of trees at the very top of the timberline, catches the transient glow of the few rays that have found their way through the mountain passes to this remote and silent spot. The painting exploits the tension created, on the one hand, by the sharp upward thrust of the mountain and, on the other, by the contrast between the perpetual stone and snow of the forbidding heights and the softer greens of the gentler slopes below.

When the Paynes returned to Paris in the fall of 1923, they did so with Edgar's reputation well established there. Two of his paintings, *The Great White Peak* and *High Sierra* had been accepted by the Paris Salon the previous April, and the first had been awarded Honorable Mention. The Paynes' friend and fellow-California artist, Jesse Arms Botke, reported that she had seen both Payne paintings at the Salon, with award tag, remarking, "Isn't that fine? And they looked great."[77]

In the same month of April, 1923, there was the exhibition of 26 of Edgar's paintings which had been shipped from Rome to the Stendahl Galleries at the Ambassador Hotel in Los Angeles.[78] Anthony Anderson, art critic of the *Los Angeles Times,* wrote of this show that either Edgar Payne "has grown in distinction as a painter or I have advanced in the . . . art of appreciation and understanding. Perhaps both." He particularly praised Edgar's mountain landscapes, noting that "Payne left Los Angeles after conquering the High Sierras in paint, with the avowed purpose of vanquishing the Maritime Alps with the same medium. His exhibition proves that he has apparently done it off the bat." A week later, in a second review, he wrote particularly of Edgar's color "in the sea of ultramarine blue, in the towns climbing in red and yellow splendor up the green hillsides from the bays below, in the boats whose sails flare with color till they resemble pirate ships on a campaign of conquest." More than picturesque, the scene is enhanced in Edgar's work, "because it's nature's beauty plus an artist's feeling about it."[72]

On the Paynes' return to Paris, they enrolled Evelyn in a French school as a day student, but as she felt isolated and apart from her classmates she asked to be a boarding student, to which her parents acceded. With their daughter provided for, Edgar and Elsie began to see something of the night life of Paris — the Folies Bérgères, the Moulin Rouge, and the Beaux Arts, all frequented by the city's artist community. This was a particularly happy time in the life of the two artists. They were busy, productive, and part of an interesting and stimulating circle of friends.

Painting by artificial light was not possible in those days, which is why a studio with a large north window was so important to a painter. When the light faded, the working day was over; quite early in wintertime. In Paris the Dôme Cafe was a regular evening meeting place for American artists, among whom the Paynes had many friends. In addition to evenings at the Dôme, there were occasional studio parties which provided relaxation and plain old fun. The Paynes most frequent companions were George and Alma Evans, old friends from Chicago days. George was a commercial artist who painted when he could, a man of easy disposition and a delightful

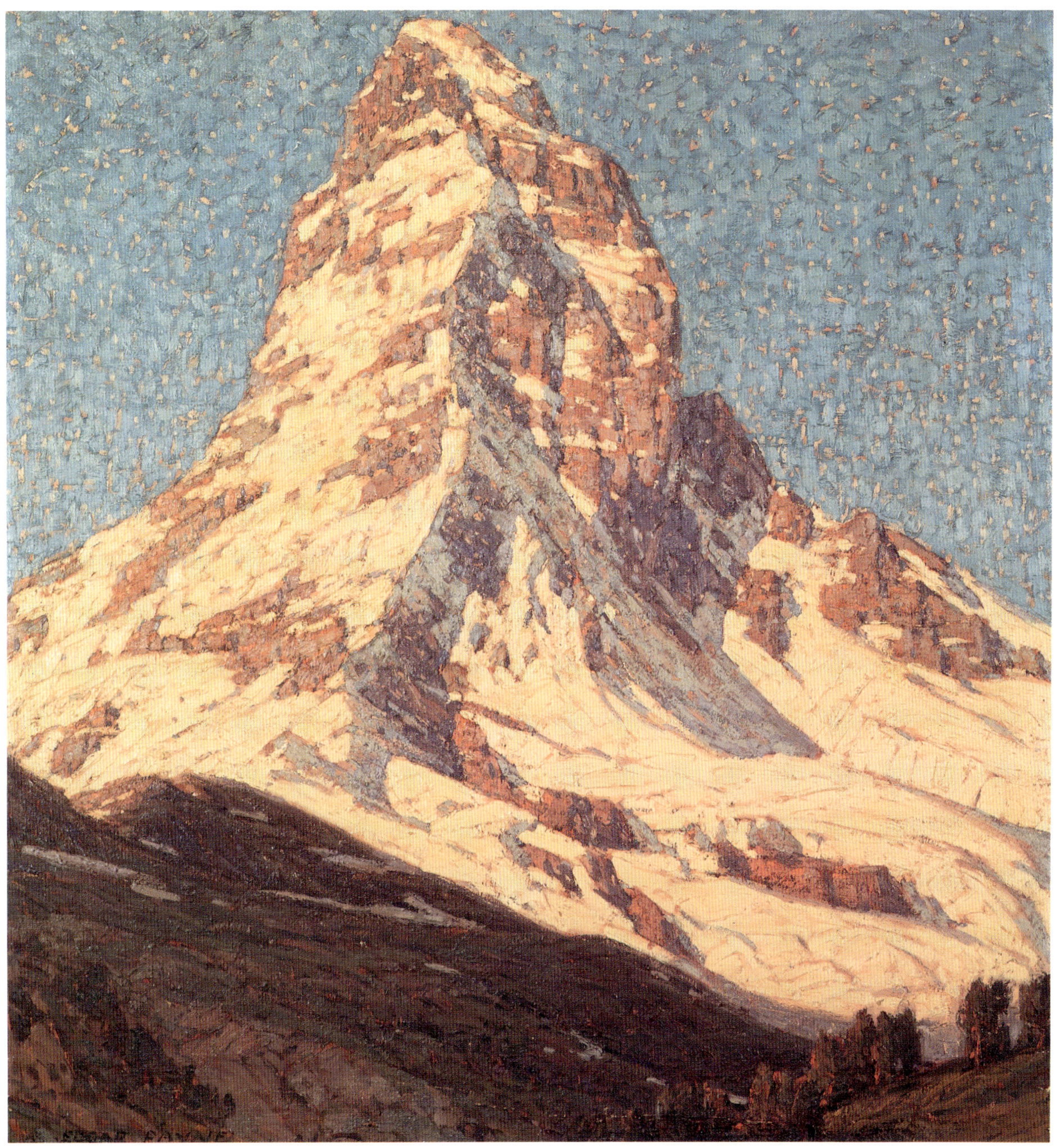

Fig. 5.12. The Matterhorn from Zermatt, by EAP.

sense of humor. He greatly admired Edgar's work and could deftly handle any social situation or difficulty. Their good times included a particularly memorable New Year's Eve celebration that extended into January 1st, 1924, at the Cafe du Dôme, with their friends and many of the artistic element and celebrities of the foreign colony of Paris.

But life in Paris had its serious side as well. Early in the New Year there was an exhibition of the American Art Association in Paris, opening on January 27th at No. 4, Rue Joseph Bara. Edgar's *Boats, Chioggia* and *Glacier* were among the paintings that hung there.[79] At the same time Edgar was also getting ready for another important exhibition, the second to be shared with an old friend from Chicago, the sculptor, Nancy Cox McCormack. This show, which ran from March 15th to April 1st at the Jaques Seligmann Gallery on the Rue St. Dominique, featured several of Edgar's mountain scenes for which he had already acquired a special recognition. They included *Eternal Snows (Mt. Blanc), The Sierra Nevada of California,* and *Mt. Cervin. Venetian Waters* was among the Payne marines also shown at the Seligmann exhibition.[80] The Payne paintings elicited a favorable, indeed enthusiastic, response. A correspondent for *Le Revue Moderne des Arts et de la Vie* wrote of Payne's mountain landscapes that, while other painters of the Savoie Alps strove for grandiose effects, making themselves small in confrontation with the mountains, letting nature dominate them, Edgar, in his pictures, dominated nature:

> "He composes on a grand scale, conscientiously but without minutiae. His colors are vigorously applied with a firm brushstroke that is knowing and sure and distributed with a rare mastery. Distant fogs, light mists, heavy skies, menacing clouds, dark rocks, bright snows, and audacious peaks — this is the captivating poetry of the high summits expressed in his work. He feels the poetry, comprehends it profoundly and interprets it in a way that sings to our memories and dreams in the majestic tones of a powerfully expressive largo."[81]

The Paynes were now living at 48 Rue Varin with a separate studio on the Rue Saint-Jacques for Edgar.[82] With Elsie quietly maintaining her place in the background, Edgar was very much a part of the American-artist-in-Paris scene. He was photographed in his studio with Nancy Cox McCormack against a background of a large laid-in sketch of his second painting of Mt. Blanc, a photograph that was to appear in the Chicago Daily News.[83] His name is included among the honored guests at a dinner on March 31, 1924 tendered by the Comité France-Amerique to members of the newly formed American Artists Association under the Triumvirate leadership of Walter Grey, a painter of domestic interiors, Alexander Harrison, who specialized in marine subjects, and Paul W. Bartlett, a well-known sculptor.[84] The American Ambassador to France, Myron T. Herrick, presided, as the guests, who included Elsie though she is not specifically mentioned, dined elegantly on consomme deslignac, filet of sole florentine, chicken paysanne, artichoke hearts, ices and pastry.[85]

Edgar also entered the Paris Salon in the spring of 1924, where, according to later newspaper accounts, two of his mountain landscapes, including *Snow Clad Heights* were hung.[86] For some reason, these paintings are not listed in the Catalogue for the 1924 Salon of the Societé Nationàle des Beaux Arts, and they won no awards. In some disappointment at not having achieved even the "Honorable Mention" of the year before, Edgar took off on a sketching and painting trip with Cornelius Botke and George H. Evans while Elsie stayed in Paris to be near Evelyn.[87]

One weekend day at St. Cloud, not far from Paris, while Evelyn and Billy Botke ran around the park, Elsie painted the formal pond, with her friend Jessie Arms Botke at the other end sketching, and providing a spot of color (Fig. 5.13). Mrs. Botke, who was to become well known for her decorative pictures of birds and other crea-

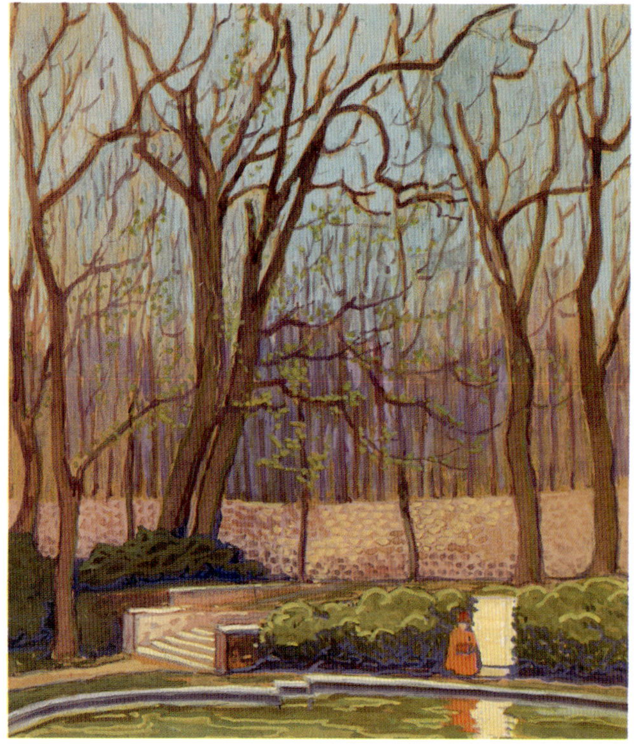

Fig. 5.13. St. Cloud, France (Jessie Arms Botke sketching), by EPP.

tures, is seen as a tiny figure of undifferentiated features holding a sketch pad in front of her as she sits at the far side of the pond. Alone in the scene, she appears dwarfed by the tall, early spring trees which, with their interlaced branches just coming into leaf, create an ornamental screen above her. She must have liked the picture because both she and Elsie valued the decorative patterns evident in the painting as opposed to the transient, illusionistic landscapes of both their husbands.

The summer sketching of 1924 was to be in Brittany, and the Paynes left Paris with three white mice, survivors of a group acquired earlier by Evelyn and her friend Billy Botke. Before the summer's end, the three white mice had become 23 — not counting the many of their number who had escaped from their box and vanished in the corridors of various country inns or into the Breton countryside. The Paynes (and the mice) travelled first through the Valley of the Loire, where both Edgar and Elsie painted a number of the ancient castles on the way. Elsie's picture of the *Chateau Josselin* (Fig. 5.14) is typically flat and decorative, carefully delineating the French Renaissance architecture with its many dormers and ornamental line of corbels. The castle is seen as a backdrop to the river which mirrors, in graceful ripples, the old stone building on its bank. Edgar's view (Fig. 5.15), taken from the other side of the castle, shows it rising, foreshortened and dominant, above the village rooftops. Unlike Elsie, he creates a sense of enveloping space, capturing with a quick brush and a simple directness, the romance of a subject that had appeared in the decorative murals and triptychs of his earlier career. Thus, where Edgar's view shows the castle receding into the space of the composition, emphasizing its three dimensionality, Elsie's speaks to the stylization of an illustration, focusing on the chateau not as a volumetric mass but as a flat backdrop for the busy life on the river.

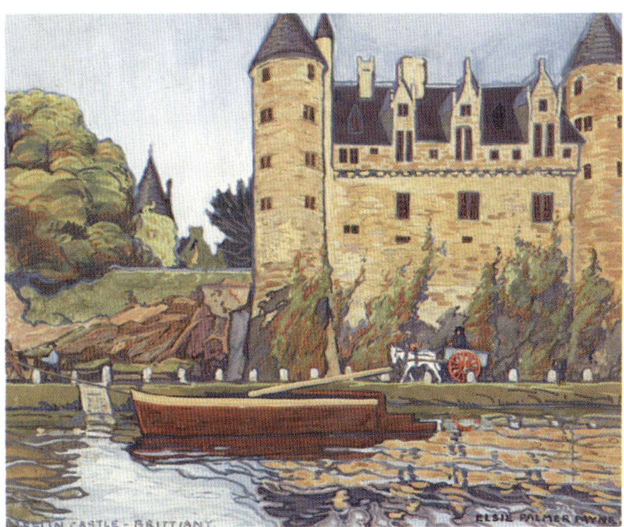

Fig. 5.14. Chateau Josselin, Brittany, by EPP.

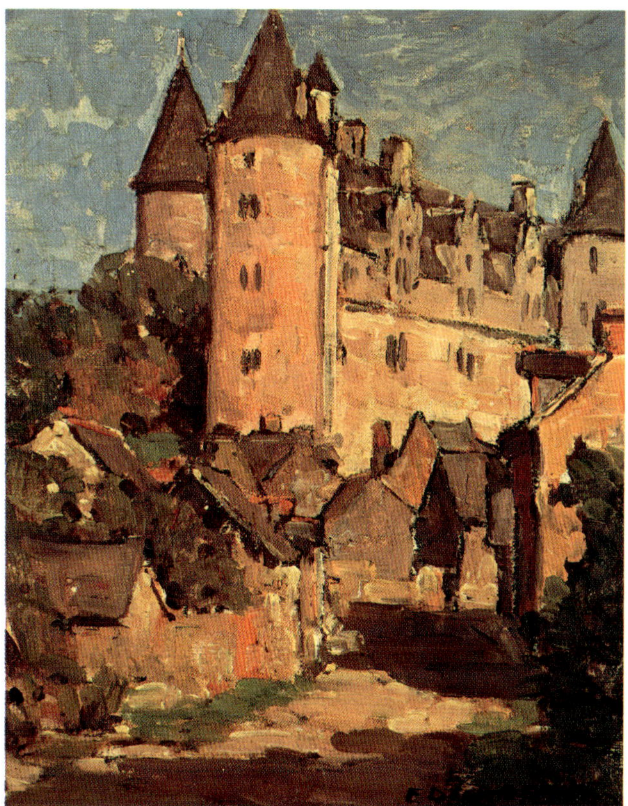
Fig. 5.15. Chateau Josslyn, by EAP.

The Paynes' destination on this trip was the coast of Brittany, particularly the fishing towns of Douarnenez and Concarneau. They discovered on the Breton coast the same unspoiled environment combined with down to earth practicality that they had admired in Chioggia. They loved the place and Edgar painted the French fishing boats with joyful freshness and vitality evident in *Breton Tuna Boats: Concarneau* (Fig. 5.16). Meanwhile, of course, Elsie focused on the life of the

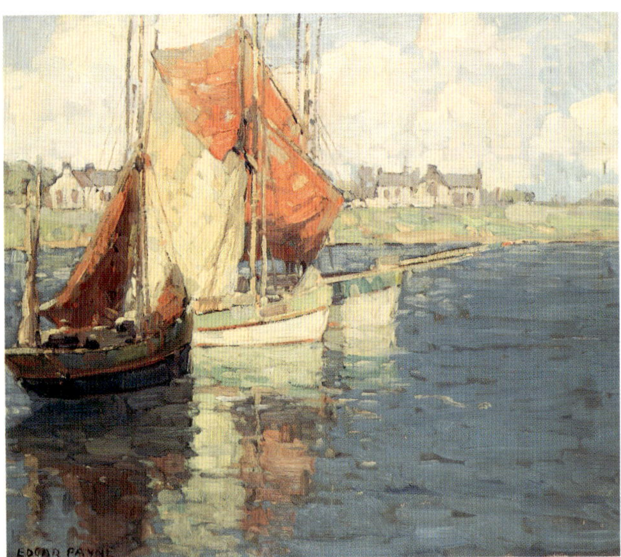

Fig. 5.16. Breton Tuna Boats, Concarneau, by EAP.

townspeople, their cottages, the quays, and the fishermen and their wives. "We went mad over those Breton scenes," she later wrote. "I painted the villages and the quaint houses and left the boats to Edgar."[1]

Many of Edgar's boat pictures were actually painted later, sometimes many years later, in his studios in the United States, but they were based on photographs and sketches made in Brittany. The sketches are themselves vivid pictures, often distinguished by a buoyant spontaneity that still retains the freshness of the scene (Fig. 5.17). But

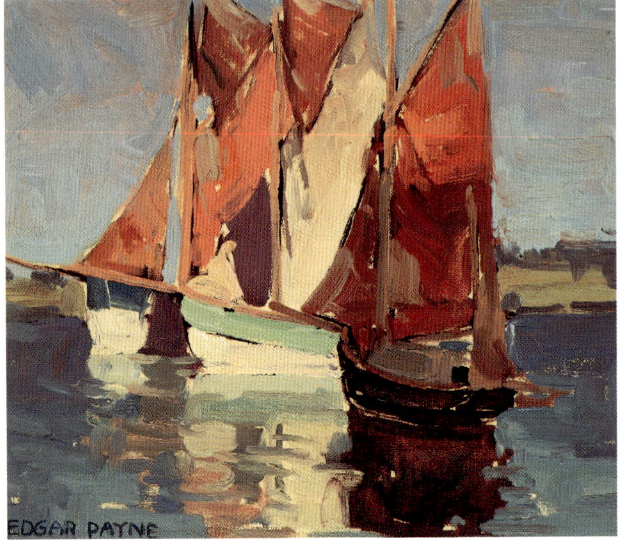

Fig. 5.17. Summer Afternoon, Breton Boats, by EAP.

Edgar was intent on the detailed and accurate representations of the boats and their rigging; his notebooks contain many exact measurements. Though a simple block in the rigging would never appear as more than a single stroke in a painting, he knew and sketched its actual construction. Later in the United States he was to make accurate, detailed models of the Adriatic and Breton boats, for he loved to carve. In making such models, he had the help of his friend, George Brandriff, a dentist who also liked to model boats, and who was a week-end painter until 1928, when he closed his dental office to paint full time.[88] As a dentist he had the perfect tool for making the tiny scale model pulley blocks for the boats — a dentist's drill. Indeed, when the boats were later displayed at a show of Edgar's paintings at Earl Stendahl's gallery in Los Angeles, there were eager customers for them. "What price shall I put on them?" Earl wired to Edgar, then in Westport, on February 24, 1927. Edgar's terse reply, wired back two days later, was "Boats not for sale. Paintings are."[89]

Elsie's picture *The Captain and the Crew* (Fig. 5.18) is also a painting done much later from sketches and memories of Concarneau and the Breton coast. Although it is a water color, a medium frequently associated with a more transient and casual vision, Elsie's brush captures the solid figures of the Breton fishermen, who assume a monumental, even heroic pose that echoes the massive stanchion beside them. The Captain, a commanding figure in dark blue, projects an air of authority over his more modestly dressed companions, but all of them suggest the simple dignity and courage of a life dedicated to the sea.

The memorable summer of 1924 also included two weeks in London where Evelyn hurt her ankle in a seesaw accident. Since walking was painful, Elsie spent the mornings riding with her on London's double-decker buses to all parts of the city, with the understanding that the afternoons were to be devoted to museum visits. Thus the Paynes familiarized themselves with the art masterpieces in the British Museum, the National Gallery, and the South Kensington (now the Victoria and Albert) Museum, while Evelyn

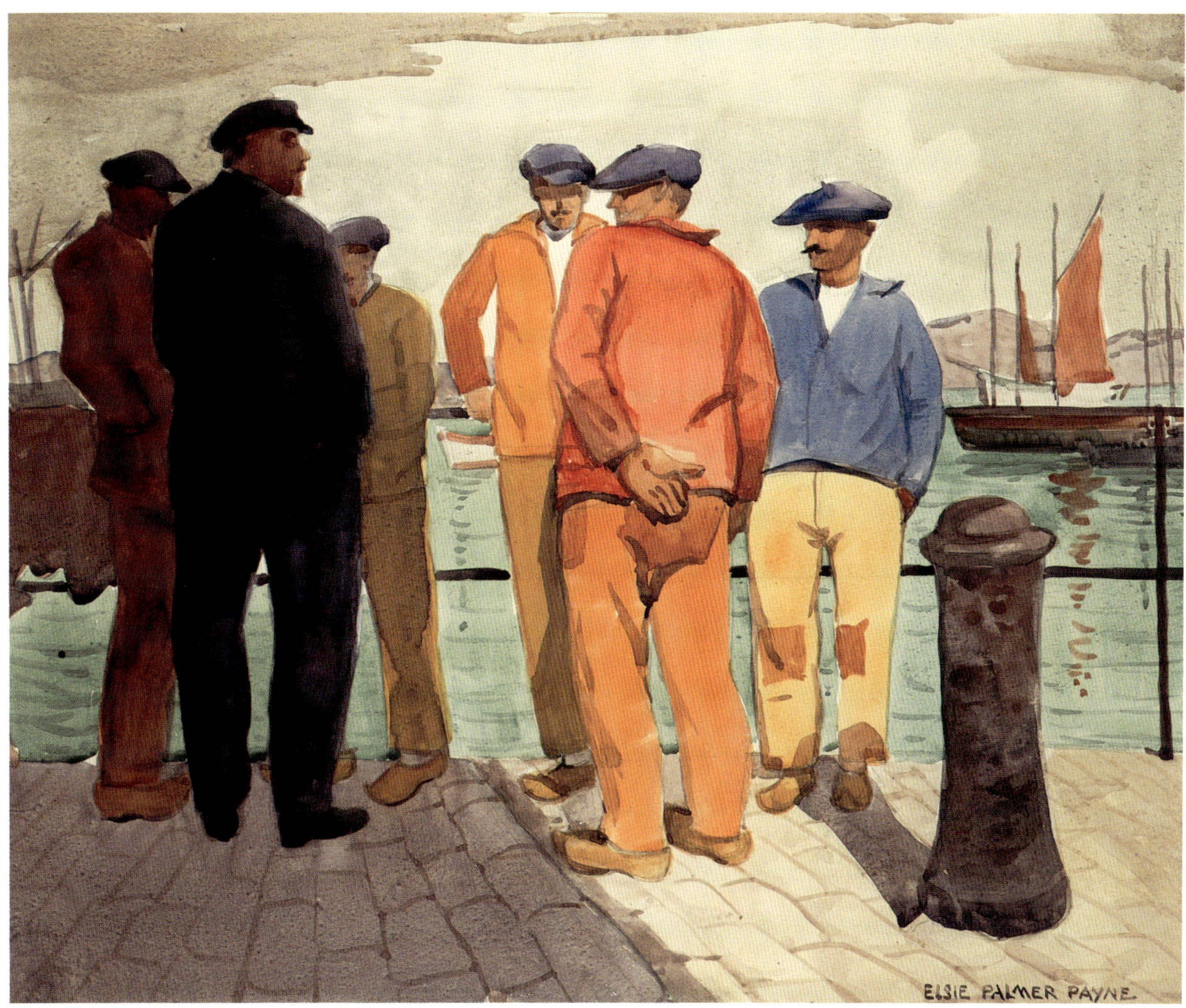

Fig. 5.18. The Captain and the Crew, by EPP.

waited patiently, either reading or entranced in her favorite section of the museum.

But the good times in Europe were drawing to an end. Having exhausted their funds, the Paynes booked passage on the SS Leviathan and returned to the United States in the fall of 1924.

Though they never again took up residence in Europe, as they had on the 1922-24 trip, the Paynes did return for one much shorter visit in the spring and summer of 1928. Sailing from New York in May of that year on the SS Minnikhada, Evelyn later remembered its commander, a Captain Jensen, who told them he was "the chauffeur of the ship." He was quite impressed by fourteen-year-old Evelyn's knowledge of ships and everything that pertained to them and invited her to spend much of the voyage on the bridge. On this trip they spent little time in Paris, quickly pushing on by train to Chioggia. The trip had been the result, at least in part, of Edgar's insistence on accuracy in his paintings of the Adriatic (and Breton) sailing vessels and he wanted to further study their construction, their rigging, and the disposition and patterns of their colorful sails. This time he actually sailed out to sea on a number of these boats and also took extensive photographs to be used as a reference source in later paintings.

While Edgar was out to sea or in the harbor sketching and painting the fishing vessels, Elsie again spent her time on the quays and in the back

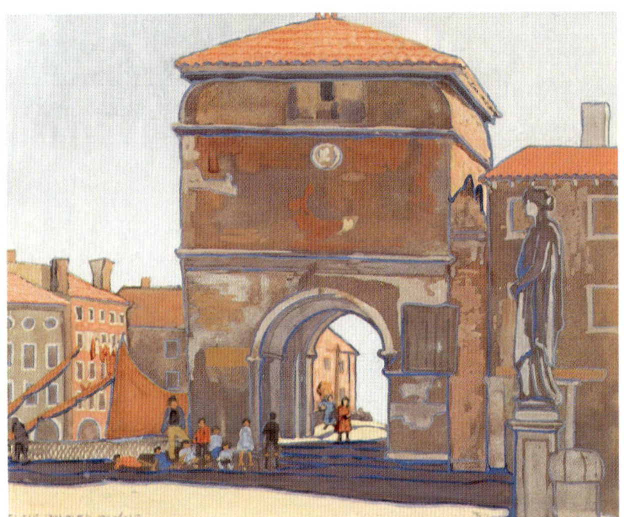

Fig. 5.19. Old City Gate, Chioggia, by EPP.

streets and alleys of Chioggia. There she painted in her own personal style, its old brick *City Gate* baking in the hot afternoon sun (Fig. 5.19), its lively copper and tin market (Fig. 5.20), or young lace makers sitting in disciplined ranks at their tables, learning the traditional women's craft of Chioggia in the shade of a covered alley (Fig. 5.21). Always interested in the family life of the people around her, whether at home or abroad, she painted a thoroughly genre scene, *The Airing* (Fig. 5.22) in which a woman holding a baby on one arm works at a laundry press, while more children investigate the contents of the laundry baskets, sit on the lap of a grandfather, or simply

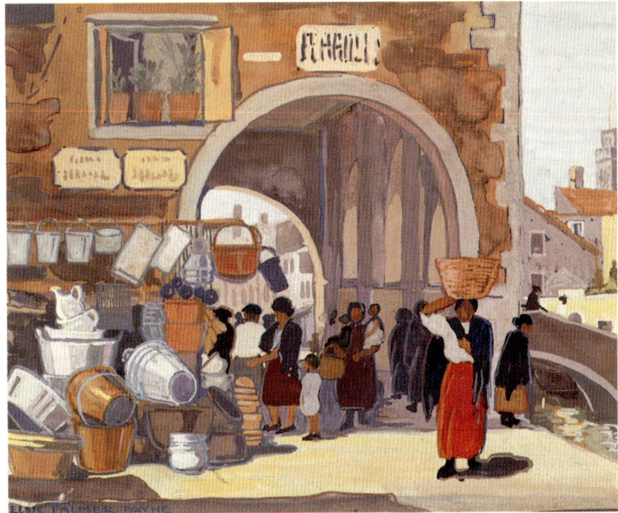

Fig. 5.20. Copper and Tin, Chioggia, by EPP.

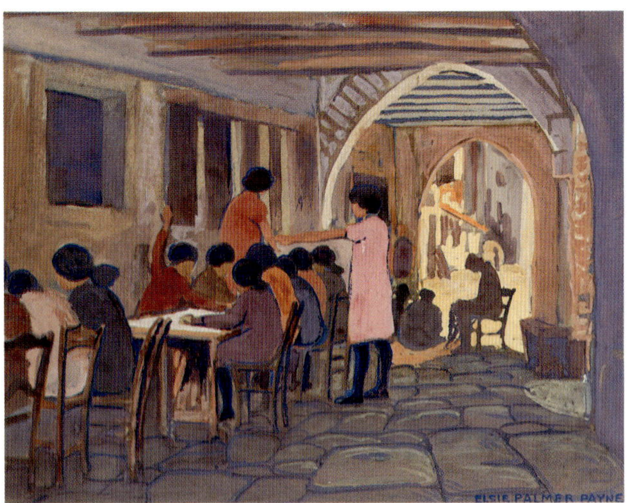

Fig. 5.21. Young Lace Makers, Chioggia, by EPP.

stand and look at the artist. A spill of white defines the linen hanging out of a window to air, providing a note of the transient and contemporary in the life of the ancient town. On these outings in Chioggia, Elsie was frequently accompanied by Evelyn, who would sit some distance away from her mother and start drawing. This had the distinct advantage of drawing the children away from Elsie, thus leaving her undisturbed by their excited curiosity and uninhibited comments.[74]

Towards the end of July, in Nice, Edgar registered another Ford Model T[90] and drove the family back to Concarneau and the Breton coast which they had so much enjoyed on their previous trip. In Brittany, as in Chioggia, Edgar devoted

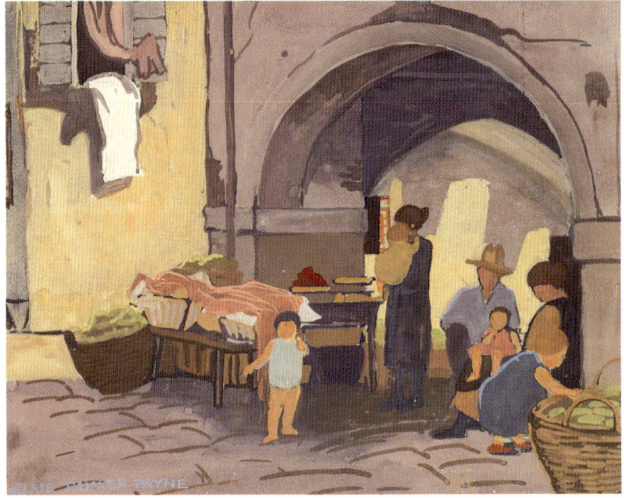

Fig. 5.22. The Airing, by EPP.

his attention to the fishing boats at sea or riding at anchor at the harbor, and Elsie concentrated on the townsfolk, especially its women. *Fishwives' Quarrel* (Fig. 5.23) that Elsie painted at this time reflects her commitment to "painting the women's side of things" and her ever-present interest in the foibles of ordinary people. There is a vivacity of spirit here, a briskness and liveliness that speak of an alert and not unsympathetic observer. *Coifs and Cabbages* (Fig. 5.24) similarly observes the local scene and records it in a series of flat, round shapes that heighten the decorative aspect of the subject and at the same time exploit the ornamental qualities inherent in the cabbages at the market and the headdresses of the Breton women.

Though many of Edgar's and some of Elsie's European pictures were actually painted later in their Chicago, New York, or California studios, they have a vivid immediacy that suggests a sight just recently experienced. Even Elsie's patterned representations of peasants and fisherfolk have some of the spontaneity of Edgar's more impressionistic views. It should be noted that even in Elsie's patterned paintings the execution was often quite spontaneous. Most of her European scenes were composed on the spot as she painted them, and she very much enjoyed snatching something from the scene in such a way as to enhance the design. She often said that if she needed something to balance a composition near the bottom of a picture, a dog or a child would conveniently come by, providing just the element she needed. She worked in this manner in the United States too, of course, but the encounters and adventures of the European sojourns were for both Edgar and Elsie the high point of their artistic life together. Europe nourished their imagination, inspired their brush, and remained in their memories forever.

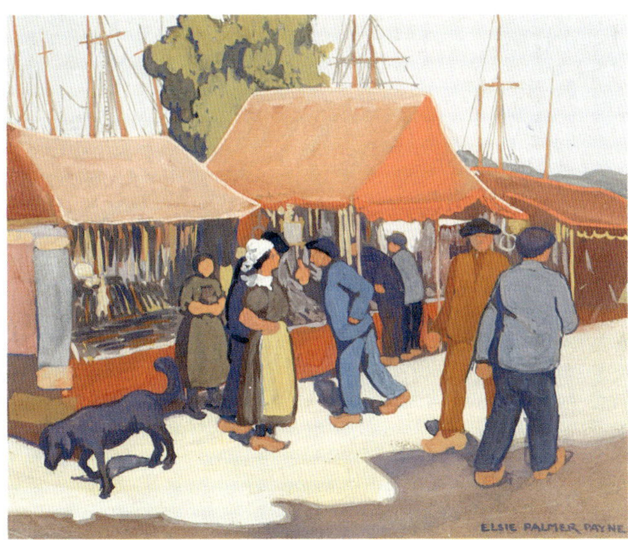

Fig. 5.23. Fishwives' Quarrel, by EPP.

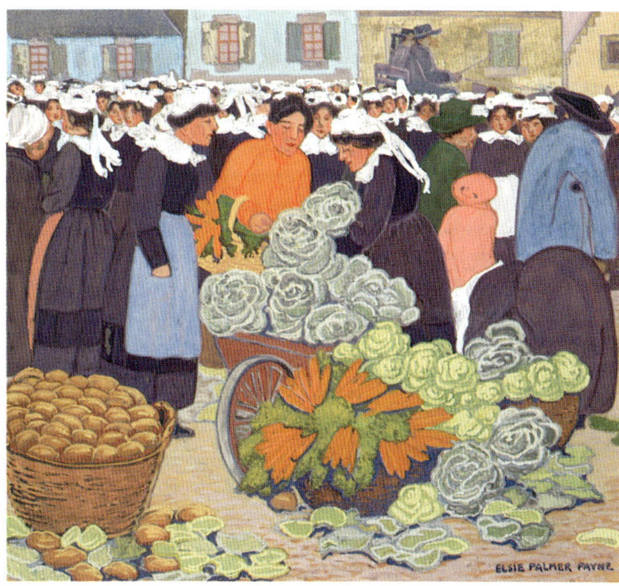

Fig. 5.24. Coifs and Cabbages, by EPP.

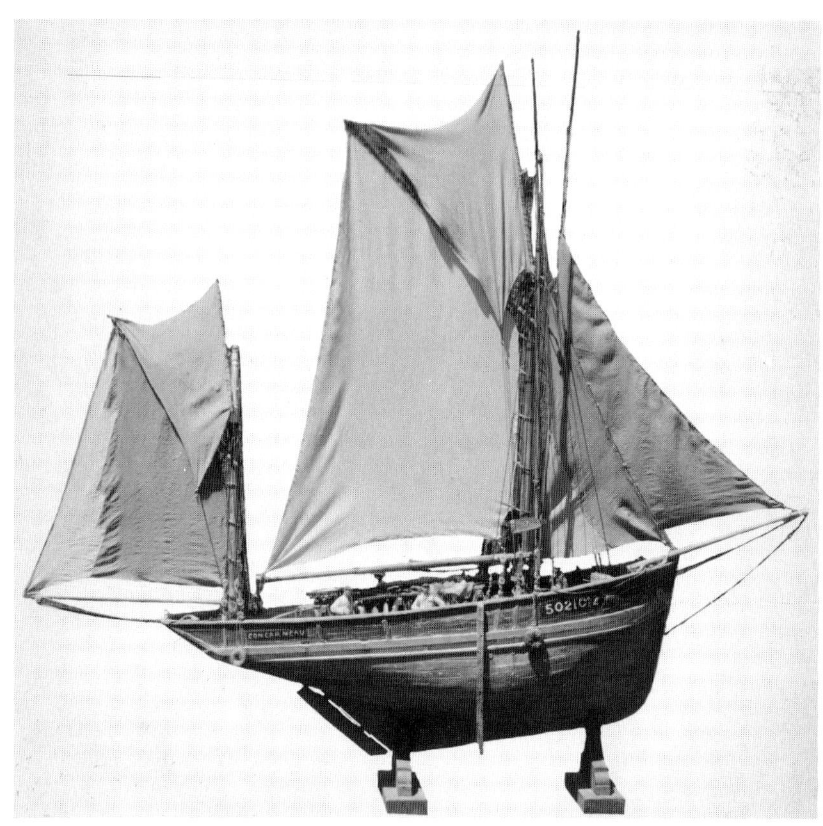

Fig. 5.25. EAP's Breton Tuna Yawl Model. Sails by EPP.

Chapter 6: At Home in the U.S.A.

When the Paynes returned from Europe in the fall of 1924, rich with the memories of their European adventure but with family fortunes at a very low ebb, they planned to spend a few months in Chicago where Edgar would finish a few paintings, re-establish contact with dealers he knew, and collect money owed him from previous sales. Elsie went to work painting "beaded" lampshades in a factory. Pay was by the piece, and as she could paint fruit and flowers freehand, she made more than her fellow workers in the sweat shop. Edgar continued to work at his easel pictures, translating his European sketches into larger studio paintings and preparing for a number of exhibitions. His pictures sold so well that he was soon able to pay off their debts. Unfortunately, however, he did not remember to tell Elsie of that fact and she continued the hated work in the lampshade factory. In point of fact, Elsie later proved to be a much better financial manager than Edgar, but as he seldom let her know the state of the family finances, she had to guess at them and manage the household on whatever Edgar doled out. Typically, during their life together, Edgar and Elsie would spend whatever savings they had managed to accumulate on travel and special efforts connected with their work.

Even in periods of economic depression the Payne household and studio, wherever it was, contained many art objects, and paintings by other artists who had traded their pictures for Edgar's. Most furniture was temporary and merely serviceable, although there were plenty of oriental and Navajo rugs for the floors. When they left winter quarters, they often put many of their things into storage. Sometimes not all of these possessions were recovered, for example, some very fine things from the Paris studio that went for storage charges.

Fortunately both Edgar and Elsie were confident about their art and optimistic about the future, enjoying to the full their periods of prosperity and adapting, of necessity, to their periods of economic depression. They lived, in their daughter's words, a very "upsey-downsey" existence, even though Edgar was unusually successful at selling his paintings as the source of the family income. To this end he continually entered his work in exhibitions and kept his dealers supplied, hoping to attract wealthy and influential patrons and accounting, in no small part, for his constant travels from one part of the country to another.

As a matter of fact, during the time they lived in Chicago — from the fall of 1924 to the spring of 1925, Edgar's paintings were receiving considerable exposure. The Art Institute of Chicago had exhibited both *High Sierra* and the 1923 Paris Salon piece, *Great White Peak* in the twenty-eighth Exhibition of Chicago Artists from February 1st to March 11th, 1924. The following year, from January 30th to March 10th, 1925, *Bernese Peaks* and *Tuna Fisherman* were shown in the twenty ninth exhibition of the same name.[91] There was also a very successful exhibition in late March, 1925 at Newcomb-Macklin's Gallery where five of the paintings shown were sold the very first week.[92] It was noted of this exhibition that all but two or three of the paintings were of European scenes, but that the exhibition "is very American in character. There is a bigness, a feeling for the sweep of space, a grasp of fundamental features and an absence of unessential detail that mark the work of the great American landscape painters." And though, the reporter continued, "Mr. Payne's love of the mountains is patent from the number of paintings he made of them, the sunnier and softer pictures of Italian and French fishing boats, cutting through the blue Mediterranean or at anchor in harbor with their yards and sails aslant in graceful lines across the cloudless sky . . . exhibit the same attention to the passing mood of what he paints . . . They are far in character from the more somber studies of rock and pine but equally evident of power."[93] The same ability to please his audience is demonstrated by the fact that at about the same time as the Chicago shows, Edgar's *Sails of Cameret* and *White Dome* were on display at the Pennsylvania Academy of Fine Arts[60] and some of his European scenes that had been shipped to Stendahl's from Rome were now on exhibit at the Los Angeles galleries of Cannell and Chaffin.[94]

In May 1925 the Paynes set out for California in the new Pontiac they had acquired, accompanied on the trip by George Hurrell, a friend of Edgar's who later became a well-known Hollywood photographer. The car was damaged in an accident near Denver, but fortunately no one was hurt, and after a brief delay, they arrived in California at the end of May. They spent the first part of the summer at Laguna Beach, welcomed back by old friends, and staying as guests at Buck Weaver's studio[95] where there was an open-house exhibition of Edgar's recent paintings. They were also honored at a large party, with games and fireworks given by Anne Mason, a local resident patron and a founder of the Laguna Beach Art Association, before they left Laguna Beach in early July.[96]

From Laguna the Paynes set out on the usual summer sketching trips. This time they first went to San Francisco for a brief visit; here Elsie made a speech to an audience of artists that included her former teacher, Alice Best. From San Francisco the Paynes went to the Sierras for part of their summer sketching, ending up finally at Thoreau, New Mexico, for Southwest sketches. In the fall the Paynes established residence in Los Angeles at 134 North Reno Street, with a studio at 550 South New Hampshire Street. Here Edgar immediately started work preparing for the exhibition of his European paintings to be held in the spring at the Stendahl Galleries in the Ambassador Hotel, not far away. Edgar was at the peak of his career, gathering awards and honors for his paintings. In August the Laguna Beach Art Association had awarded its prize for marine paintings to Edgar's *Fisherman, Concarneau.*[95] In October his *Peaks and Shadows* won the gold medal given by the California Art Club for the best landscape in its sixteenth annual exhibition at the Los Angeles County Museum.[97] Just a month later, his painting *The Harbor* won second prize (after Oscar E. Berninghaus' *Haytime in Taos)* at the California State Fair.[98]

Such recognition blossomed even further with the major exhibition of Edgar's paintings at the Stendahl Galleries from May 15th to June 15th 1926. Sixty canvases (and two boat models) were shown in this retrospective, encompassing the full range of his subject matter, from the snowy peaks of the Sierras and Alps to the fishing boats of Italy and Brittany, including also marine paintings of Laguna and its environs. An extended and well-illustrated hardbound catalogue contained a biography and an appreciation of the artist by Antony Anderson who was listed as "Art Critic of the West" and an essay, "Edgar Alwin Payne and his Art" by Fred S. Hogue, chief editorial writer of the *Los Angeles Times.* Their praise of the artist was whole hearted. "Payne sees nature in a big and comprehensive way," wrote Anderson, "and something of this bigness of outlook he communicates to us . . . " There were, he added, "poetry and beauty in the pictures at Stendahl, and a vitality that is amazing." Hogue's essay went even further in his comparison of Payne's paintings to ancient literature. "Payne painted as Homer sang," he wrote, "wandering from place to place [like] . . . the rolling stone, the floating cloud, the vagrant bee. Wherever there is warmth and variety in color, a contrast of plastic and static form — wherever nature has unfolded one of its divine masterpieces, Payne had made a pilgrimage as the faithful to a shrine; and he writes on canvas with pigments his symphonies as Homer sang them to the tune of his lyre.''[68]

The summer of 1926 was spent again sketching and painting in the High Sierras. There were two different kinds of trips involved in these expeditions. In one case they simply travelled by car to various remote areas and either set up their own camp or stayed in local accommodations, providing their own food. For such trips they found it most useful to have a large, hinged box mounted on the running board of the car. It was painted black on the outside and white in the interior, with a drop-leaf shelf that could serve as a kitchen table. The box itself provided storage for the family provisions, such as bacon, beans, carrots, potatoes, powdered milk (Klim), and cocoa (Fig. 6.01).

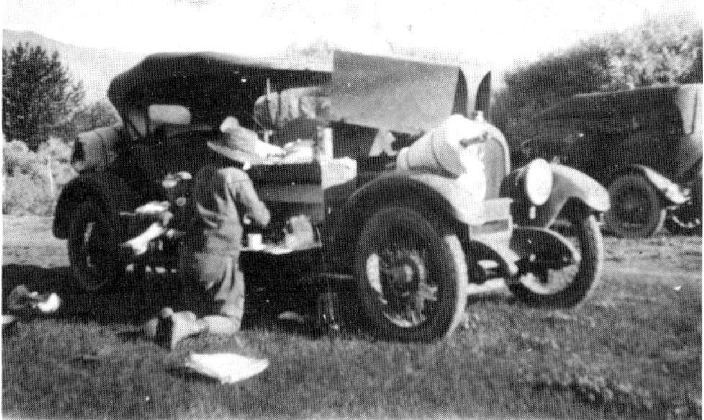

Fig. 6.01. A lunch stop while the Marmon cools, about 1920.

Other trips, especially to the higher mountains, were pack trips. On these, besides any painting materials, what went into the camp was only what could be carried by a couple of pack animals. Once the packers left to go back down, the camp was completely isolated for a week or more. In the early days the pack trips were long. As time went by and more roads to higher elevations were bulldozed in, the pack trips became shorter. Many of the sites they visited can be reached by car today, but at the time the High Sierras were really a wilderness area, remote and hard to reach. For the Paynes, of course, this added to the freshness of their experience in the mountains and their delight in the unspoiled scenery. Their camping accommodations, though primitive by today's standards, were typical for that time and comfortable enough. A small canvas lean-to tent with a flap for a door, contained a single wide bed made up of pine boughs, springy willow branches, and a top layer of pine needles which was both comfortable and fragrant. Elsie's cooking was done over an open fire, and thirteen-year-old Evelyn caught her mother in the act with some pencil drawings (Fig. 6.02).

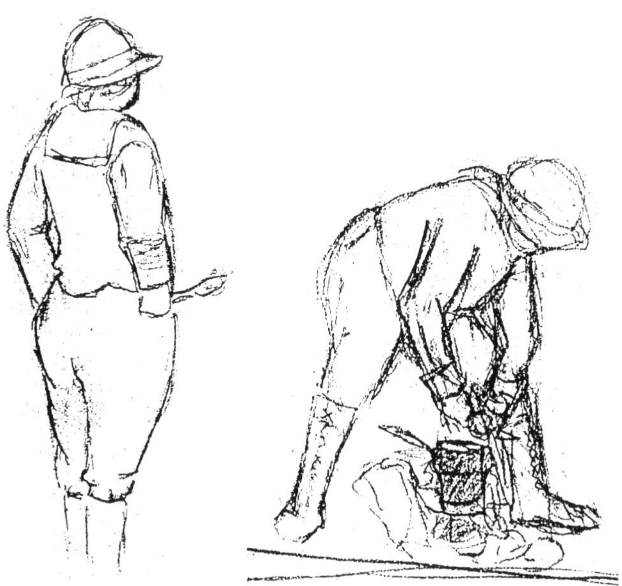

Fig. 6.02. Elsie cooking in High Sierra Camp, Sketch by her daughter.

As the summer expeditions continued year after year, some refinements were gradually added to make the living arrangements a little less spartan.

Evelyn provides a first-hand glimpse of the Sierra trips in the 20s: ''On the sketching trips . . . he [Edgar] liked to drive slowly, and where there was anything sketchable a pleased smile would come on his face, and a sense of anticipation, and he would look over the country, and see some things, or some shadows on the hills and say 'Hm-m-m, nice' and wave his hand toward them . . . He usually made one sketch in the morning, and another in the afternoon . . . By the time a trip was over, the back of the touring car would be piled high with the wet oil sketches put together in stacks with double pointed push tacks — the sketches were distressing to me, as my space in the car got smaller and smaller.''

There is only one known painting that records the Sierra campsites, and this is a sketch by Elsie (Fig. 6.03) of a very untypical one in 1932, when Edgar had taken along a fair-sized group of students as well as a cook and handyman. Her picture depicts a group of people gathered at a large canopied table in an aspen grove. As always,

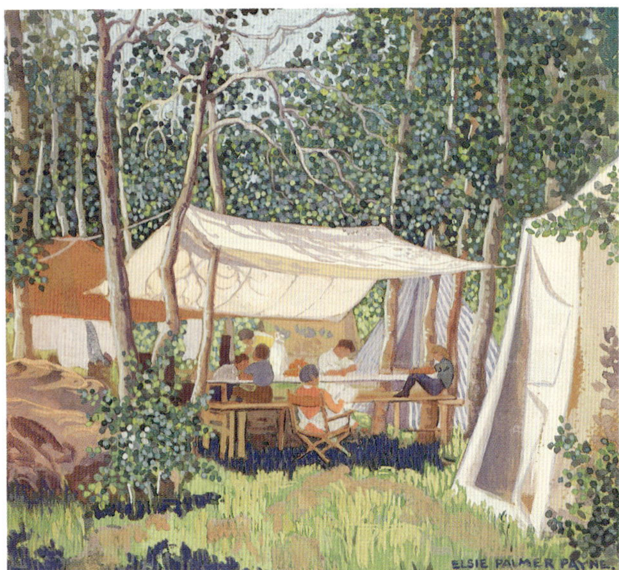

Fig. 6.03. Camping in an Aspen Grove, High Sierras, by EPP.

it was the human touch that interested Elsie and she endowed the scene with the comfortable familiarity of a backyard picnic. In fact, her picture has more to do with paintings of genre activities au plein air by artists such as William Merritt Chase than it does with the rugged austerity of Edgar's Sierra scenes.

With the success of the 1925/26 exhibitions in Chicago and California, it seemed to Edgar that the time had come to expand his markets in the East, and so the family moved to Westport, Connecticut, arriving there in October, 1926. Here they rented the Bean Studio on Kings Highway, a fine old prerevolutionary house with an added studio. Edgar may have made a few attempts at painting out of doors in the area, but somehow the landscape of the northeast did not inspire his brush and no pictures of the region exist today. He did, however, appreciate the autumnal colors of the Northeast, writing that "the countryside is wonderful, all red, yellow and brown. Such a contrast to California." But with the cold of winter there was little if any outdoor sketching, and as usual Edgar painted his larger easel paintings from the accumulated sketches of the High Sierra and the Breton and Italian fishing boats.

The sailing ships of the American past also interested him, and he acquired scale models of the U.S.S. Constitution and the Santa Maria in addition to his own models of European boats. A small but vigorous picture of a square-rigger under full sail (Fig. 6.04), a subject to which Edgar had devoted several larger paintings, is testimony to his continued fascination with all forms of navigation that depended on sail and wind and the skill of the mariner rather than on the steam-driven engines that drove the behemoths of the modern era.

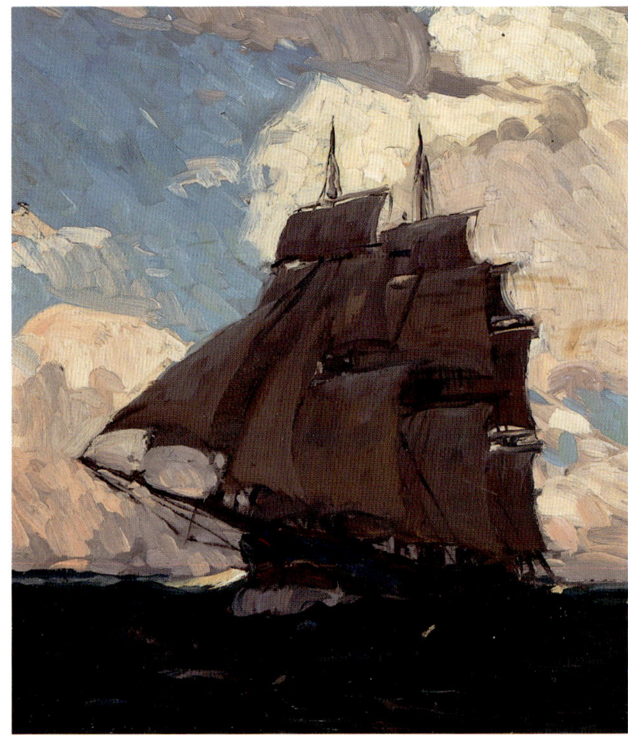

Fig. 6.04. Square Rigger, by EAP.

Edgar stayed in Westport through April, mounting an exhibition for the Women's Town Improvement Association in the YMCA.[99] He then left for Chicago and California, while Elsie and Evelyn moved into an apartment until Evelyn finished the school year, when they joined Edgar in California. There was another Stendahl exhibition of his work in May and early June 1927, following which the Chicago Galleries in Chicago were to mount a similar show. Both exhibitions were again highly successful and much praised in the local press. Sonia Wolfson in her *Art and Artists* column, writing of the esthetic and scenic delights of the canvases at Stendahl's, particularly liked the "fine mass formation" of the Breton tuna boats whose sails deepened in color from yellow to glowing orange as the boats sailed steadily toward the observer and the French coast. But France has no monopoly on maritime loveliness, for the artist "gives us so entrancing a glimpse of Italian boats on the Adriatic, that we promptly become all yearning to board them and cruise eternally over like green waters . . . Coral sails billow out so fulsomely we sense the breath of strong winds and the tang of salt air and decide never again to be landlubbers." Patriotic fervor, however, gave the edge to *Sierra Twilight* which caused the critic to "breath an unconscious prayer of thanksgiving for the beauties of our homeland and the artists who, knowing the glories of other lands, are big enough to convey them to us and still bring us to a realization of the beauties close to us."[100]

Another project of 1927 that Edgar undertook was a commission, brokered by Earl Stendahl, to do eight large decorative paintings for the new St. Paul Hotel at Sixth and St. Paul streets in Los Angeles. The subjects of these separate paintings, "murals" in the sense of permanent incorporation into the walls of the hotel lobby, covered the full range of Edgar's themes, from the fishing boats of France and Italy to a covered wagon train crossing the plains (reminiscent of his earlier murals in Chicago). There was even one called *High Sierra Peaks,* a large painting of his favorite subject during this period.[101]

The end of the 1920's was a period of busy commuting back and forth across the country, essentially on business, with sketching trips to Europe, the Canadian Rockies, and the Southwest. In the late fall of 1927 on their return to the East from sketching in the Sierras, the Paynes rented an apartment at 3127 Netherland Avenue in Spuyten Duyvil, just north of Manhattan, while Edgar also maintained a studio downtown at 1930 Broadway. Sputyen Duyvil was a charming residential area in Riverdale, where their lifelong friends George and Alma Evans had built a home. The Paynes bought a lot a few blocks away, planning to build a studio home there. They drew many sketches and designs for the house, and traded paintings for such items as steel sash windows and tiles, which they stored in a sturdy shed on the lot. Unfortunately, the dream house never materialized, and the building materials stored in the shed were lost.

Soon after moving into the Spuyten Duyvil apartment, Edgar fell ill with pneumonia. The doctor forbade him to go to his studio, and he was confined to the apartment for what was to be — before the advent of antibiotics — a long convalescence. While recovering, Edgar used Elsie's tempera materials to translate many of his European sketches to paper. His handling of this medium was most unusual — he used the paint as though it were oil, with impressionistic short brush strokes. They are, in effect, miniature versions of his studio oils (Fig. 6.05).

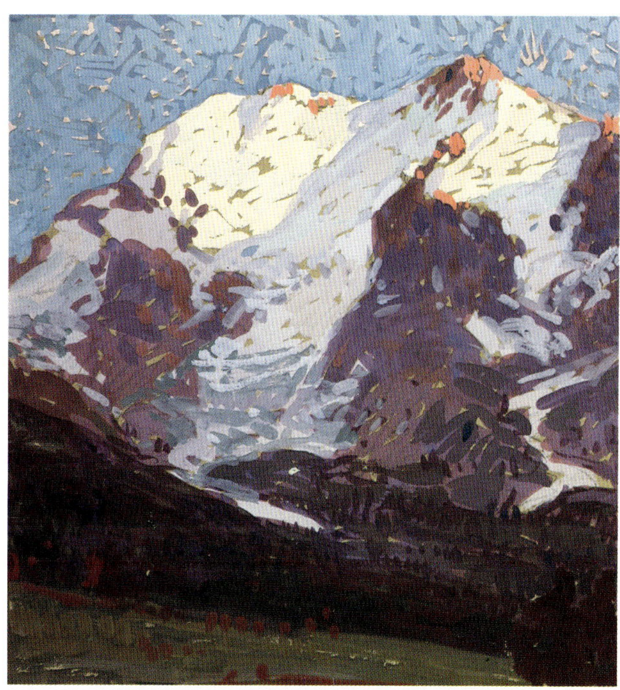

Fig. 6.05. Swiss Mountains, by EAP.

By early the following year, he was sufficiently recovered to make arrangements for a January exhibition at the Wilshire Galleries in Los Angeles.[102] He also visited Ogden, Utah early in the year to arrange an exhibition for the following July.[103]

By the time of that exhibition, however, the Paynes were again in Europe on a five-month return trip to Chioggia and the Breton Coast. They had decided, earlier in the spring, to use the $5,000 from the St. Paul Hotel commission for a shorter trip to Italy and France in the summer of 1928. The expected money was not immediately forthcoming, however, and a rift between Edgar and Earl Stendahl developed. Edgar's letters to Stendahl in the spring of 1928 are increasingly importunate. From his studio at 1931 Broadway hc wrotc to the Los Angeles dealer on April 4, 1928 regarding the money owed him: "Please understand this is not a debt. You owe me merely my money you are using for other purposes. As I wrote you before, I need this cash and must have it." Stendahl replied by return mail that "I have been hoping to send you a check for $5,000 long before this. I didn't write you about it for I wanted to hand you a surprise. But last week my principal had all of his money tied up in such a way that I had to cancel my deal. This set me back considerably . . . but I will try and get some money right away so don't worry . . . Payments are coming in slowly," he continued and "I still owe the bank $15,000 so you see I have my worries also." Edgar was not impressed. "I am sailing on the Minnikhada June 9th," he wrote Stendahl on May 31st 1928. "Wish you would make an effort to get some money to me before that time . . . I feel that further discourtesy is not only unbusinesslike but unfair to me." On June 5th Stendahl sent Edgar a telegram, "Saw my banker yesterday for a loan of $5,000 to settle account in full STOP . . . traded some paintings for land which proved a bad deal for me STOP . . . Other sales have been very disappointing STOP . . . Wish I were going over too STOP Regards to Mrs. and Evelyn." On June 9th the $5,000 was deposited in Edgar's bank, and the Paynes sailed for Europe on schedule the same day.[89]

After a summer in Chioggia and Concarneau that refreshed their memories and renewed their spirits, the Paynes were back in New York, with Evelyn enrolled as a scholarship student at the Fieldston High School run by the Ethical Culture Society. With this scholarship and entry to high school, Elsie promised, and kept her promise, that Evelyn would be able to graduate in four years without having her school years cut off at the beginning and end. By the time Evelyn had finished eighth grade, she had attended ten different schools in different countries, typically starting after classes had already begun, and only once finishing the entire year before leaving with her parents on their sketching trips.

Early in 1929 Edgar again travelled to Los Angeles, via Chicago and Ogden, Utah, arranging exhibitions. The first showing was at the Allerton House in Chicago on May 14th.[104] Here Edgar proudly included a "smaller interpretation" of his Sierra painting *Fifth Lake, Big Pine Creek* (Fig. 6.06) which had been purchased by the Ranger Fund for the National Academy of Design the previous December,[105] and which became in 1957 part of the permanent collection of the National Collection of Fine Arts.[106] In Ogden Edgar arranged for a later exhibition at the Hotel Bigelow Gallery, and in Los Angeles for still another showing at the Biltmore Gallery beginning June 23rd.

When school was over, Elsie and Evelyn joined Edgar in Laguna Beach, renewing old friendships and admiring the new Laguna Beach Art Gallery, located on a scenic bluff overlooking the Pacific Ocean. It had opened a few months earlier, on February 15, 1929, and was built in a modified Spanish style with large double doors copied from those leading to the Padres' garden at the old mission of St. Juan Capistrano; the lobby was also in the Spanish style with a dark, beamed ceiling. The new exhibition space, 60 by 36 feet, was lit by over eleven hundred square feet of glass in the roof. In contrast to the original gallery of 1918, it was a veritable exhibition palace.

About July 1st the Paynes departed for their regular summer trip to the mountains, but not,

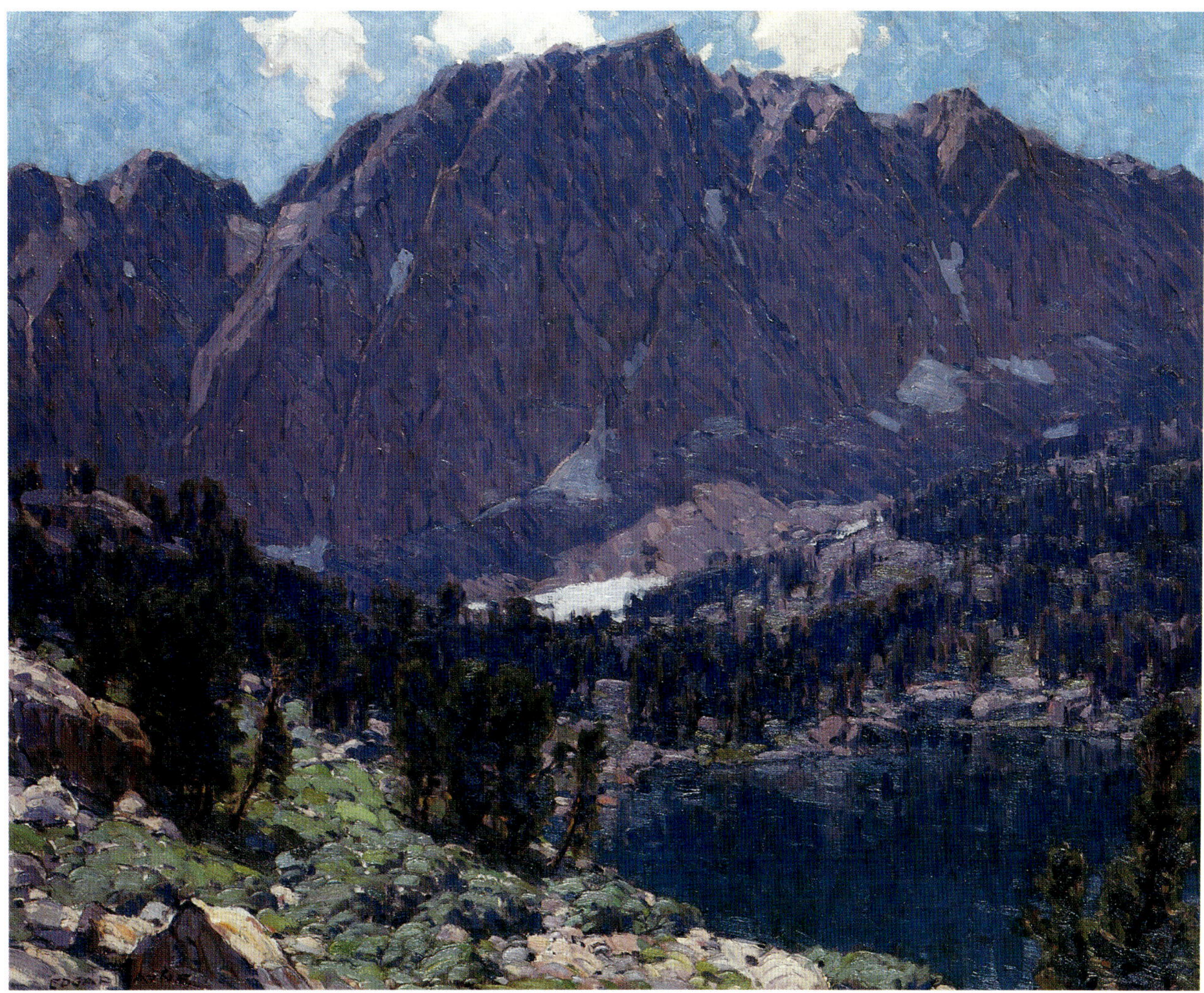

Fig. 6.06. Fifth Lake, by EAP.

this time, for the California Sierras, and for the first time, without their daughter. She stayed in Laguna Beach with friends while Edgar and Elsie went to the Canadian Rockies. The pictures resulting from this trip preserved the spirit and style of Edgar's Sierras scenes, as in *Lake Louise, Canadian Rockies* (Fig. 6.07), just as Elsie's *Lake Louise* (Fig. 6.08) maintained hers.

Edgar rarely dated his mountain landscapes (or any of his other work, for that matter), but a very rough chronology can sometimes be established through his brushwork. This changed from an early, subdued, relatively careful style to one that was "chunkier," paint brushed on the canvas with a broader and looser stroke, thus becoming increasingly impressionistic. Ever sensitive to the nuances of nature's changing moods, his "impressions" of the High Sierras are particularly alive, earning him his earliest and most enduring recognition as a premier American landscape painter. The whereabouts of his *Rugged Slopes and Tamarack* which was painted in 1919 and won the Cahn prize the next year is not known today. But judging from old photographs of it, it is very similar to the still extant *Shadow Slope, Inyo County, California, Near Bishop* (Fig. 6.09) also painted in 1919. It is evidence of Edgar's mastery at revealing the mountain scene in all its rugged massiveness and thrusting power, together with a sense of isolation and remoteness from the everyday world. Its cold blue glacial lake and stony crags, the snowy patches clinging to the mountain ridges,

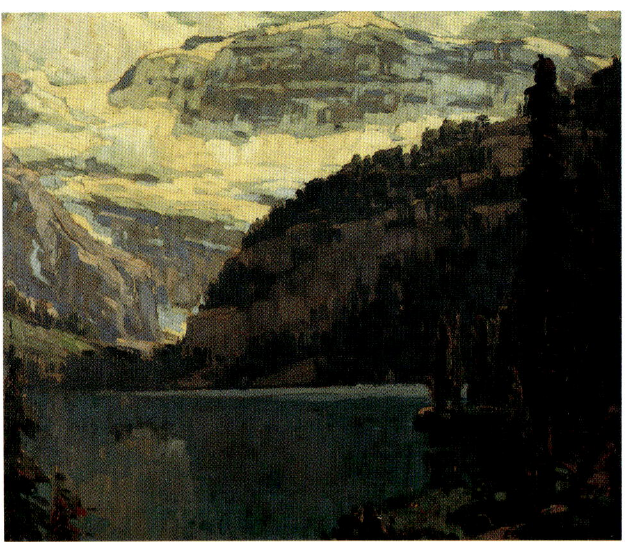

Fig. 6.07. Lake Louise, by EAP.

the dark green firs struggling to the top of the timber line combine to effect a contrast of color and mass that became a part of Edgar's artistic vocabulary. Since such pictures were very popular and sold well, Edgar turned them out by the score. Nevertheless, in spite of the frequency with which he produced them, the best of them are unsurpassed in their energy and formidable power.

Though these mountain pictures seem a spontaneous evocation of the mountain scene, in his 1941 book, *The Composition of Outdoor Painting,* Edgar revealed how much thought and studied

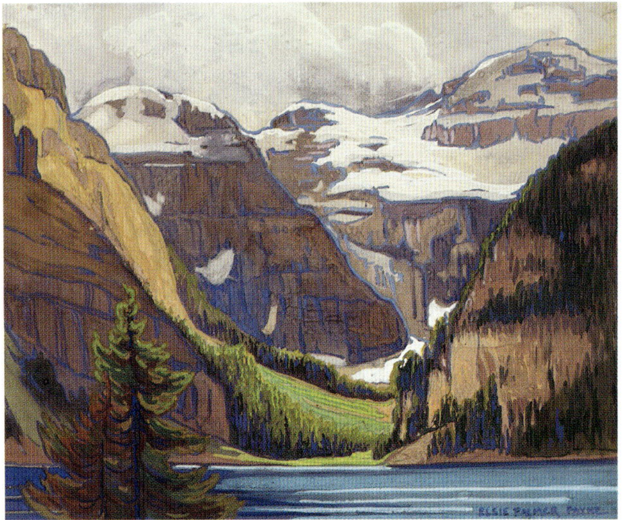

Fig. 6.08. Lake Louise, by EPP.

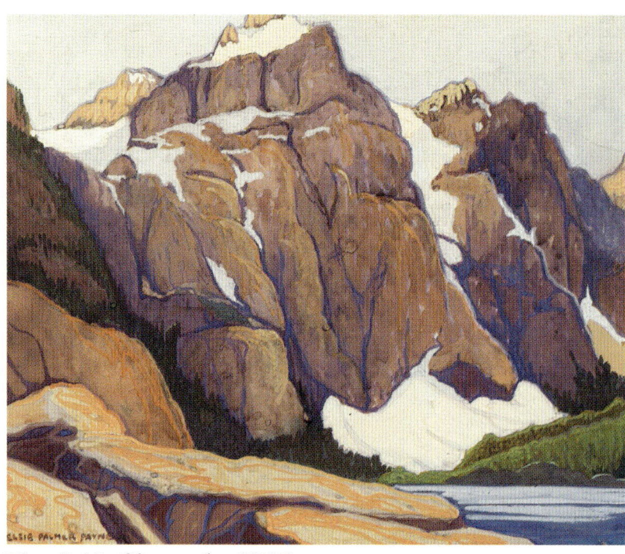

Fig. 6.10. Sierra, by EPP.

observation preceded the actual painting on canvas. The painter of mountains, he wrote, should first of all "study their characteristic forms as the figure painter studies the human figure." He went on to observe: "Height is one of the strongest points in hills or mountains [and] they are also massive and suggest solidity and permanence." Ever responsive, furthermore, to the effects of light in the out of doors, he advised the painter of the mountain scene to locate his easel in a place where the mountain is either mostly in shadow or mostly in light "since equal measures

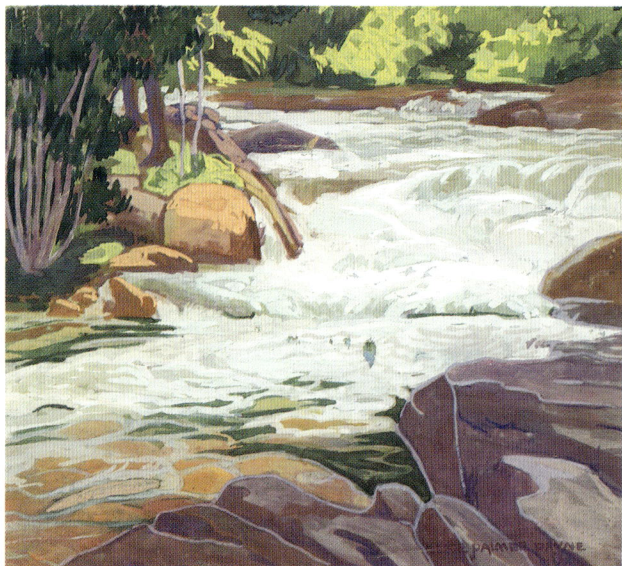

Fig. 6.11. The Creek, Sierra, by EPP.

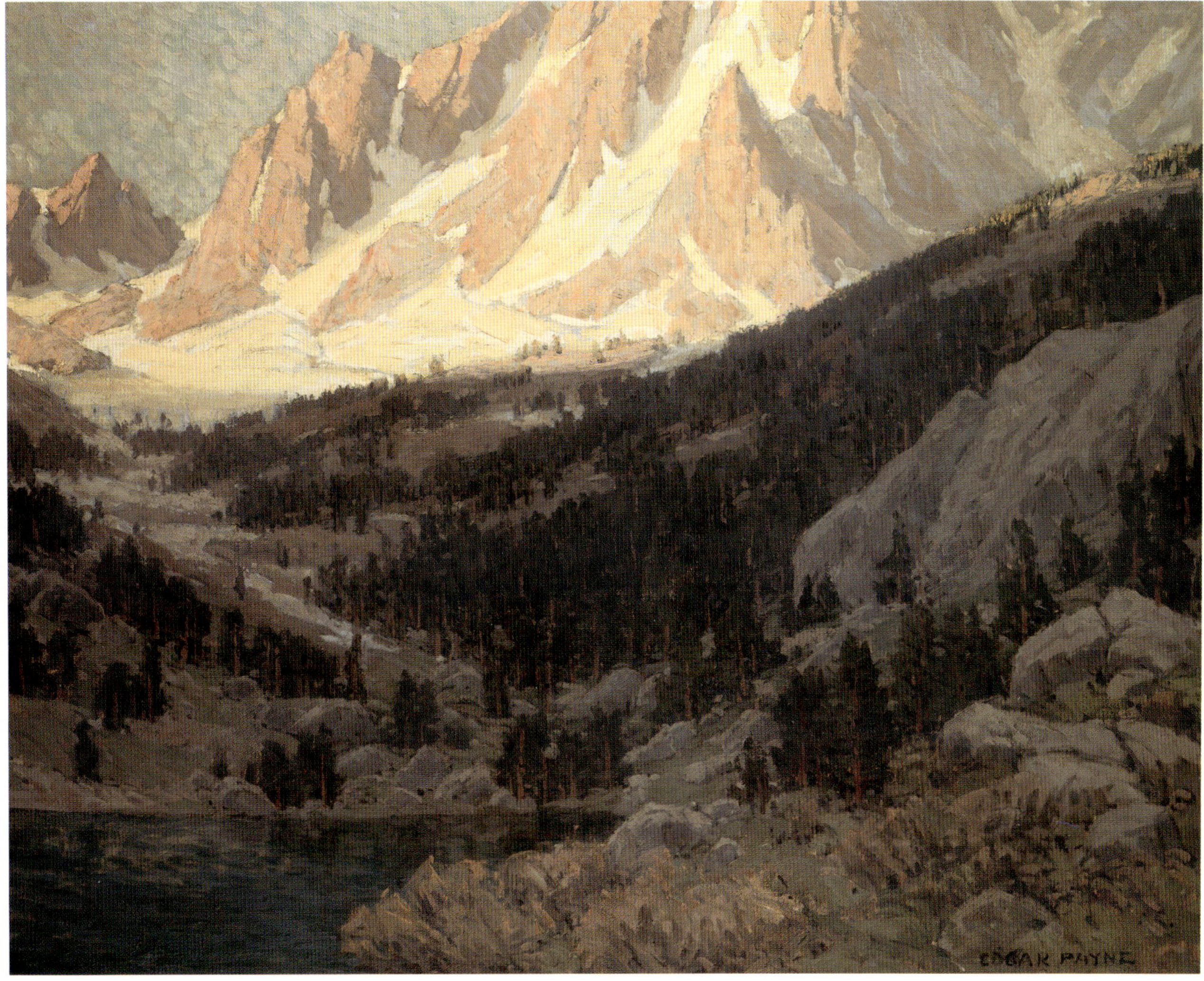

Fig. 6.09. Shadow Slope, Inyo Co., Calif., near Bishop, by EAP.

are particularly disastrous in this kind of subject.'' But balanced arrangement of forms is important too, and, ''In composing hills and mountains, unity may depend on an all over atmospheric condition, or the contrast of haze in the distance, and strong foreground values; or still further, on patterns of cloud shadows or those cast along canyons or ridges.'' However, ''preceding and transcending all visual appearances . . . are the great, invisible qualities to be felt when viewing hills and mountains — their nobility, height and grandeur — those fine, abstract qualities that exhilarate and lift the mind even from visual appearances.''[107]

Elsie, though she preferred to concentrate on human activity, was equally moved by the nobility and grandeur of the mountain scene, though again her approach was entirely different from Edgar's. Where Edgar warned students of the ''deceptive'' quality of the ridges and canyons of the mountains and the tendency of the massive rock formations to create a flat, planar appearance, Elsie capitalized on just those qualities in such pictures as *Sierra* (Fig. 6.10). She saw in those ridges and canyons an opportunity to develop the very patterns of mountains and snow patches that her husband had found deceptive. Not as concerned as Edgar with the illusion of three-dimensional space and the foreshortening of form to create recession into the picture plane, she chose instead to study the intricate convolutions of the mountains' ribs and seams and to deliberately

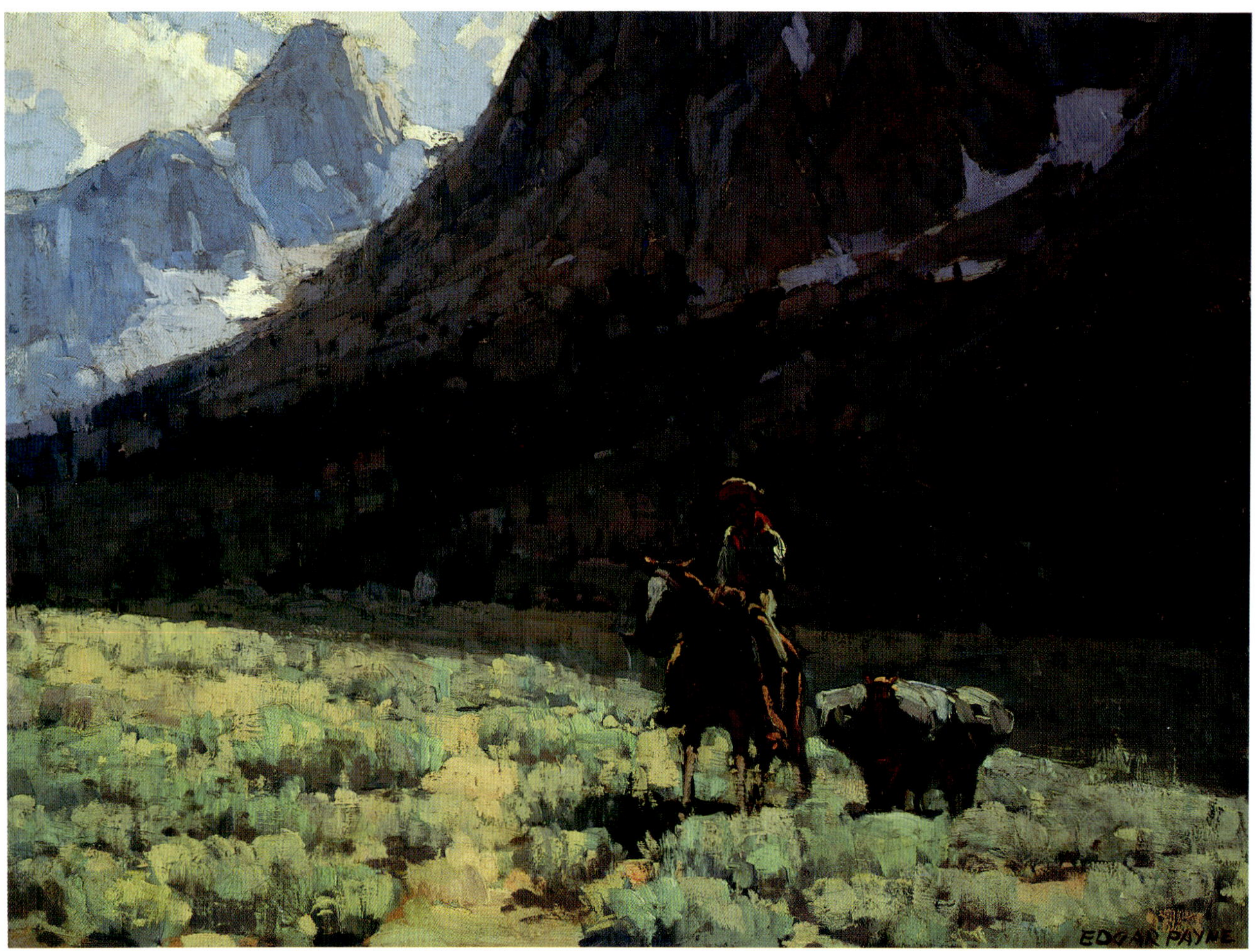

Fig. 6.12. Teton Country, by EAP.

emphasize their decorative designs. The muted palette of blues, browns, and greys that she used to follow the hilly contours and emphasize their linear design, further flattened the composition and stressed its more abstract pictorial qualities. Nevertheless, the illusion of depth is still frequently present in her mountain landscapes, as *The Creek (Sierra)* (Fig. 6.11) clearly reveals. Choosing a low vantage point, in contrast to Edgar's focus on the heights, she exploits the patterns of rocks and water, combining her flair for the decorative with a sophisticated design that allows the scene to recede in pictorial space as the mountain stream rushes towards us, splashing against the boulders in its way.

Though Edgar was primarily a landscapist, some of his pictures include horsemen or packers, as in *Teton Country* (Fig. 6.12). They add movement, color, and a sense of scale to the mountain vastness. Amid just such a group of packers Edgar himself would travel to the more remote and isolated areas of the California mountains, in his never-ending quest for the most dramatic manifestations of nature's authority. In time, he developed a packer's familiarity with the Sierras as well as an expertise at invoking them on canvas.

Indeed Edgar studied the "anatomy" of mountains as intensively as that of boats or horses, so that no matter how much the peaks were softened in color by distance, they are not softened in structure. His oil sketches included studies of rock formations, sometimes detailed in pencil in his notebook. He also took a great many photographs of them, as he did of boats, horses, and other landscapes, for reference. His daughter remembers:

> "He sometimes planned his studio painting in the evening; he very often sketched penciled compositions as he sat, perhaps listening to the radio. They were little composition sketches, working out artistic problems. It was interesting to watch him draw; his hands moved very rapidly, and he held his Venus 6B pencil in the same fashion as he would hold a piece of charcoal when drawing on a canvas. He always cut his pencils, very soft ones, into two or three pieces."

The principles he developed from such studies were to be captured in his book, *Composition of Outdoor Painting,* that provides instruction on both the techniques of landscape art and what he considered equally important, its proper motivation. "A painter," he wrote, reflecting his own experience, "needs to study, meditate and experiment and practice interminably" in order to produce a painting that would have "nobility in its concept, variety, rhythm, repetition, unity, balance and harmony in its composition." Acutely aware, however, of the necessity for artistic freedom and the importance of avoiding dogma in the pursuit of art, Edgar went on to observe that though the artist demands "that his imagination and creative power have minimum restraint," yet " 'liberty under law' is not only an axiom of both democracy and of art, but also an essential of each."[108] The text that follows is a skillful balance of rules of harmonious composition with a sensitive respect for individual creativity and esthetic judgment. But the picture required more than mere technical virtuosity, for Edgar insisted that in outdoor painting, the view must present "a worthy motive . . . and a quality that lifts the mind beyond the mere making of a picture . . . Entirely separate from the mechanics of painting . . . art has a deeper and more significant meaning. It must touch the innermost depths of feeling from which comes all esthetic enjoyment or appreciation."[109] The reproductions of his quick, outdoor color sketches that are included in the book clarify the artist's observations and illustrate his text. A typical example is a small oil sketch, *Sierras* (Fig. 6.13) which reveals the same combination of studied composition and bold, spontaneous execution that his book recommends.

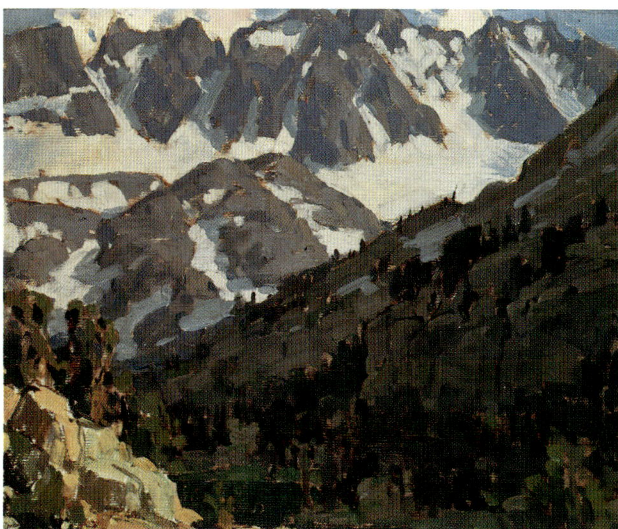

Fig. 6.13. Sierra, by EAP.

The book text provides a great deal of insight into how Edgar thought about art, and particularly about composition, which, unlike many artists, he was able to articulate verbally. In addition, Edgar also drew many pages of illustrations in which basic organizational principles are made clear in tiny simplified, almost diagrammatic, drawings. These are a tribute to Edgar's skill in reducing complex compositional ideas to simple demonstrations.

But while Edgar was contemplating nature in the isolation of the High Sierra peaks or distilling his experiences in the quiet of his studio, he was also a participant, and an important one, in the American Impressionist movement. Landscape painting, with a special reverence for nature, had, of course, been the focus of American art since the early nineteenth century when the work of Thomas Cole and his followers in the Hudson River School depicted the American wilderness as a new Eden. It was believed by contemporary philosophers and painters that this paradise had been bestowed on the American people by a transcendental and benevolent deity whose love for mankind was especially expressed in the "sublime" beauty of its deep, virgin forests, its mountain cliffs and chasms, and its mighty rivers and streams. The response of the earlier artists to such sublimity in a tight, rather literal style derived from European academic realism, gradually gave way to a new style in which nature was described in terms of light, color and atmosphere. This "modern" way of revealing nature on canvas had been developed in the 1860's, 70's and 80's by a group of French painters at whom the term "impressionists" had been derisively flung. But many artists, including Americans who had been trained or who had travelled abroad, fell under the spell of its seductive color and luminosity. By the last quarter of the nineteenth century, Impressionism was a favorite style and technique among many of our native artists, who depicted the beauties of their own surroundings in as vivid and spontaneous a manner as the French Impressionists had celebrated theirs.

A concern with light was not new to American landscapists, but its manipulation to heighten the visual impact of a scene through a bold brush stroke and a broken color technique, represented, for the Americans, a break with the traditions of the past. The new style abolished neutral tones and the blacks and greys traditionally used to suggest shadows and to enhance the illusion of three-dimensional modelling that had been the goal of academic practice for many generations. Instead, through their use of intense color and by replacing firm outlines and smooth surfaces with a thick impasto, the Impressionists achieved a vibrant atmosphere and an immediacy of recognition that was the style's essential characteristic. Like other Americans both before him and contemporary with him, Payne saw in Impressionism the perfect vehicle for suggesting, with a new freedom, the vast and varied American scene.[110]

Edgar used an impressionist palette that excluded black and saw color in even the darkest tones. Though he himself discovered that a combination of vermillion and ultramarine to portray shadow in the California hills would result in a vibrant description of the scene, his independent discovery was a typical impressionist response. He differed somewhat from the Impressionists, however, in that while he often used broken color, he did not adopt the technique of using pure color unmixed on the canvas, although he was well aware of it. On the contrary, he achieved harmony by "previously mixing a large amount of dominant shade then injecting it into every color used."[111] This "soup" was by no means necessarily a dark tone, and the more brilliant ones added richness to the shadowed areas. Moreover, Edgar always sought to combine a sense of the structure and solidity of the mountains with the feeling of light and air achieved by impressionist techniques.

Edgar's Impressionism came toward the end of the manifestation of that style in the United States. By the 1930's, European avant-garde styles were considered the new and "educated" way to look at the world, and Edgar's Impressionism became old-fashioned. Nevertheless, he continued to practice it, criticizing the "insanity" of the new abstract movements. He believed that art should be about nature, and the human relationship to nature. His paintings of the High Sierras most clearly show the American tradition of finding spiritual qualities in the wilderness. It was here too that he expressed most explicitly his quiet, personal patriotism, for, as he told Fred Hogue, chief editorial writer for the *Los Angeles Times,* he did not get the same feeling of communion with nature in the Swiss Alps that he did in California. In Europe, he complained, shelter huts are found even on the peaks, "the slopes are cultivated to the snow line [and] the hotels follow you everywhere. Here it is different . . . I have stood on the banks of fifty mountain lakes that are neither charted nor named. I have sketched in the shadow of mountains that would be famous in Europe, but that are known here only as units of the Sierra range" even though "there is more color in the High Sierras than in the Alps, and more atmosphere." "A hundred years from now," he predicted, "people . . . will be coming to California from all over the world, just to visit the lake country that those living in the great industrial districts . . . have not yet discovered."[112]

Edgar was also taking extended sketching trips into the American Southwest, to New Mexico and Arizona. Here he sought the same "noble poetry of silence, living and passionate,"[113] that he had found in the High Sierras, but that was also to be seen in the deserts, canyons and mesas of another part of the West. Here, both Edgar and Elsie were to find equal inspiration for the brush and new ways of expressing their separate visions.

Chapter 7: The Southwest

Edgar and Elsie first visited the southwestern states of New Mexico and Arizona in 1916, but on their many trips between Chicago and California they had undoubtedly admired what they could see of the area through the train windows of the Atchison, Topeka and Santa Fe Railroad. Though they may not have been aware of it at first, the railroad company was, in fact, an important patron of American artists, having been a pioneer in the corporate purchase of works of art. Since the beginning of the twentieth century, the railway lines serving the Southwest, particularly the Santa Fe Railroad Company, had been encouraging artists with free transportation and lodging as well as by the purchase of their paintings, to depict the scenic attractions of the areas served by it, both to promote tourism along its line and to provide color for their advertising in the absence of color photography.[114]

Many of the artists patronized by the Santa Fe were members of the Taos Ten, founders of the later well-known Taos Society of Artists. As early as the first decade of the twentieth century, these artists travelled to the Southwest, taking advantage of the free transportation and fulfilling commissions for pictures of its desert landscape. Once there, many of them elected to stay, drawn not only by the unique character of its scenery but by the colorful Southwest Indian populations and their unique cultures. The patronage of the railroads thus not only supported the development of art in the Southwest but made the region well known beyond its borders. It also laid the foundations for some important collections of Western art. The steady support and enthusiasm for the artists' work of such backers, for example, as William H. Simpson, General Advertising Agent for the Santa Fe, who had established the railroad's advertising department in 1896, resulted in the valuable collection of southwestern art that the company began to accumulate more than eighty years ago.

Edgar Payne never actually joined the Taos group of artists but he was acquainted with many of them as well as with others like Conrad Buff (1888-1975) and Frank Tenney Johnson (1874-1939) who knew and painted the southwest scene. Within the Taos art colony itself, Edgar's friends included some who eventually became well-known: Ernest L. Blumenschein, Victor Higgins, E. Martin Hennings, Nicolai Fechin, and Walter Ufer. Irwin O. Myers, who was, like Edgar, peripherally associated with the Taos group, was a special friend of the Paynes, having been a member of their group on Santa Cruz Island during the memorable trip to California in 1915, and had exhibited in Santa Barbara with Edgar.

For the Paynes first trip into the Southwest and Navajo-Hopi country, the arrangement with the railroad was that Edgar would receive $100 cash and $100 in "hotel and livery" bills at the El Tovar Hotel at the Grand Canyon together with free transportation. In return he transferred to the Santa Fe his painting *Montecito Way,* which was to be redeemed for one of Canyon de Chelly on his return.[115]

And so, armed with appropriate letters of introduction from Advertising Agent Simpson, Edgar arrived in Gallup, New Mexico, on June 25, 1916, "with wife and baby in good condition". They were met there by Roman Hubbell, who operated trading posts and automobile and stage connections from Gallup, and who sent the Paynes out by special car to the Canyon de Chelly.

While the record suggests the Santa Fe anticipated a relatively short trip which included the Grand Canyon, the next record of the Paynes after the Canyon de Chelly is their arrival at the El Tovar on October 15th, nearly four months later. This was quite a surprise to C.A. Brant, manager of the hotel, especially since the Paynes only stayed a day and a half and purchased Indian artifacts, such a Navajo jewelry, rugs, Mariaware, etc., against the $100 credit.

During that four month "disappearance" the Paynes lived near the Navajo and Hopi Indians, observing at first hand their way of life. It was a fascinating adventure for the Paynes, one they repeated in later years, for, aside from their taste for adventure, they both had an innate sympathy and respect for these ancient peoples of the Southwest. It was a lesson for them too, in the arrogance of White civilization, for Elsie later recalled her irritation at the sight of Navajo girls, famous weavers of rugs in their own native tradition, being taught by the White mission schoolteachers to make rag rugs on sewing machines! Also vivid in her memory was the mission school's insistence that their charges abandon their colorful native dress and wear instead the drab cotton dresses deemed proper attire by the teachers.

As was the case with many of the artists who visited or came to live in the Southwest during this period, the Paynes particularly admired the arts of Indian peoples. They recognized the artistic merits of the "curios" available for sale, and considered them works of art, testimony to the creativity of Indian peoples as artists.

During their first visits in the area, Elsie and Evelyn would usually stay at nearby trading posts, such as Chinle, Ganados, or mission stations on the reservation, while Edgar made short trips, typically in a buckboard wagon with Indian guides, in the canyons (Fig. 7.01). He particularly admired Canyon de Chelly, a desert canyon, winding eighteen tortuous miles in northeastern Arizona and forming a spectacular gorge of sheer red sandstone cliffs, rising at their highest point to almost a thousand feet above the canyon floor. It is the main part of a set of canyons that join to provide a total of over 60 miles of canyon walls that are the sites of hundreds of prehistoric cliff dwellings, whose ancient ruins attract not only archeologists but illegal pothunters. The Canyon became one of Edgar's favorite landscape locations in the area on his many return trips over the years.

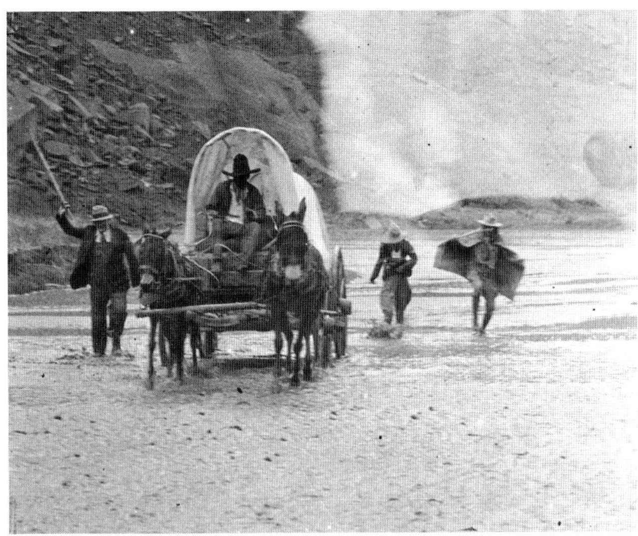

Fig. 7.01. In Canyon de Chelly. Wading the stream for the 30th time.

From his sketches of this trip Edgar did several paintings of Canyon de Chelly and Canyon del Muerto, and showed them to Mr. Simpson and Mr. Butterfield of the Santa Fe. They chose two of them. The first, *Sunset, Canyon de Chelly,* fulfilled the agreement and the Montecito painting was returned; a second, titled *Navajo Country,* was also purchased for an additional $250 to be paid in installments. Both of these were first displayed in the office of T. R. Henry, General Agent in Detroit, but about a year later the *Navajo Country* was transferred to the new El Navajo Hotel in Gallup where it remained for many years.

Edgar's excitement at his early exploration of the canyon is revealed in *Sunset, Canyon de Chelly* (Fig. 7.02), which the Santa Fe later reproduced on its 1971 calendar, and which is now in the Anschutz Collection in Denver. By far one of Edgar's most dramatic paintings of the Southwest,

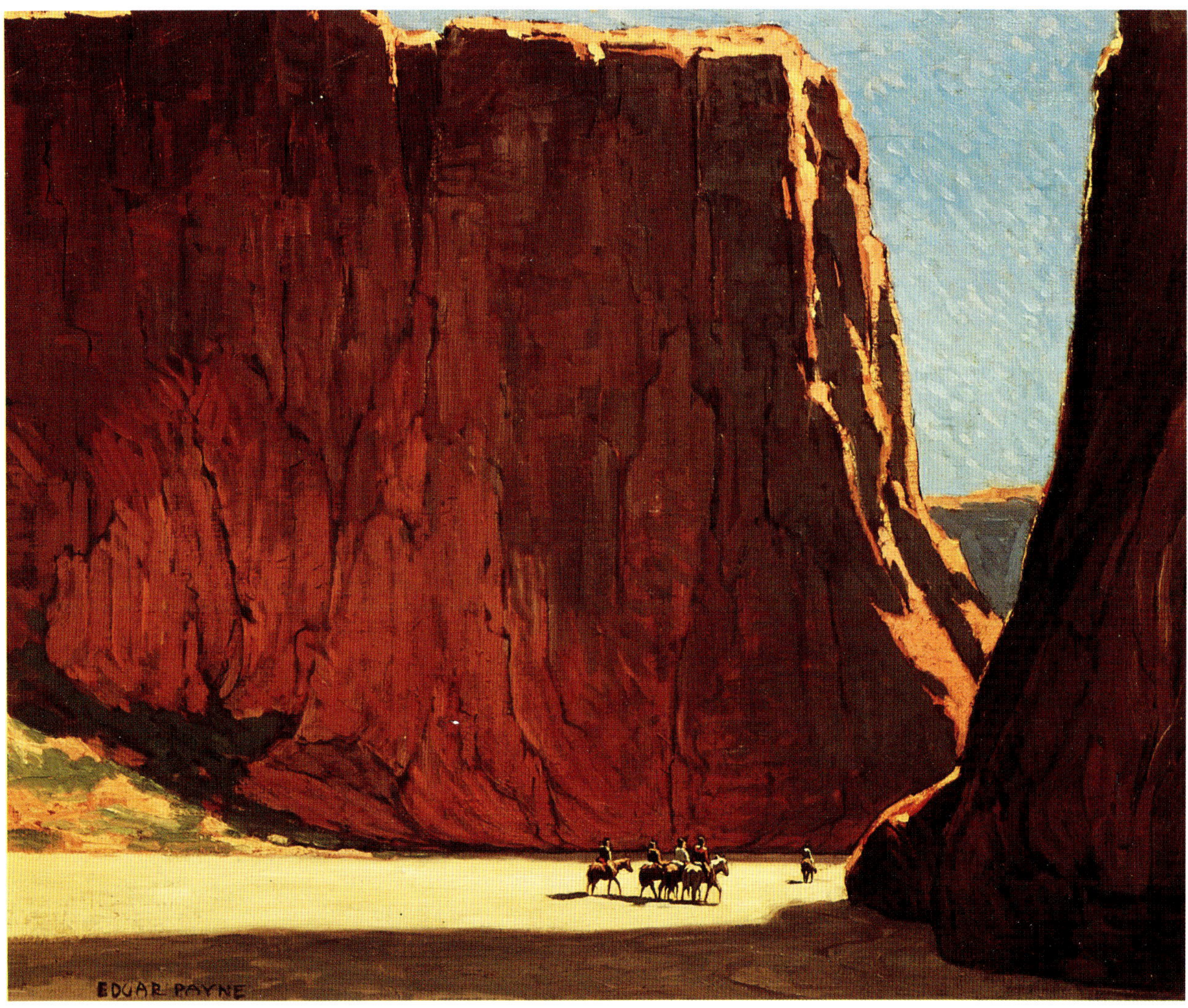

Fig. 7.02. Sunset, Canyon de Chelly, by EAP.

it depicts the high, steep cliffs of the canyon walls outlined against the sky by the intense sun of Arizona. The golden glow edging the cliffs also floods the canyon floor in a shining carpet of gold, upon which a few horsemen, diminutive in scale, ride below the towering walls. Though the blue sky, barely glimpsed through the narrow canyon, is brushed in with the bold strokes of the Impressionist painter, the canyon ridges are traced in a more linear pattern, one that exploits the random designs created by the weathered ribs of the desert mountain. Indeed, *Sunset, Canyon de Chelly* seems diametrically opposed to the Impressionist style, conforming once again to the "glare esthetic" of post-Impressionist American painting, which, as has been seen, sometimes characterized Edgar's work. Instead of the true impressionist's use of a shimmering light that dissolves form and records only the ephemeral character of the outdoor scene, Edgar's painting manipulates light in order to reinforce form and thus stress its permanence. By contrasting the dark, shadowy cliff face with the intense light at its edge, the artist emphasizes the strong planar surfaces of the composition and thus heightens its dramatic power.

There are many paintings of Canyon de Chelly by Edgar, some based on the sketches of this first trip. There is no record, however, of Edgar's important paintings of other aspects of the area scene or of the Navajo, either on this first trip, or on a later brief visit in 1925. The full impact of Edgar's relationship with the Southwest becomes clear only with a consideration of all of his work, much of which dates after 1930, when a family stay in Thoreau was perhaps pivotal in providing a focus for his work and friendships important in his personal and professional life.

In the spring of 1930 the Paynes travelled from New York to Chicago, where there was a May-June exhibition of Edgar's works at the Illinois Women's Athletic Club,[116] and then on to the University of Illinois[117] and another exhibition of Edgar Paynes. Here they stayed a few days, in the house of the President of the University, who was away, while Edgar varnished the murals in the School of Architecture where his exhibition was held. The next stop was Ogden, Utah,[118] where they were royally entertained by Mr. and Mrs. Frederick Gray Ruthrauff, for Mrs. Ruthrauff, the director of the Hotel Bigelow Gallery was a great admirer and enthusiastic supporter of Edgar Payne's work and had arranged the big Payne exhibition at the Hotel Utah in Salt Lake City in 1928. Her husband was the local agent for the Union Pacific Railroad and was himself an amateur artist and a friend of the Paynes in Paris, where he had studied the pointillist technique. In Ogden the Paynes were joined by Buck Weaver, a family friend from Laguna, who drove there in his new Model A roadster. By this time Buck was making a name for himself as a painter of desert landscapes which he had studied with another master of the desert scene, Maynard Dixon.

After putting on a big barbecue in Ogden Canyon, to which all of the many people who had entertained the Paynes were invited, the Paynes and Buck took off for the Southwest in their two cars. They went by way of Zion and Bryce canyons, staying in cabin courts along the way, but the Paynes did not do much sketching until they got to Thoreau, New Mexico. When unpacking in the cabin court in Thoreau, Buck dropped his six shooter, and the slug went the length of his upper leg. Edgar drove him the 30 miles to the nearest medical help in Gallup, where Buck stayed in the hospital the rest of the summer, unable to sketch with Edgar as they had planned.

In Thoreau the Paynes stayed at the cabin court just across from Lloyd Ambrose's trading post, which was visited by both Indians and Anglos. Ambrose, who was to become a close friend of the Paynes, was a well-liked trader, honest and appreciative of fine Indian artifacts. He insisted, in his trading, on the high quality Indians could provide and would not buy poorly woven blankets, for example. It was here that Edgar later met both Gladys Reichard, professor of anthropology at Columbia University's Barnard College and a pioneer in the study of Navajo art, and Oliver La Farge, whose 1929 novel about the Navajo, *Laughing Boy,* won the Pulitzer prize.

The Navajos who accompanied him on excursions to the Canyon de Chelly were of a people who had occupied that region since the middle of the eighteenth century. They were sheep and goat herders as well as famous craftsmen in silver and woven wool, essentially a nomadic tribe, compared to the more settled Pueblo Indians of New Mexico and Arizona. For that reason, perhaps, Edgar felt more at home with them than with other Indians, or, for that matter, with some of the more conventional and sedentary members of his own race. He painted many pictures of them, for the most part sketchy figure studies showing them conversing as they lean on a buckboard wagon, seated beside their small, covered wagons, or mounted on their horses, as in *Navajos Pausing* (Fig. 7.03).

In his Southwestern paintings, as in all his work, the theme of the relationship between man and nature is an important one. Pirates and fishermen, packers and Navajo on horseback all move within a landscape to which they are closely related, both artistically and conceptually. In some works the conception seems romantic, but in others a profound philosophical and spiritual awareness is clearly conveyed. That his concern and respect for the natural world was neither unconscious nor automatically reflected we know from his writing. Very often it is in the desert paintings that this relationship is most clearly expressed, with Indian horsemen often shown as very small figures within a dominating landscape. There were, however, some exceptions to the

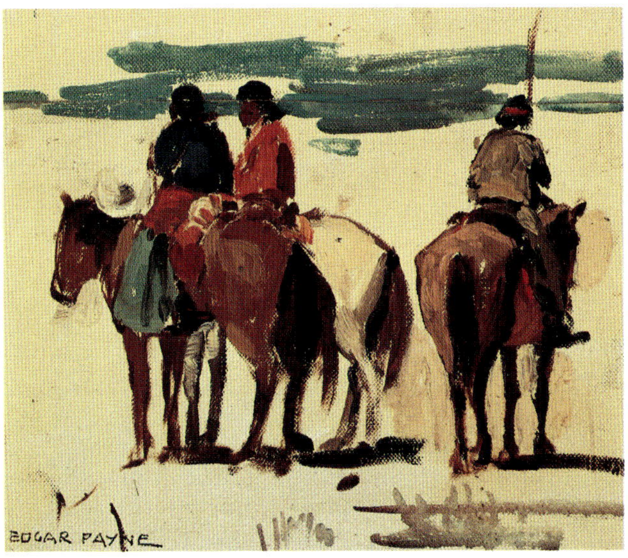

Fig. 7.03. Navajos Pausing, by EAP.

general pattern that horses and men are subordinate to the landscape. His daughter remembers:

> "There is one painting that I know of that he did of just horses, and I do not know if it still exists. I went to his studio, about 1940, and there on his work easel was a large spectacular scene of the Southwest, with a whole herd of horses, and great thunderclouds in the sky and a dramatic fight between two stallions. I thought it was terrific, and I said so, and he said, 'Too melodramatic.' That was all he said. I would guess from this that he probably destroyed it, and it *was* melodramatic, but he was getting away with it, and I hope it still exists. This makes me suspect that every once in a while he did paint a very dramatic picture, a painting with the kind of expression of more violent emotion than he ordinarily allowed himself. But these were for his own satisfaction, and I wonder how many times he said 'Too melodramatic' and scraped it off."

Edgar not only drew many studies of Indian people in pencil and oil but took photographic notes as well. He studied Indians, their horses and wagons just as he did the packers of the Sierras or the European fishermen and their boats and gear. These were the notes to be used for easel paintings later, and also a way of learning. This contrasted sharply with Elsie's way of working. In her painting of wagons and camps near a trading post, or at the Ceremonial at Gallup, Elsie's sketches were compositions organized as she went along, while Edgar's were more often single horses or persons done simply as studies. His sketch that was later titled *Navajo Portrait* (Fig. 7.04) was a study of this kind. He would have been surprised to have it considered a fine portrait seen within the historical context of American Indian portraits. For Edgar's portrayal, though somewhat differently conceived than the "noble savage" in all his glory, is still a part of that expression of myth and nostalgia that had marked the image of the American Indian in literature and art since the earliest white settlement of North America. Particularly in the nineteenth century, as the reality of the disappearance of Indian life and culture became all too apparent, the association of the native American with heroic strength and dignity, as well as with the exoticism inherent in a rapidly vanishing race, had been a symbolic constant in the representation of the Indians of the west.

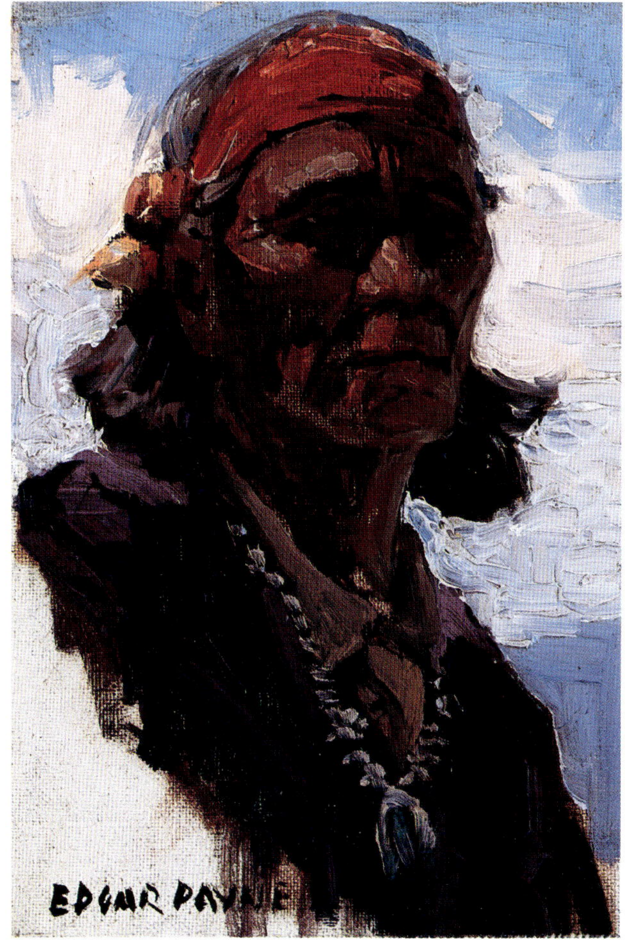

Fig. 7.04. Navajo Portrait, by EAP.

Edgar's *Navajo Portrait,* though unusual within the body of his work, demonstrates that his paintings of landscapes were a matter of choice and not the result of an inability to capture the person behind a portrait. The painting is a small one, brushed onto the canvas with a few sure strokes and showing only the head and shoulders of the subject, who wears one of the heavy, beautifully crafted silver necklaces made by Navajo silversmiths. The Indian in the portrait, strong of feature and heroic in demeanor, rises prominently against the cloudy sky as he looks out at us and at his rapidly changing world. The picture may remind one of the monumental portraits of Renaissance dukes and princes, thrust forward in the picture plane and dominating their surrounding space. Both pride and dignity are apparent in Edgar's portraits of the valiant, almost mythic hero so frequently associated with the American West.

Elsie's pictures of the Navajo, on the other hand, were, as always, a product of her human interest and basic social instincts. When she accompanied Edgar to New Mexico in 1930, she painted a Navajo camp (Fig. 7.05) as a genre scene in which women and children tend a cooking fire while their horses graze nearby. Though the shapes of the figures are simplified to conform with the essentially decorative purpose of the composition, there is, nevertheless, a social

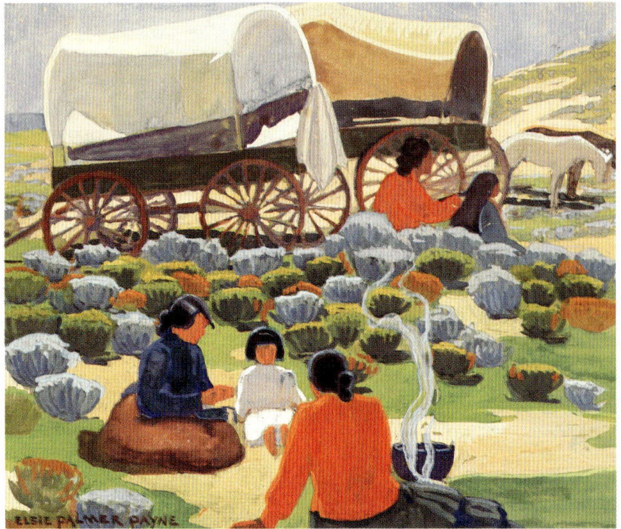

Fig. 7.05. Navajo Camp, by EPP.

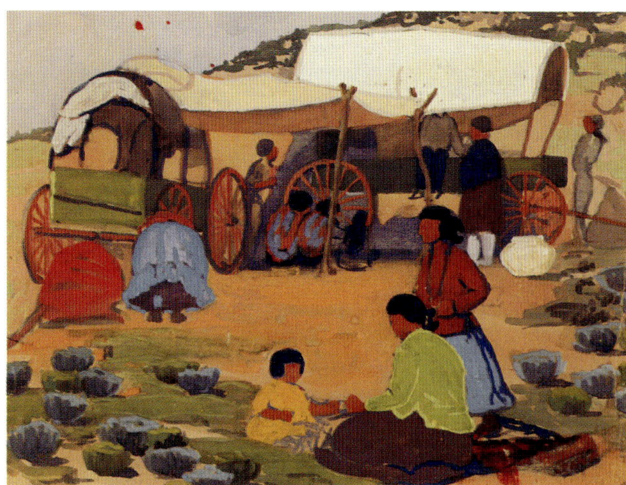

Fig. 7.06. Sketch for Trading, by EPP.

exchange taking place among the figures, both the seated ones in the foreground and the more distant one who engages in the ordinary activity of combing a young girl's hair. The colors of the sagebrush clumps, blue and green tinged with orange, are repeated in the women's clothing, while the rounded tops of the bushes are echoed in the canvas covers arched over the wagons. Even the cooking pot beside the near fire carries out the shape of the desert plants in a harmonious repetition of their basic design. Similarly, in a preliminary sketch for a painting entitled *Trading* (Fig. 7.06), Elsie concentrates on the domesticity, the simple everydayness of the scene, expressed always in the flat, simplified forms that she preferred.

Although Elsie also painted landscapes, the pictures of the Southwest painted by Edgar and Elsie are particularly revealing in their contrast of the two artists' style and purpose. The rugged life of the Paynes' summer painting expeditions usually translated for Elsie into an attentive observation of the ordinary human accommodation to the conditions of life, whether in a fishing village in Europe or on a Navajo reservation in the Southwestern United States, while for her husband it was the remote and untamed, either in the landscape or in man, that caught his attention and captivated his brush.

Sometime after 1930, as their daughters began to attend high school, the Ambroses moved to

Gallup. Their Casa Linda motel there became Edgar's headquarters on his many return visits to the area, the source of more light-filled paintings of the Southwest. Though he continued painting the Canyon de Chelly, other aspects of the desert landscape also attracted him. *Arizona Tablelands* (Fig. 7.07) probably dates from this period. It is typical of Edgar's southwestern landscapes in its depiction of the flat desert, rimmed by distant mesas and anchored under high-piled clouds that

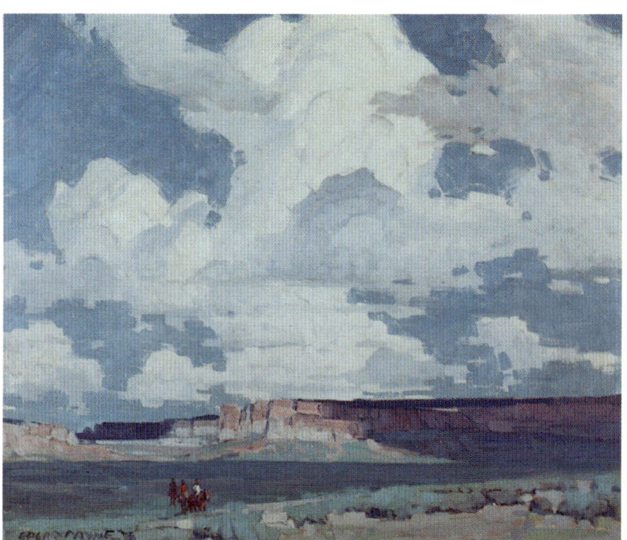

Fig. 7.07. Arizona Tablelands, by EAP.

sail across the southwest sky. A few horsemen provide a sense of scale in this expansive landscape though more usually, as in *New Mexico Vista* (Fig. 7.08), no humans intrude into the isolation of the scene or disturb its desert solitude.

It is very difficult to precisely date many of the works, including a later painting of the Canyon, titled *Canyon Portals* (Fig. 7.09), which is more subdued, or perhaps subtle, in color and a good deal less theatrical in effect than the 1916 picture *Sunset, Canyon de Chelly.* It retains the artist's characteristic sense of isolation in nature and his admiration, even reverence, for its power. Indeed, Edgar's consciousness of man's insignificance within the cosmic order, so evident here, ties him directly to the artists of the Hudson River School who, over a hundred years before, had exhibited a similar veneration for the American wilderness. Edgar Payne was a true heir of that tradition in

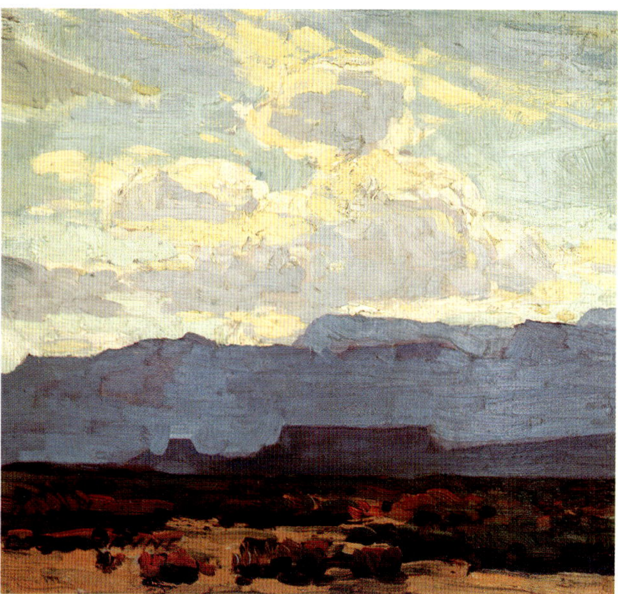

Fig. 7.08. New Mexico Vista, by EAP.

the homage he paid to the virgin land, though he transferred its focus from the forests and streams of the northeastern United States to the arid, weather-shaped monuments of the West.

In the Grand Canyon of Arizona, Edgar discovered still another spectacular landscape subject and he painted it, too, over a period of years and from different points of view. A fine example is his picture entitled *Grand Canyon, South Rim* (Fig. 7.10), where Edgar's gift for suggesting the power of nature, so evident in his paintings of the California mountains, is transferred to this desert locale. Like many of the Sierra pictures, this one is a study, at once analytical and descriptive, of the distinctive rock formations of the canyon as they recede in measured steps toward the horizon. Here too Edgar manipulates light to create a dramatic tableau of the canyon region, contrasting the patch of foreground brightness against the shadowed crag that rises at its side. But it is not so much the light that dominates this composition as the steady rhythm of the scene, creating a clear, visual unity between the near rock masses and the farther ones fading in steady cadence into the subtle lavender blues of the distance. Edgar instinctively recognized the elemental human need for an organizing rhythm in pictorial composition and he compared its function in painting to music

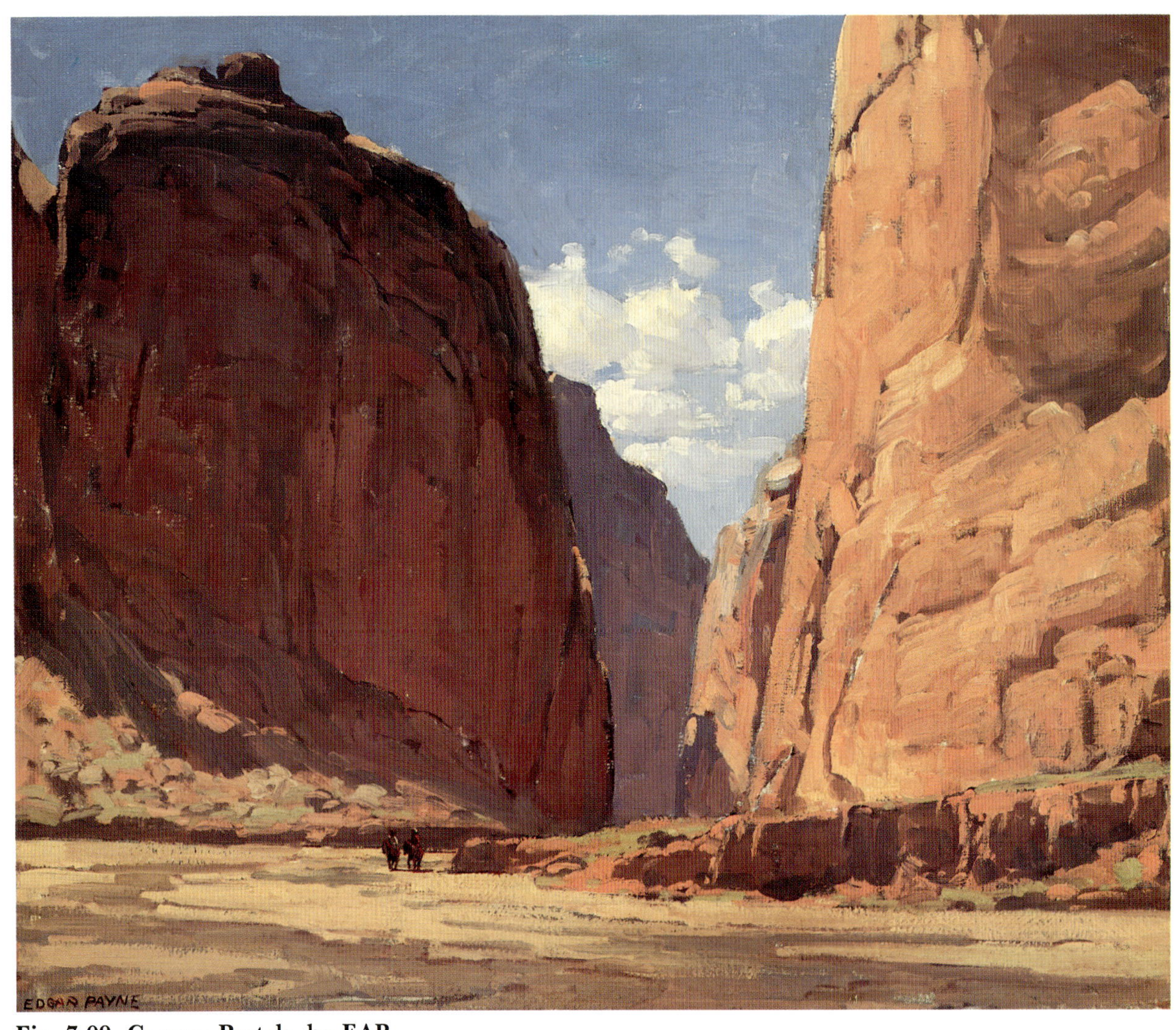

Fig. 7.09. Canyon Portals, by EAP.

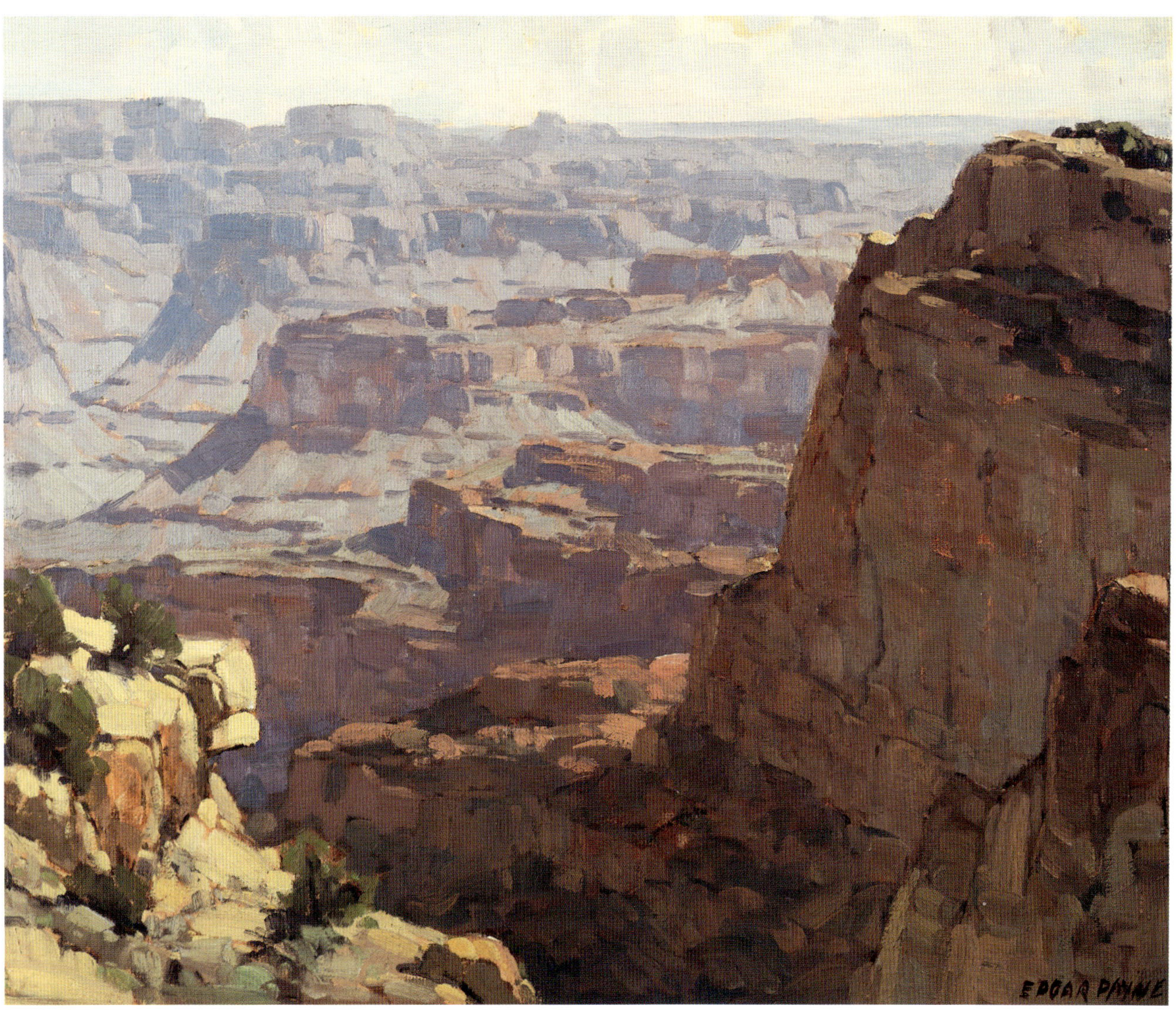

Fig. 7.10. Grand Canyon, South Rim, by EAP.

and dance. "As the dancer uses rhythm to integrate time, space and movement," he observed, "so too does the painter utilize this element to integrate the factors in art." But, though "rhythm symbolizes harmony, activity, energy or movement, it calls for . . . solid footing as a balance . . . to hold movement to proper speed. In art it needs some attachment to the more stabilizing elements to create an artistic visual unity." Above all, in the southwest as elsewhere, the artist must be in tune with nature, for "to feel the spirit of nature is to feel the rhythmic, spiritual flow which encircles animate and inanimate nature — the rhythm of life and the universe."[119]

While thinking so deeply, however, about the rhythms and harmonies of nature, Edgar was ignoring, or perhaps escaping from the disharmonies rising in his own household. After spending the winter of 1930-31 in New York, Edgar took off in the spring for the west coast, while Elsie and Evelyn stayed in New York. During the late summer, Elsie received a telegram from her husband, instructing her to close up the apartment they had been renting in Spuyten Duyvil, store the furniture, and meet him in Los Angeles in ten days. Elsie obeyed, but before she left, arranged for Evelyn to room and board with a neighbor family so that she could finish her last year at the Fieldston school and graduate from there — which she did the following Spring.

Having to miss Evelyn's graduation because they could not afford the trip, Elsie painted a picture of the graduation bouquet from a description of it. Indeed, the uses of art for both Paynes included a way to deal with their feelings, and an escape from confronting their differences.

Edgar was subsequently to return to the Southwest over a period of years to paint again in the vicinity of Thoreau, the Canyon de Chelly, and the Grand Canyon of Arizona, but in the summer of 1932 he, Elsie and Evelyn went back to the High Sierras. This camp was the last time the whole family lived together until Edgar's final illness.

Chapter 8: Separation

Elsie and Edgar separated in 1932, after a serious confrontation between Evelyn and her father that took place in the summer Sierra camp. On this trip Edgar took a group of students, as well as a cook and a handyman who worked for their "room" and board. For most of the two weeks things went very well — good sketching, stories around the campfire, and pleasant relationships. But Evelyn had brought a friend from the East, which turned out to be a mistake, for the girl had never slept out of her own bed before and was homesick and bored. Edgar thought the girls should not go away from camp at all, especially with the two young men students, and he and Evelyn clashed over his authoritarian dictates.[120]

This confrontation, however, was just the spark that led to separation. Elsie had always been willing to be overshadowed by her husband, to go where he wanted to go, when he wanted to go there. Though he admired Elsie's art, he never promoted it as he (and she) did his own, and he tended to slight her career throughout their marriage. His was the generally accepted view that, no matter how talented or able, a woman's place was to be at her husband's beck and call. Elsie had swallowed her irritations and resentments, and waited out his black moods for the sake of his good ones, and a life that was interesting and full of drama. But she would no longer permit her daughter's life to be dominated by Edgar. After he said, in anger, that he would no longer support Evelyn, both Elsie and Evelyn left to start a new life on their own.

After the breakup of her marriage, Elsie moved into a bungalow court apartment in Los Angeles while Evelyn took a job as a live-in mother's helper, earning enough to support herself while attending classes at UCLA. The following winter, while Evelyn had a short fling at art school, Elsie rented a small hilltop cottage on Hanscom Drive near South Pasadena which she and Evelyn repaired and repapered in exchange for a rent of five dollars for two months. Memorable to both was a Laurel and Hardy-like adventure entangling them in yards of pasty wallpaper and gales of laughter.[121]

Elsie was beginning, with the aid of a psychological consultant, to forge a new life for herself, emerging slowly from her husband's shadow and discovering inner resources she had scarcely been aware of during her married life. Indeed, in the years following their separation, Edgar's work settled into a repetition of the themes he had previously developed, the Sierras, the Southwest, the fishing boats of Italy and France, while Elsie's career, after a period of reorientation began to blossom and develop in new directions. She resumed, for example, giving instruction in art, finding herself an excellent teacher. She had had some previous teaching experience when the Paynes were living in Westport, Connecticut,[122] and also in New York, where she had been asked to give a course of instruction in art. At the time she was amazed to find, as every good teacher eventually does, that she herself had learned more in preparing the lessons than in all her years of study and experience. In marshalling her knowledge into definite, concrete shape so that it could be simplified and organized into transmittable form, she had discovered that "if you want to make something your own, teach it to others."[123]

Elsie's teaching was organized into a series of "basic principles" in ten lessons, with a second set of ten to take up each again in a more advanced way. In practice she seldom followed this plan closely, however, as she was so responsive to the needs and interests of each individual student that she would modify the lessons accordingly.

She used as a starting point Cezanne's advice to look at nature in terms of cubes, cones, and cylinders, and she observed that "if the arrangement is not good in the beginning, the painting will never be good no matter how wonderful the drawing, color, and the elements may be."[124]

The topics included were the familiar ones of proportion, perspective, rhythm, the color wheel, color harmony, notan (chiaroscuro), the human figure, dynamic symmetry, etc. It was the exercises she worked out to assure understanding of each topic separately before trying to put it all together that made the approach so effective.

Elsie was also rediscovering organization talents that had been evident when she and Edgar were founding members of the Laguna Beach Art Association, and she developed them now in her own studio-gallery-school in Beverly Hills. Most important of all, however, she began to paint much more steadily than she had while living with Edgar, exploring new directions in art as well as her life. In talking of her career many years later, she remembered another artist couple whose relationship had been quite different from hers and Edgar's. The devoted husband, Elsie was told, had waited on his wife "hand and foot and did other things for her and thought she was so wonderful because she could paint. Mine," she remarked with a note of bitterness, "never gave me time to paint! I was always busy waiting on him, packing and unpacking."[125]

On June 1, 1934 Elsie opened, with Marie H. Kann, a studio gallery at 332 N. Canon Drive in Beverly Hills. The Payne-Kann studio, the initial announcement promised, would feature changing exhibitions by contemporary California artists and craftsmen as well as classes offering instruction in various branches of art, including puppet-making. The latter was the specialty of Evelyn Payne, who joined her mother's new enterprise as a teacher of puppetry and producer of puppet shows for children's parties.

Elsie, however, who had never completely severed her emotional ties to Edgar, made it clear from the very beginning that the contemporary California artist to be most frequently shown in the gallery would be Edgar Payne. Not surprisingly, a special exhibition devoted to his work was held when the Payne-Kann studio and gallery opened on June 1, 1934.[126]

This support for Edgar's paintings continued even after the Payne-Kann studio and gallery became the Payne-Pegler studio when, a few months later, Virginia Pegler replaced Marie Kann as Elsie's partner in the gallery. Neither of Elsie's associates had any experience in art, besides a general interest in it, but they paid half the rent and thus helped Elsie get started in her own gallery.

Edgar and Elsie were together at the Payne-Peglar Studio Gallery on February 9, 1935, when their daughter, Evelyn, was married in the gallery's garden to John Burton Hatcher, a student of chemistry at the California Institute of Technology. Edgar, conforming to tradition, gave the bride away at the simple ceremony.[127] Though Elsie still harbored ambivalent and conflicting emotions at her separation from Edgar, the happy occasion of their daughter's marriage did not affect a reconciliation and they continued to live apart. The bond between them was strong enough, however, that the two artists never formally divorced, and when, in 1946, Edgar fell ill with cancer, Elsie moved back in with him and nursed him through the last year of his life.

The Payne-Pegler association was to prove as temporary as the Payne-Kann partnership, and on September 14, 1936 Elsie held an opening reception at her own Elsie Palmer Payne Art School and Gallery at 9419 Wilshire Boulevard in Beverly Hills.[128] There she offered classes for both children and adults in drawing, painting, art principles and clay modelling while others taught commercial art, interior decoration and costume design. Edgar was invited to teach extra classes in outdoor sketching.

Meanwhile, Edgar had established a studio at 1142 North Seward Street in Hollywood (Fig. 8.01), where he too lectured on art, specifically on

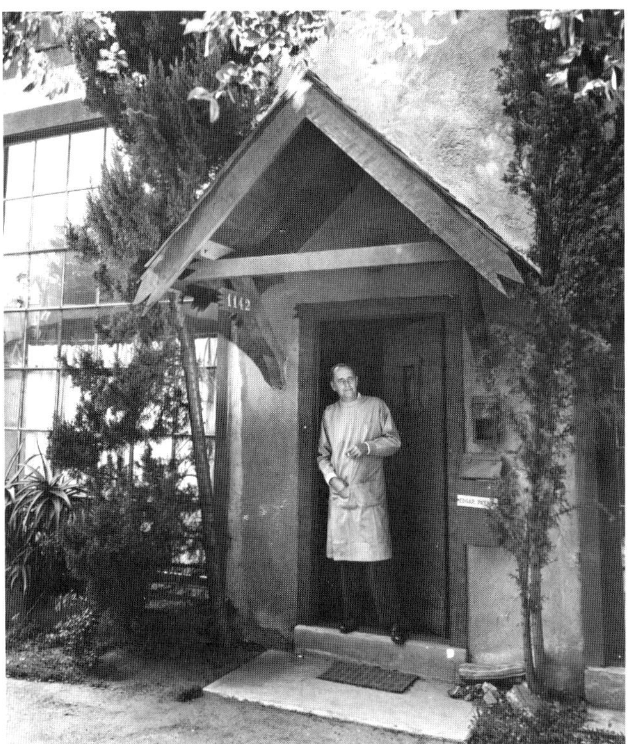

Fig. 8.01. Edgar at his Seward Street studio.

the principles of landscape painting. The ideas he organized into these lectures were gathered and published in 1941 in his book, *The Composition of Outdoor Painting,* which he published himself and illustrated with sketches and paintings of his own as well as by other artists he admired. The preface to the books opens with the statement that "The most important ally in the study of painting is the art of thinking . . . [while] individuality in thought is . . . the greatest single factor in creative work." But, he went on, as certain "forms of composition and other principles of art . . . are generally accepted by most painters . . . I have endeavored to bring out the main essentials and their contributing factors as clearly as possible according to my own way of thinking." Aware of the difficulties of teaching art through the printed word, Edgar nevertheless felt that "in study, theory or practice, knowledge is undoubtedly the keynote to individual thought and originality in painting," and therefore, he wrote, "to those who are looking for suggestions which might aid them in developing their own ideas, skill or appreciation, this little volume is fraternally presented."[129]

Edgar's teaching was more often in the form of advice on a sketching trip than in formal studio lessons. One of his serious students was Karl Albert, now a well-known western painter, who recalls Payne's silence as he looked over the young man's work, and how long it was before he finally said that he would "take him on."

Once in a while Edgar accepted a Sunday painter as a student. One story holds that a well-known surgeon who had worked with him for a while came in excitedly and said somebody wanted to buy one of his paintings: "What should I charge?" "Doctor," Edgar replied "if I studied medicine for six months, what should I charge for an operation?" This sense of humor sometimes took visual form as well. Fig. 8.02 is a wry comment on the sketching trips that were so much a part of Edgar's life.

Though Edgar did not enjoy teaching as much

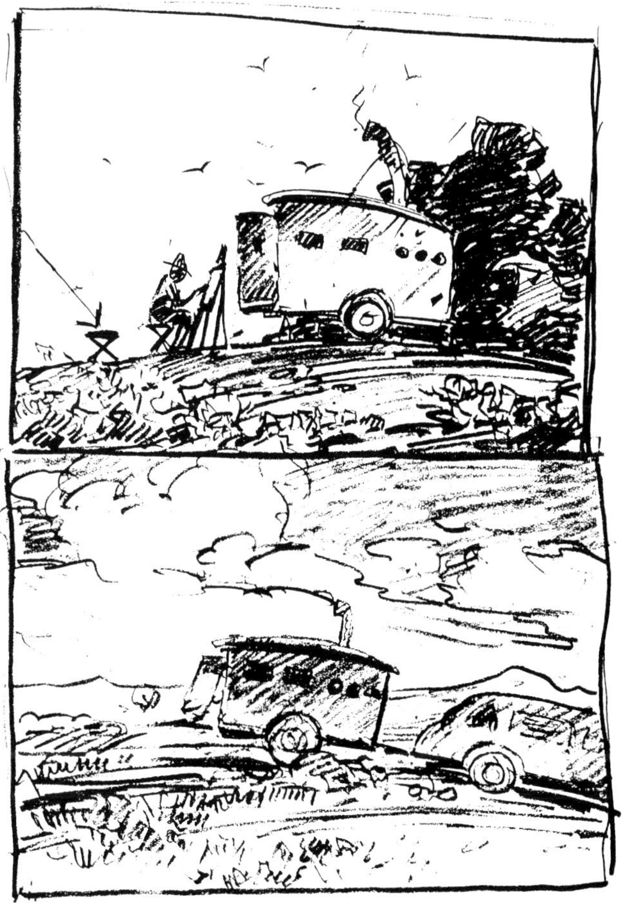

Fig. 8.02. Artist and Trailer, by EAP.

as Elsie did, his lectures on art helped augment his income during the Depression when hard economic times severely restricted the market for art and made the sale of his paintings, however much admired, increasingly difficult. But Edgar, always enterprising, managed to trade his pictures for various goods and services, ranging from a 1935 Oldsmobile Touring Coupe to free meals at the Gotham restaurant on Hollywood Boulevard — "said allowance," according to the agreement, "not to exceed five dollars per week,"[130] a generous enough sum for those depressed times.

It was not, however, just the Depression that was making the sale of Edgar's paintings increasingly difficult. During the 1930's, with the growing influence of avant-garde European styles on American painters, and the spread of abstract and nonobjective art, the Impressionist landscape style practiced by Edgar not only fell out of vogue but was frequently derided. Banding together to fight the trend toward what they viewed as "insanity" in contemporary art, a group of southern California artists met on October 4, 1939 to form a Los Angeles branch of the Society for Sanity in Art, Inc., a national organization that had been formed in Chicago by Rudolf Ingerle, a prominent Chicago landscape painter. Among the charter members of the Los Angeles chapter, which elected Charles Bensco as its president, was Edgar Payne, who served as the Society's first secretary and wrote the introduction to the catalogue of its first exhibition in Exposition Park, Los Angeles, April 1st to May 1st, 1940. The objectives of the Society, expressed in a constitution which sounds as though Edgar wrote it, were ". . . to encourage . . . an art that is based on sound, fundamental principles." The Society would endeavor to "uphold, practice and teach those essentials which translate quality in nature and create quality in craftsmanship. To display, exhibit and publicize works of art that are sane, understandable and built upon tradition and precedent of the past as well as new, contemporary ideas." Finally, the Society would "give to the present and leave for future generations an art that is built upon noble conceptions and skillful craftsmanship."[131] These ideas, of course, echo those articulated by Edgar in his book as a summary of his life's artistic experience. The Society later evolved into the Artists of the Southwest, with similiar aims, but a less belligerent title and tone.

Elsie's name is significantly absent from the Society for Sanity in Art. Though she rejected the more extreme vocabulary of the new language of art that had been formulated by the cubists and the fauves in Paris, the futurists in Italy and expressionists in Germany, she nevertheless sympathized with their explorations of new approaches. Indeed, she found some merit in the abstract direction of their painting, for she herself, like many modernist artists, had a taste for strong pattern and expressive line. But abstract art, she said, was interesting as a form of experimentation and for art school assignments. Otherwise it was better suited to decorative applications of art such as textiles than to easel painting. Painters, she felt, should have content *in addition to* the abstract pattern. She developed an art that was more insistently two dimensional than Edgar's had ever

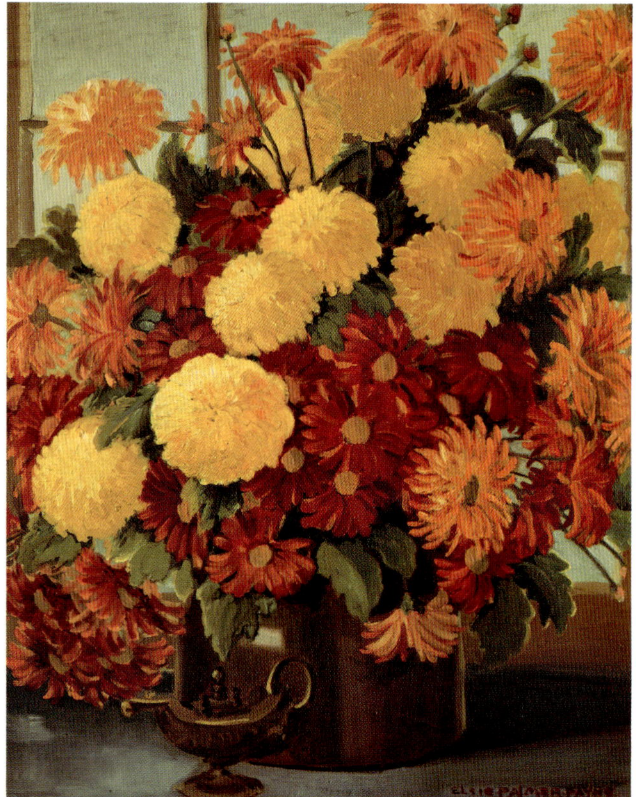

Fig. 8.03. Bright Flowers, by EPP.

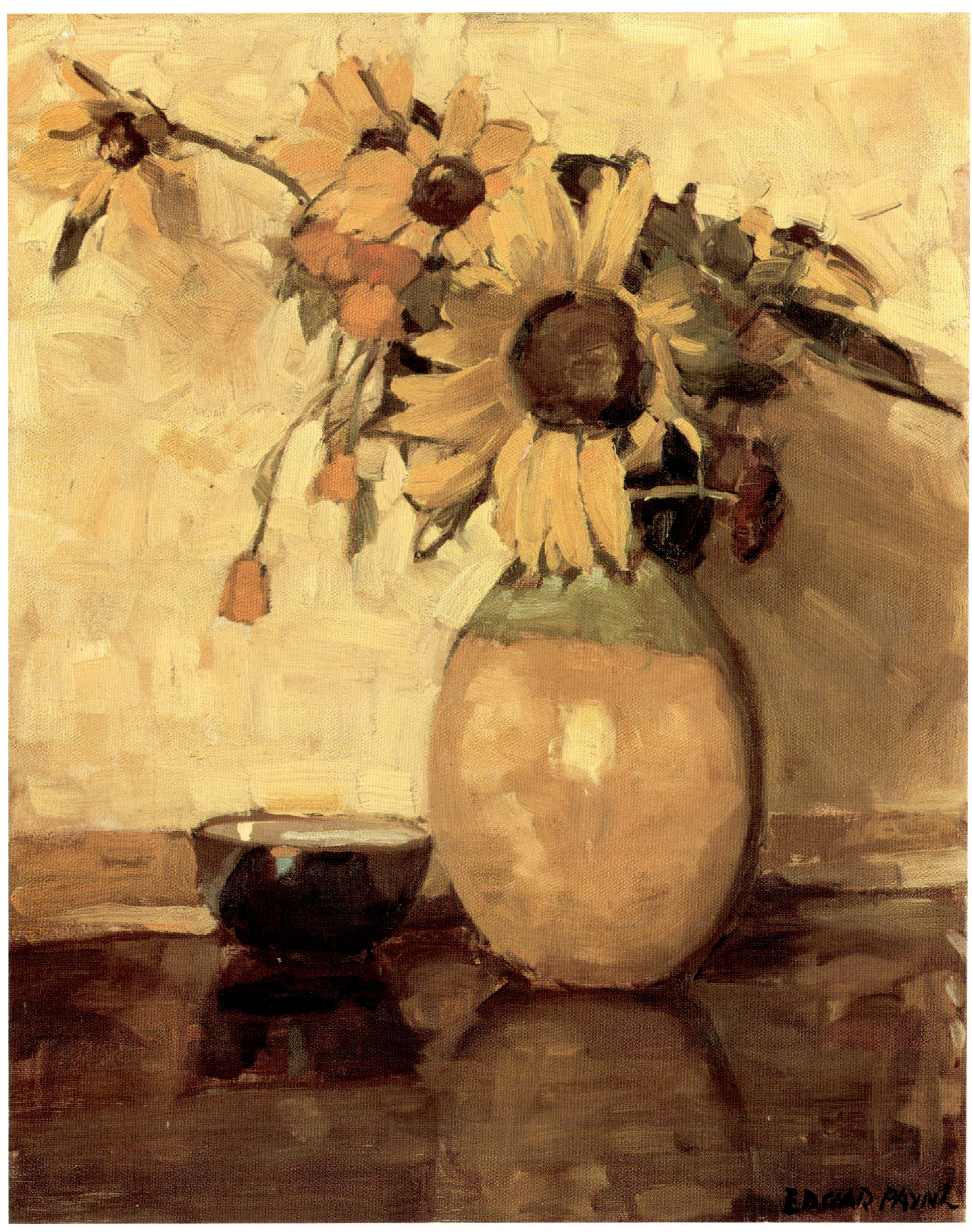

Fig. 8.04. Sunflowers, by EAP.

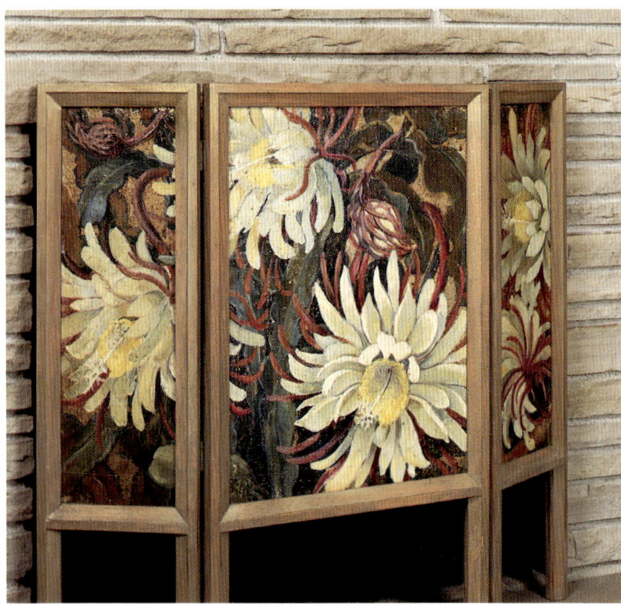

Fig. 8.05. Fireplace Screen, Night Blooming Cereus, by EPP.

been, one that stressed the decorative design of the composition rather than its illusionistic, trompe l'oeil effect. In *Bright Flowers,* (Fig. 8.03) for example, another still life of unknown date, she presents a bunch of chrysanthemums in a bold pattern close to the surface of the painting. It contrasts significantly with Edgar's painting of still life. There are only two still life paintings by Edgar known, both of uncertain date. Edgar's *Sunflowers* (Fig. 8.04) while maintaining a perfect balance in the off-center composition of sunflowers, vase, and small round bowl, depicts the subject in the painterly manner of the impressionist whose broad brushstrokes and rapid technique suggest the transience of the large blooms. Just so does the subdued color harmony of browns, yellows, and creams suggest the end of summer and the transitory season of autumn.

Elsie's flair for the decorative echoes, however distantly, the work of Arthur and Lucia Mathews whose ornamental style in painting and book and furniture design was dominant in San Francisco when Elsie was growing up there. Though she did not, as far as is known, study in the school the Mathews established, it is quite likely that she had seen their work and admired it. The fire screen she painted with a design based on the large flowers of the night-blooming cereus (Fig. 8.05) is so close to the Mathews that one is tempted to see a direct connection. The subject appears, however, in her easel paintings too, as in *Night Blooming Cereus* of 1945, a still life of large, drooping blossoms hanging gracefully from their stems, and it may be that the parallels in much of Elsie's work and that of the Mathews was a matter of similar taste rather than influence.

Elsie's preference for bold pattern and expressive line to enhance the figurative subjects and their import is particularly clearly shown in the watercolor *A Decent Burial* (Fig. 8.06), one of the figural subjects she turned to more than once. It was painted in Los Angeles in 1942 but based on memories of a scene she had witnessed many years before in Italy. In her re-creation of the event, however, Elsie transferred it to the coast of Brittany, whose cold and windswept shore, she felt, would morc appropriately echo the tragic subject. A tall, thin woman is depicted striding purposefully after a priest and altar boy who hurry on ahead. The woman carries on her head a small coffin topped by a modest bouquet of flowers, a gentle note that contrasts with the harsh reality of the occasion. No other mourners attend the Decent Burial of her infant child or gather to share her grief. Rather than pathos, however, there is a grim determination in the scene whose dark tonalities emphasize the darkness of its mood. Shortly after witnessing the small procession, Elsie made a statuette of the woman carrying the coffin but she sold the only casting of it in Paris.[132] Still, she was haunted by the memory of that lone figure until, many years later, it came to life in this boldly patterned composition.

The painting was well received, earning for Elsie three major prizes, including the first prize for watercolor in the Women Painters of the West show in the fall of 1942, and the first prize for water color at the California Art Club's spring, 1943 exhibition.[133] It was also shown at the Bowers Museum in Santa Ana and, by special invitation, at the Riverside Museum in New York City.

With a new self confidence, inspired by such recognition and fostered, too, by the success, modest though it may have been, of her gallery

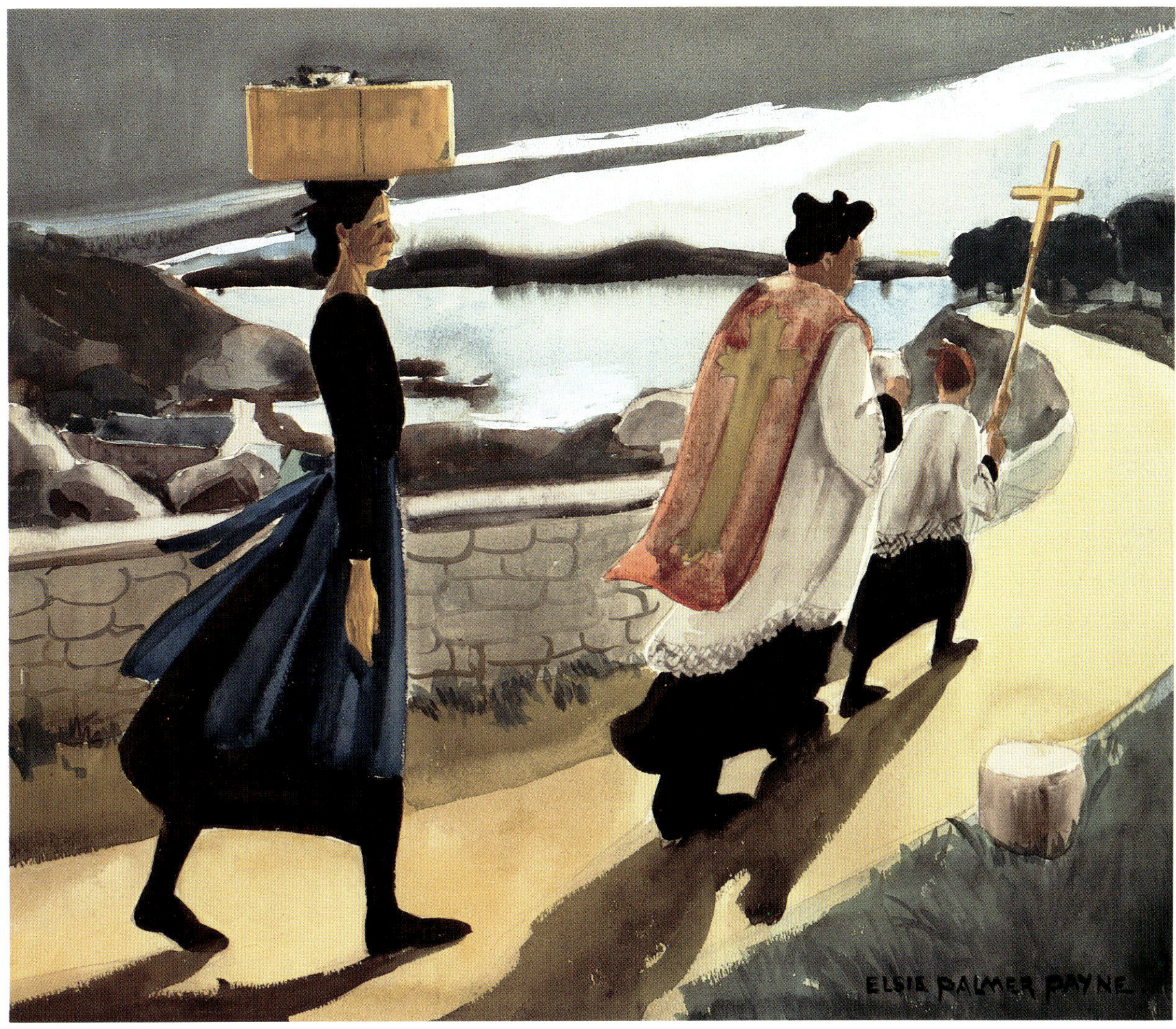

Fig. 8.06. A Decent Burial, by EPP.

and school, Elsie increasingly involved herself in civic activities, raising money for the War Chest Fund and for the cancer society, and serving on many volunteer committees. She also found time to donate her talents to the American Legion and to the United Service Organization of World War II. Every Sunday afternoon during the war years, she would show up at the USO, and in the evening at the American Legion, to draw pastel portraits of the young servicemen who were regularly entertained by these organizations. She gave these portraits to the soldiers, sailors, and airmen as gifts to send home to their mothers, wives or sweethearts.[134]

While busy with such civic activities, Elsie was also exploring new ways of expressing her ideas in art. She was, indeed, a versatile artist, far too alive to the varied possibilities of her medium to stick exclusively to one style. Thus a major painting of 1945, *The Thrifty Drug Store* (Fig. 8.07), announces a new sense of direction in her work and offers testimony to her increased self-confidence and painterly authority. The picture depicts the lunch counter of a local drugstore where Elsie frequently took her meals. With an oblique view into the busy scene, she reveals, once again, her primary interest in genre paintings of ordinary people doing ordinary things. The young waitress who looks directly at us as she mops up the counter with one hand and offers a salad with the

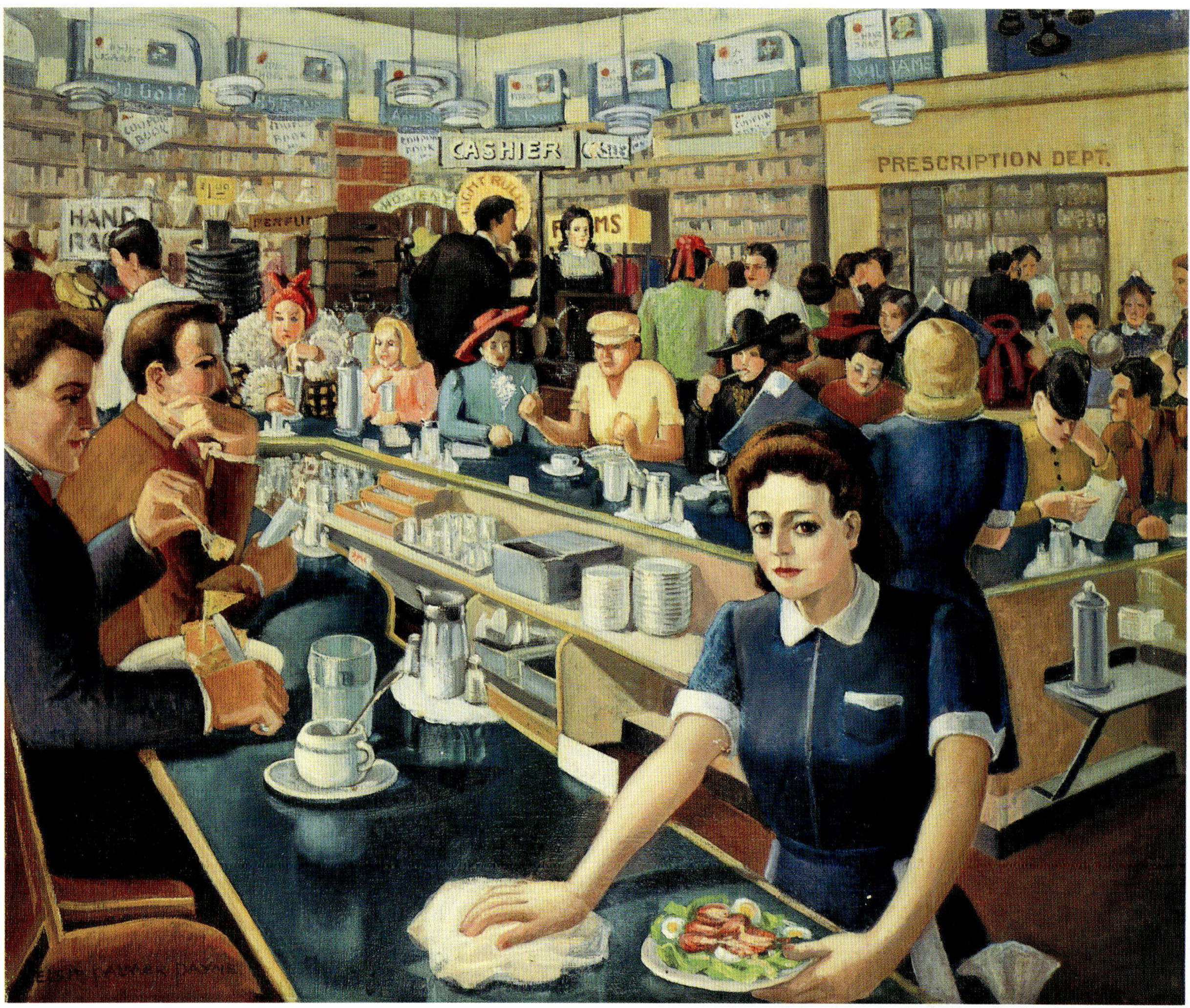

Fig. 8.07. Thrifty Drug Store in the 30's, by EPP.

other is likely the very one who served the artist's own lunch. The scene is crowded, lively and familiar, bearing the unmistakable air of something habitually seen. Indeed, it invites comparison with Edgar Manet's well-known painting of 1881-82, *The Bar of the Folies-Bergere,* where a mirrored image of a busy night-time Parisian cafe is separated from the viewer's space by a marble-topped bar displaying bottles of wine and compotes of fruit. Behind the bar, and presiding over it, is the monumental, strangely haunting figure of the barmaid, talking to a customer who is reflected only in the mirror behind her. But, while Manet's picture implies a comfortable, middle-class clientele and depicts a world of social pleasure and diversion, Elsie's seeks its inspiration in the everyday lives of working-class people, of whom, it is implied, the artist is one. It is more closely linked, therefore, to the genre pictures of the so-called Ashcan School of New York in the early decades of the twentieth century, as well as to the 1920's and 30's paintings of George Bellows, Isabel Bishop, Guy Pene du Bois, Kenneth Hays Miller, and Reginald Marsh. For Elsie Payne, this vein of genre subject matter, alternated with her more deliberately decorative pictures.

Los Angeles' Chinatown offered Elsie many opportunities to capture a colorful and exotic atmosphere with the added advantage of not having to travel far from home, and she profited from its decorative possibilities in much the same way that she had in the streets and shops of

Chioggia and Brittany. Indeed, *Chinatown* (Fig. 8.08) of the 1930's, reveals the same warm tonalities as her picture of the *Old City Gate,* at Chioggia (Fig. 5.19), described above. Both pictures were, in fact, exhibited together at J.W. Robinson in Los Angeles in May, 1941.[135] Even

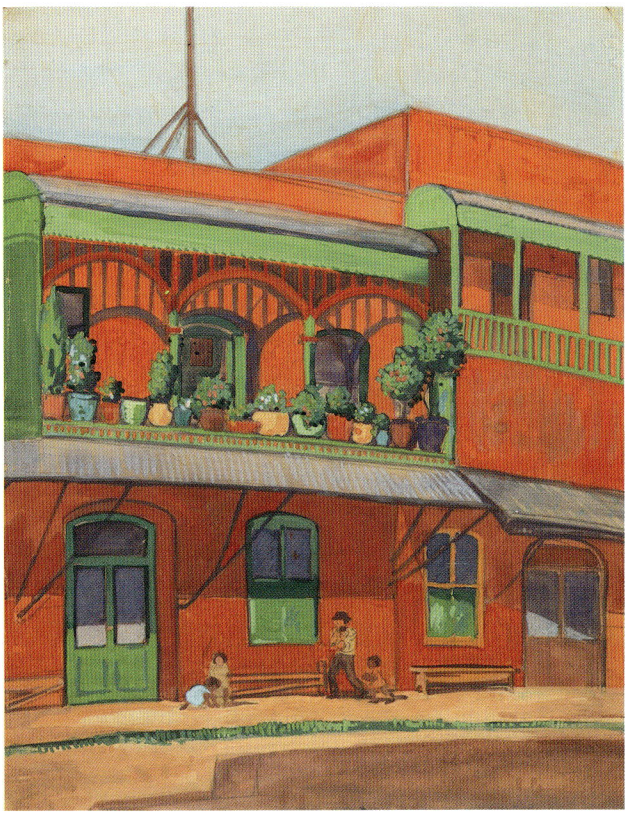

Fig. 8.08. Chinatown, by EPP.

more frankly ornamental, however, is her *Tree in Old Chinatown* (Fig. 8.09), where the bare branches of a large tree trace elegant, curvilinear patterns against a Chinatown facade. But at the same time, it is also a cheerful genre scene of everyday life, with people sitting at their leisure or strolling about, while dogs nap in the shade and children play in the street. The branches of the tree, festooned above them, act as a decorative screen dominating the picture, flattening the composition, and leading the viewer's eye back to the picture plane.

Meanwhile, Edgar too was exploring a new direction, or medium, in art. With a nephew, Ralph Payne, who was an amateur filmmaker, Edgar made a short color film, *Sierra Journey,*

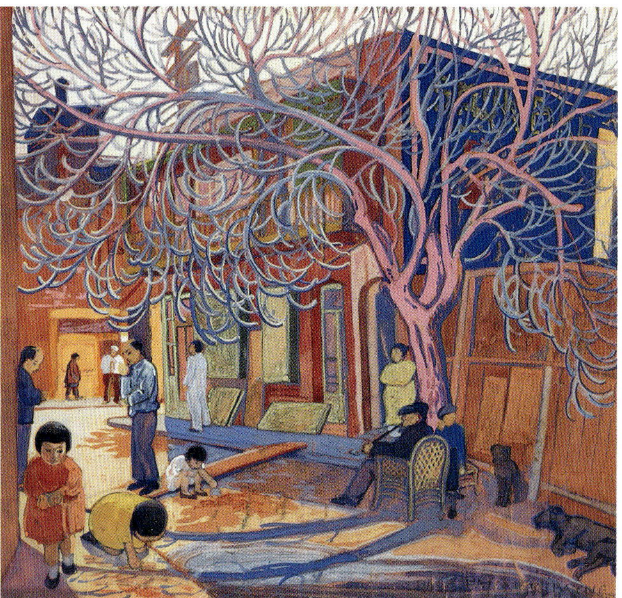

Fig. 8.09. Tree in Old Chinatown, by EPP.

depicting his beloved California mountains with narration based on his experience and knowledge of the High Sierras and his artist's love of their beauty. Ralph's suggestion for such a movie as a record of its wilderness aspect perhaps appealed to Edgar because of earlier contacts with the movie industry. Not only had he enjoyed the patronage of some of its actors and filmmakers, but he had worked as a glass painter for some of the film studios during the Depression of the 1930's. In those days studios employed artists to paint distant background landscapes on large plates of glass, which were set close to the camera in such a position that the background properly merged with the foreground and the action in the filmed scenes. Edgar could earn as much as fifty dollars a day at this, a princely sum for those days. And although glass painting may be different from scenery painting on cloth, Edgar's early experience with the latter in Chicago gave him the trained eye for dealing with the difficult perspective problems involved.

Edgar and Elsie's separation became permanent on April 8, 1947 when Edgar died after a long struggle with cancer. Throughout their years apart he and Elsie had maintained contact with each other, and she had taken care of him before at her own studio when he was quite ill in 1936.

And now, during his last year, when he was sick and alone, Elsie closed up her Wilshire Boulevard studio and moved into his Seward street studio-home.

That final year proved, paradoxically, one of the happiest in Edgar and Elsie's marriage. Edgar, no longer striving to capture the art world's attention, relaxed enough to allow his innate gentleness to emerge. Not since the early years of their marriage in Chicago had these two creative individuals so tenderly supported and sustained each other as they did in the year before Edgar's death in 1947. In the month that Edgar died, one of his paintings of the Sierras, *Temple Crags* won popular first acclaim at the Laguna Beach Art Gallery,[136] a fitting tribute to the artist who, twenty-nine years before, had helped to form the Laguna Beach Art Association and Gallery, with which he had maintained a close association throughout his life. It was a sign also of the reputation he had achieved as a California landscape painter and the preeminent painter of its High Sierras.

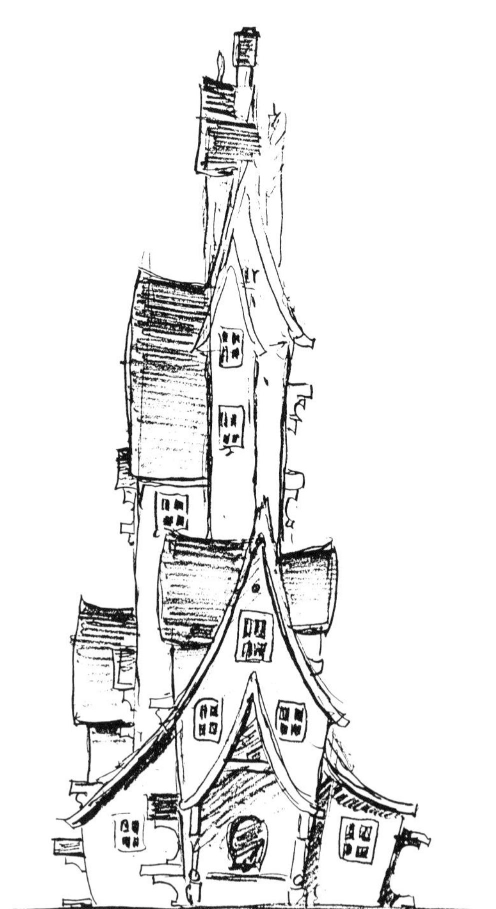

Fig. 8.10. Sketch for Birdhouse, by EAP.

Chapter 9: Elsie Alone

In the years following Edgar's death, Elsie devoted much of her efforts toward displaying and publicizing her late husband's work. Indeed, as early as August of the year he died, she chose the canvases for the combined Memorial Exhibition of Edgar Payne and his friend and fellow landscapist, William Wendt at the Laguna Beach Art Gallery. Their passing was described as the end of an era, for both had painted California "in the grand manner with reverence for nature as God had made it."[137] Other memorial exhibitions were to follow, at some of which Elsie showed Edgar's film, *Sierra Journey.* There was an exhibition at the Bowers museum in Santa Ana in February, 1948 and others at the public libraries in both Hollywood and Riverside in April as well as at the Hollywood Athletic Club in June.[138]

Elsie, however, was not neglecting her own interests in pursuit of recognition for Edgar, though she frequently managed to combine the two. While some of her own paintings hung on the walls, she would speak on Edgar's work to civic groups and women's clubs, at which she was much in demand for her informal, humorous and personal style.[139] Except when she was talking to artists and art students, specifically about principles and techniques of art, she stressed the woman's angle: how to be both artist and homemaker, life as an artist's wife, and the like. While her talks were not billed as "art appreciation" this was often a main theme — using personal anecdotes, her art principles, and examples from art history to further an interest in art.

Elsie was also continuing to teach art as a private instructor, initially attracting students who were serious about learning the principles of art she could so effectively impart. Increasingly, however, it was women from the milieu of women's clubs who came to her classes. Changing times and different contacts meant fewer serious students and more dilettantes. Finally, "I gave up teaching to a great degree. I made some very wonderful friends who have been very faithful and kind, but so many women just want to get houses bedecked with paintings for the price of a few lessons and they go from one teacher to another with the old gag, 'show me how to do that will you please — I can learn more by watching' and flatter the teacher into doing the work. One group of ten wanted to come all day for $10 and get a finished painting every time. I told them I wasn't that hungry."[140]

As a form of teaching Elsie gave demonstration lectures, painting as she talked. One such lecture-demonstration was held at the Duncan Vail Framing Shop and Gallery in February, 1957 for the American Artists Professional League. Though the paintings themselves were not major works of art, they very effectively illustrated the points she was making, sometimes with dramatic effect.

In addition to her activities in arts and civic organizations, Elsie also found time to arrange the third edition of Edgar's book, *The Composition of Outdoor Painting,* adding a short biography and filling orders that came in steadily from all over the country. The book's last edition, the fourth, was published in 1985 by Payne Studios Inc. in Minneapolis.

During all this time, Elsie was also busy pursuing her own artistic career. She showed her paintings at the Beverly Hills Women's Club and won two prizes at the Greek Theatre Exhibition of November, 1948. This show, which had several separate sponsoring organizations, awarded Elsie's oil portrait, *My Mother* (Fig. 9.01), second prize from the Women Painters of the West and a third prize for her watercolor, *The Picnic* from the Artists of the Southwest.[141] At the same time, a number of her paintings were also being shown at the Ebell Club, a social and cultural organization in Los Angeles dating back to 1891.

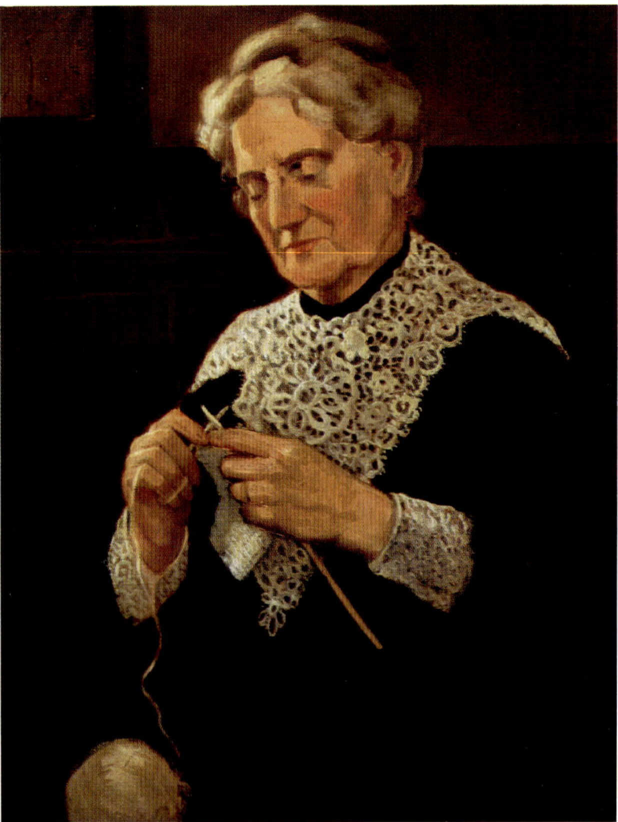

Fig. 9.01. My Mother, by EPP.

By the end of 1948 Elsie was earning enough from her teaching and from the sale of her own and Edgar's paintings to start building a studio home of her own. A Mrs. Jacoby, one of her students, had acquired three lots part way up the hills above the Sunset Strip. Two of the lots were quite standard, but the lower one was triangular, located at the convergence of two streets with a carob tree at the point. Visiting the site one day, Elsie asked about it and when told it was for sale, just asked "how much?" As the price named was almost exactly what she had in her savings account, she immediately said, "I'll take it." In spite of the difficulties posed by the odd-shaped lot, she designed her own delightful studio home on it at 1269 Ozeta Terrace. Some years earlier Elsie had seen another triangular lot, also inexpensive because of its hard-to-build-on shape, and she had tried to persuade Edgar to buy it. She thought they could build a two-studio home on it, but Edgar was not interested and she dropped the idea. Nevertheless, she had thought a good deal about the possibilities of triangular lots and was now ready to put her ideas to the test. After some searching she was able to find a sound and responsive contractor who was willing to build the house according to her design and make some inexpensive suggestions about how to deal with the rather steep slope of the land. The finished studio home consisted of a large studio, 25 by 40 feet, with a small inside balcony and adjacent bedroom, kitchen, and bath and two outside balconies. Beneath this there was a small but complete apartment and two garages (Fig. 9.02). By renting the downstairs apartment she was able to cover much of the mortgage on the house.

In her own comfortable home at last, surrounded by the paintings of two productive artistic careers, Elsie continued her busy life, painting, teaching and actively participating in many arts and civic organizations. She had been a founding member, for example, of the Women Painters of the West and now she served a term as president

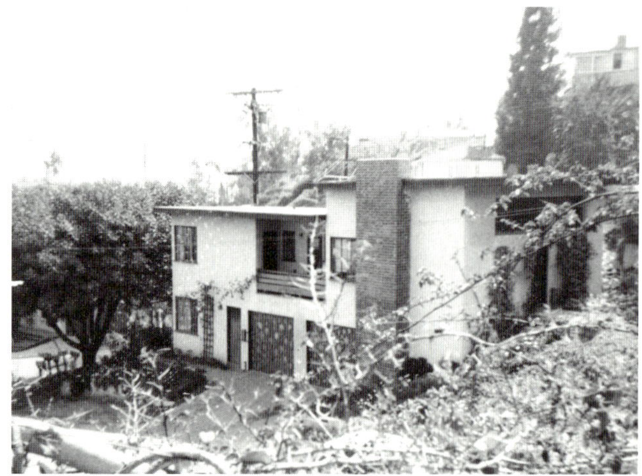

Fig. 9.02. 1269 Ozeta Terrace.

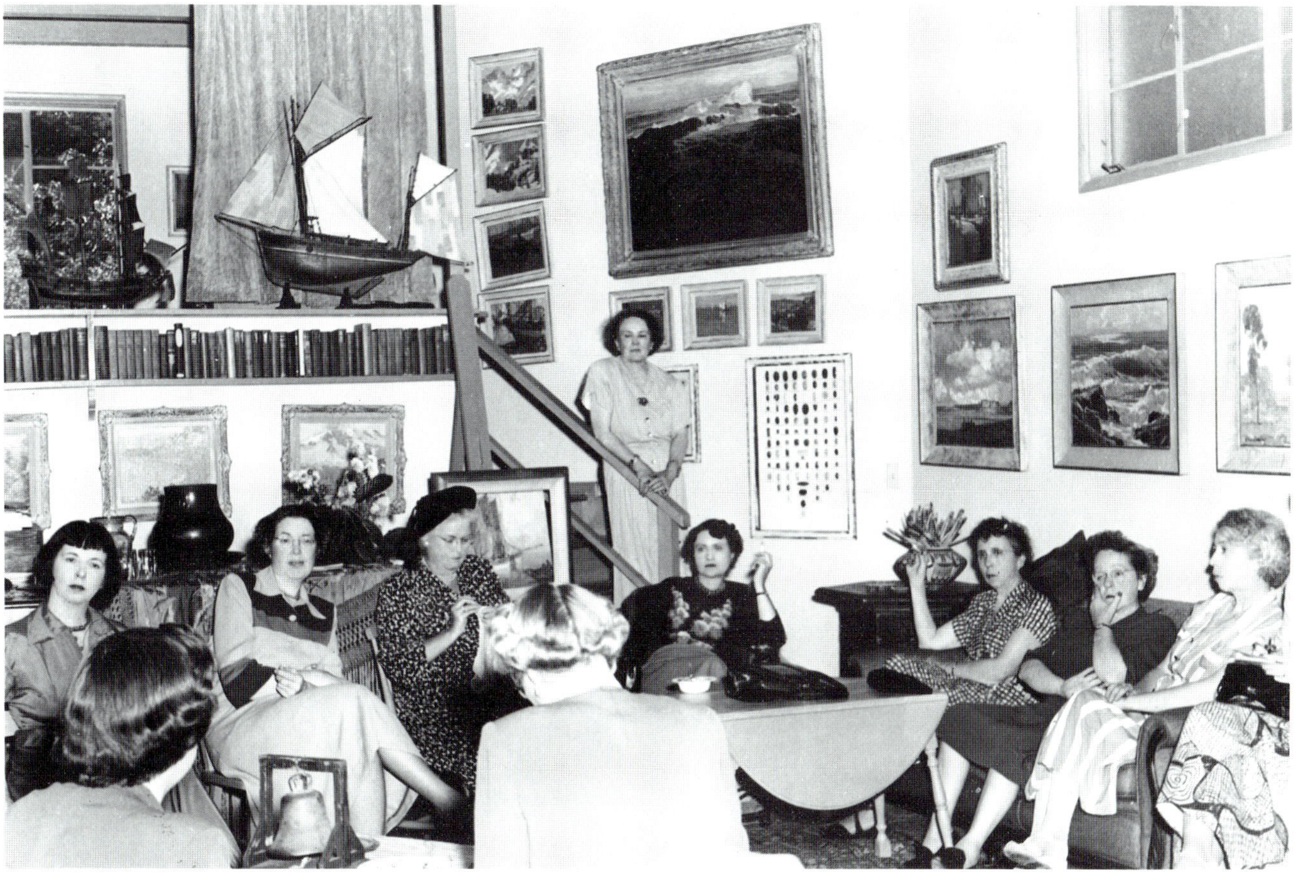

Fig. 9.03. Elsie in her Ozeta studio.

of the Los Angeles chapter of the National Society of Arts and Letters. She was a member of the American League of Professional Painters, the California Art Club, the National Association of Women Painters and Sculptors and the Artists of the Southwest.

Indeed, almost as soon as Elsie occupied her new home at Ozeta Terrace in the fall of 1949, it became a gathering place for both people and paintings (Fig. 9.03). When she was exhibition chairman for one of the various art groups she belonged to, it was common for exhibitors to bring their paintings to Elsie's for later transport to the exhibition site, and when there was a juried show, the judging was usually done there too. She held studio teas there also, making the elaborate refreshments herself, until she discovered that the guests commented more on the intricate canapes than they did on the art displayed on the walls. Through these activities Elsie greatly expanded her social horizon, meeting many people who became students, customers, and friends. Two of the gentlemen among them proposed marriage,

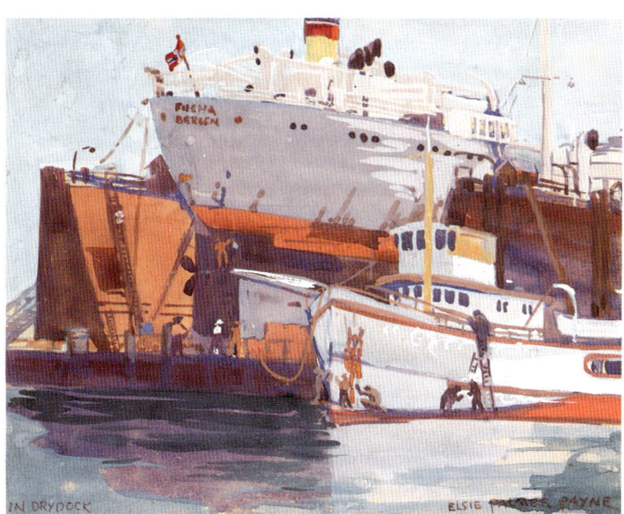

Fig. 9.04. In Drydock, Wilmington, California, by EPP.

but though she was very fond of one of them, who became a close friend until his death from cancer, she never remarried.

From the time of the separation Elsie had gone on a number of sketching expeditions near Los Angeles with a few students, on one of which she painted *In Drydock* (Fig. 9.04). She had even gone twice to Mexico with friends, sketching the local scene in the same manner as she had done with Edgar in Europe. Again she concentrated on the village life and the activities of the ordinary people. She continued this type of painting after she moved into her Ozeta Terrace home, completing some large landscapes in the studio.

One of these, *Hillside Corral* (Fig. 9.05) is a sunny domestic landscape viewed from a height that obliterates the horizon and arranges the scene, panorama-like, below us. From the high vantage point of the observer, the horses are miniature creatures, almost toylike, as they graze in a field guarded by a rickety fence. Behind them a grove of trees, rising almost to our level, constitutes the focus of the composition. Far back, a winding road that leads to a distant group of houses provides the elegant curve Elsie so much admired. The brushwork here is much more impressionistic than her usual style. But in spite of its loose, painterly brushwork, the picture has something of the cheerful domesticity and patterned arrangement of Grant Wood's stylized paintings of rural Iowa in the 1930's. *Hillside Corral* may have been the picture awarded third prize for landscape by the Los Angeles Friday Morning Club in May, 1960.

Encroaching City (Fig. 9.06), also of the 1950's, is an artist's comment on urban spread and another of Elsie's landscapes to employ a loose and brushy technique. Through the blue and smoggy haze enveloping the city as it overtakes the rural foreground, urban structures creep up on the old barn and water tower. The water tower, framed by two eucalyptus trees, is a ramshackle affair, an abandoned relic of rural life

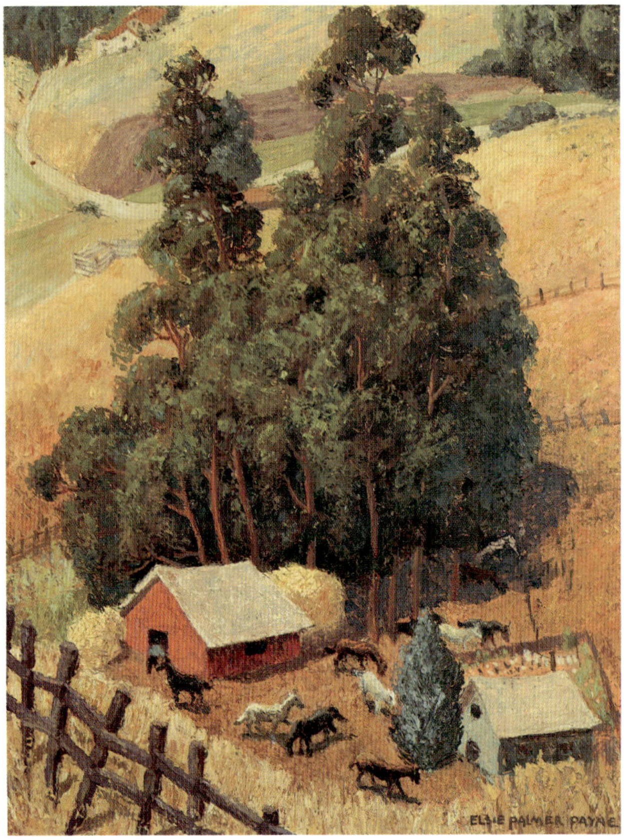

Fig. 9.05. Hillside Corral, by EPP.

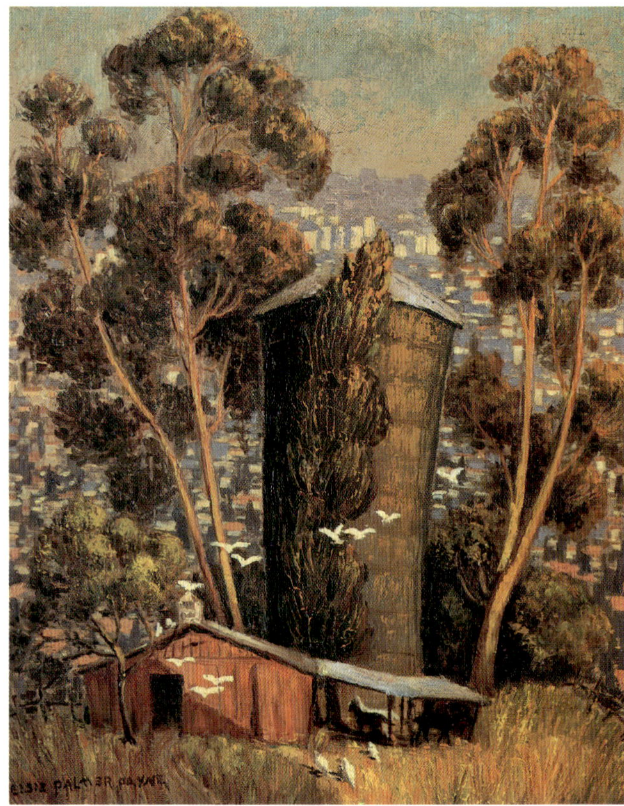

Fig. 9.06. Encroaching City, by EPP.

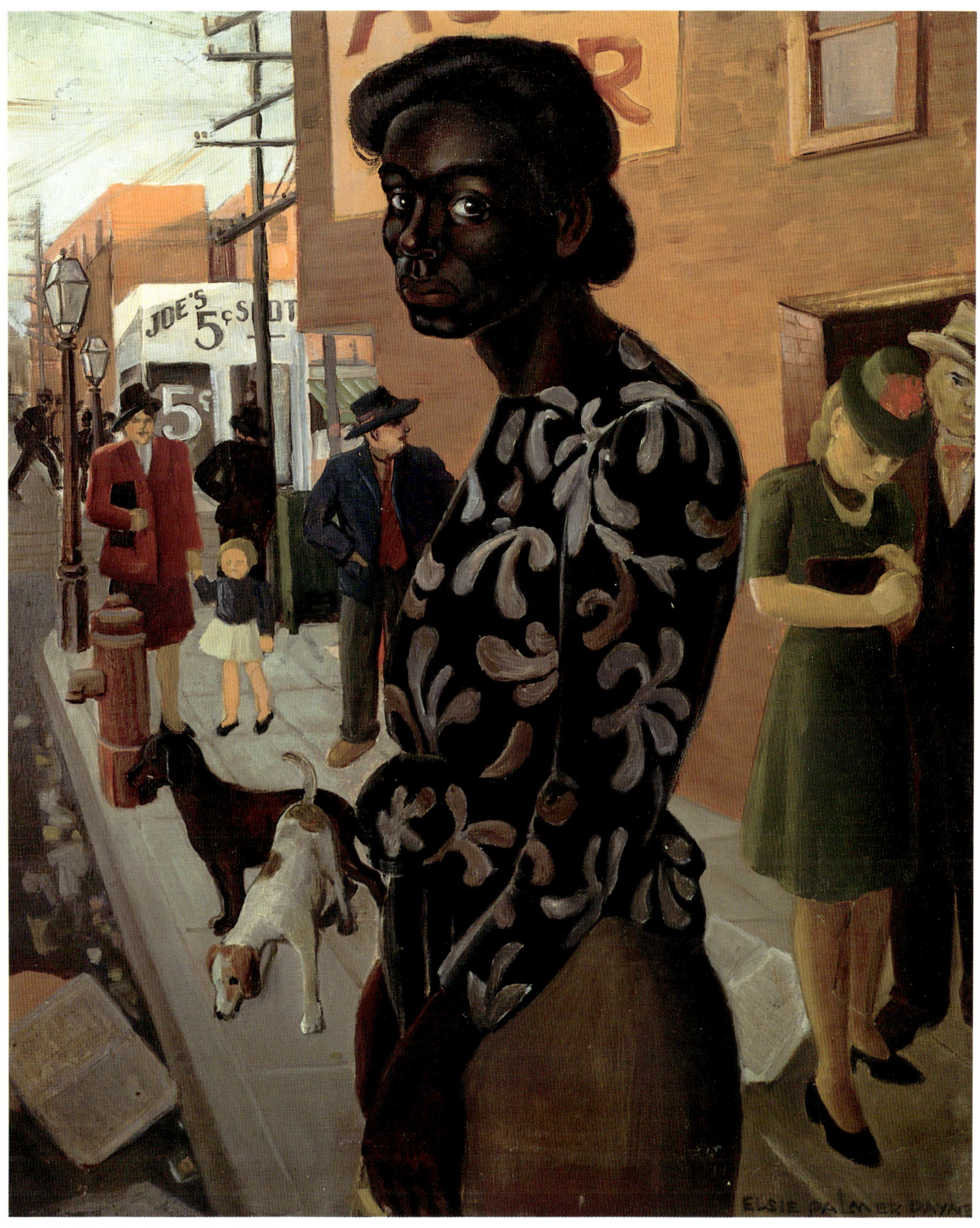

Fig. 9.07. Bus Stop, by EPP.

that seems to strain upward as though issuing a note of warning against the encroaching urban sprawl. Even the doves seem to have been startled off their perches as they flutter about the foreground, echoing a sound of alarm just as their white forms also echo the color of the high-rising buildings of the city.

Elsie also painted flower subjects, still lifes, and portraits. Some of her portraits were of professional models, but she also fulfilled portrait commissions, finding that sometimes patrons are difficult to please. She told one tale of a woman, proud of her carefully dressed white hair, who wanted every curl carefully delineated. "You know," said Elsie, "if I put in all those curls, to be consistent I'd have to put in all the wrinkles in your face," which settled the matter. When she used herself as a model, as in *The Artist as Rembrandt,* however, she was more concerned with working out a direct confrontation with herself through her art.

The variety of Elsie's media and styles tended to fit the subject at hand; neither medium nor style identifies a particular period in her work. As she did not date her paintings, it is hard, therefore, to know when they were done, unless there is a record of exhibitions or prizes.

In 1952 she again turned to sculpture, a medium she had occasionally used previously to earn extra money from modeling figurines. This time, however, with a more specific purpose in mind, she modelled in relief a portrait plaque of Edgar. She had it cast in bronze and then gave it to the Laguna Beach Art Gallery to be placed in honor of his memory at the entrance to the Edgar Payne room which formerly occupied a prominent place in that museum.[142] The relief is yet another example of Elsie's willingness to experiment, her versatility, and her assured command of many different media.

Her willingness to accept new challenges sometime had unfortunate results, however, since she did not always get around to destroying her unsuccessful experiments, and her attempts at new styles and techniques meant some unevenness in the quality of her work. While many of her sketches were unfinished; some of these have proven very attractive to recent taste. By the same token some of her paintings are overworked. She was aware of this and was quoted as saying that it takes two to paint a picture; one to paint and one to tell the other when to stop. Though she had nobody around to do that for her, there is little question that at her best she produced paintings of the highest quality.

One of these is undoubtedly *Bus Stop* of 1949-50 (Fig. 9.07), in which she again turned to the life of the people she encountered every day as the subject for a major composition. The drooping posture of the young black woman who waits for a bus to take her home vividly suggests her weariness after a long day's work. Her patterned blouse sets her off from the other, more anonymous, figures in the street, while her direct glance at the artist — and at us — creates an instant bond with the viewer. Alone in the busy street, she dominates the composition, commanding both our attention and our sympathy. The Women Painters of the West honored the picture as an "outstanding oil painting" when it was exhibited at the Pasadena Art Institute in May, 1950.

Though both Edgar's and Elsie's paintings continued to be appreciated by a few collectors, the 1950's and 60's witnessed a decline of interest in the figural art they both practiced. Abstract expressionism was the new game in town, a style that almost completely captured the attention of the cognoscenti. However, a major retrospective of Edgar's work, arranged by the Denver art dealer Wolfgang Pogzeba and others, was shown at the Kennedy Galleries in New York from April 6th to 30th, 1970. It signaled the beginning of a revival of favor, however gradual, for Edgar's paintings, a revival that gathered momentum during the 1970's and accelerated even further in the 1980's. Not coincidentally, a renewed appreciation of California's plein-air painters was also occurring with the rediscovery by museums, galleries, critics and collectors of the area's own landscape-painting heritage. Elsie's work however, did not enjoy the same renaissance of interest. Perhaps her style was too varied and also too far out of the mainstream of American art during the 1950's and 60's to be popular, for it was neither entirely impressionistic, wholly figural, or completely abstract. Like a few other artists of the time, she used pictorial reality to express humor, compassion, and other psychological and social themes as well as to explore formal artistic problems. Her style was, in fact, a synthesis of tradition and abstraction. It was graceful, people-oriented, frequently decorative, and always individual, but because it lacked an easy label it did not find a ready market.

By the end of the 1960's Elsie's activity as a painter began to decline. She was, after all, in her eighties and her eyes were failing even more than she realized. She fell prey to some unscrupulous dealers who took advantage of her vulnerability at this late stage in her life and made off with a number of Edgar's paintings, even some badly cracked and disintegrating that were stored and easily accessible in the garage beneath her studio. Later when these were badly restored and came on the market, Elsie was accused of having tampered with Edgar's work.

As Elsie's activities slowed down she became something of a "tribal elder" in the various art associations she had served so long. In more than one of these she was the sole surviving founding member. She greatly enjoyed being taken to ceremonial occasions, sitting at the head table, being made much of and introduced as "our darling Elsie."

In 1968 Elsie was persuaded to go on a group tour to the Orient. The passport photo for the trip is the last photograph of her (Fig. 9.08). After a few days in Japan, it became evident that the sightseeing was too much for her, and she was flown home, to face the fact that her enormous vitality was deserting her.

Indeed, by 1969 it had become clear that she could no longer be entirely on her own. She gave up her studio home where she had lived for so many years, and moved to Minneapolis with her daughter and son-in-law, who built for her a small studio addition to their home. Here she was a founder of Payne Studios Inc., the custodian of all the remaining Payne works and records. These

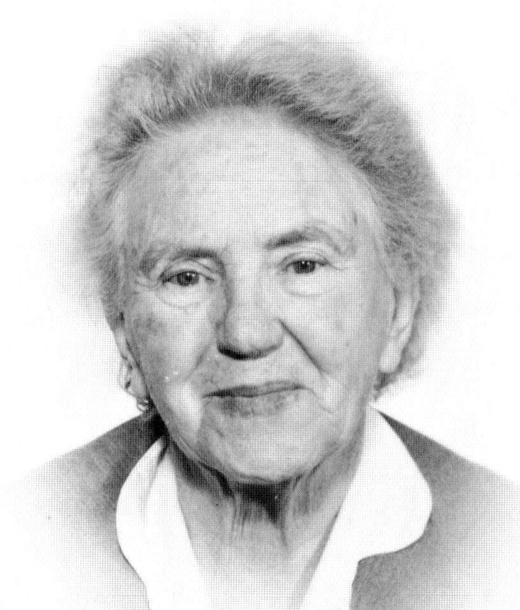

Fig. 9.08. Elsie, 1968.

included listings of the monies owed to her which had been ignored, and it became necessary to file several legal suits to collect many of the substantial amounts.

During her final year and a half in Minneapolis, Elsie found one more student to whom she could impart her "basic principles" of pattern, design, and color. She also taped her memoirs of a life devoted to art, reliving in the process her adventures, as well as her frustrations, as the wife of Edgar Payne. Feeling that she had lived her life to its conclusion, she peacefully passed away on June 17, 1971, leaving a legacy of service to art behind her. She had no publicist, as she had been to Edgar, to notify the world of her death other than a brief biography she had prepared some time earlier, as an announcement and obituary. Her memory lives on, however, both in Edgar's important place — which she did so much to assure — in the history of American art, as well as in the body of artistic work she herself bequeathed to it. Above all else, she was alive to the human condition. Her interest in, and sympathy for, her fellow man and woman particularly informs her work and shines through it.

Notes

These references provide the available documentation of the sources of much of the material; the various oral contributions of the family are not specifically noted. Some items which lack complete and proper identification at present are included with the feeling that these could be firmly identified by other scholars or future research.

1. Marquis, Neeta. *Los Angeles Times,* November 22, 1925, §2, p. 8.
2. Payne, Elsie. Unpublished biographical notes of 1930-60, §5.4.
3. *Ibid.* §10.1ff.
4. Payne, John B. Ltr. August 8, 1981.
5. Wakefield, Paul. Clipping, no source, March 19, 1916.
6. Payne, Elsie. Transcription of 1970 tapes, §4.5ff.
7. Ref. 2, §10.5.
8. Boles, Judge J. V. Ltr. March 11, 1985.
9. *San Diego Sun,* April 6, 1921.
10. Ref. 6, §7.3ff.
11. Ref. 2, §7.1.
12. *Ibid.* §7.3ff.
13. *Ibid.* §8.3ff.
14. Ref. 6, §7.7.
15. *Ibid.* §12.10.
16. Hughes, Eldon M. *Artists in California 1786-1940.* Hughes Publishing, San Francisco, 1986. p. 43.
17. Ref. 2, §11.1.
18. *Ibid.* §5.1.
19. Ref. 6, §8.11.
20. *Ibid.* §15.11.
21. *Ibid.* §20.1ff.
22. Payne, Elsie. Notes for *Who's Who of American Women,* ca. 1961.
23. Ref. 2, §13.1ff.
24. Invitation from the Union Internationale, ca. 1912.
25. *Los Angeles Times,* September 17, 1911.
26. *The Cowbell,* Palette and Chisel Club, v. 2, no. 2, February 1, 1913.
27. *Chicago Evening Post,* May 10, 1913.
28. Ref. 26, v. 2, no. 6, June 1, 1913.
29. Ref. 2, §12.2.
30. Ref. 6, §8.6.
31. McCauley, Lena. *Chicago Evening Post,* 1914.
32. Ref. 6, §20.7ff.
33. Biermann, Daisy. *San Diego Union,* April 22, 1921, p. 8.
34. Bennett, Chas. A. *The Peoria Journal,* May 31, 1914.
35. *Chicago Post,* July 1, 1914.
36. *Chicago Tribune,* June 27, 1914.
37. St. Clair, Gordon. *Inland Printer,* 1914.
38. *American Art News,* March 27, 1915.
39. *Chicago Post,* March 18, 1915.
40. Ref. 26, v. 4, no. 4, April 1, 1915.
41. Ref. 2, §14.1ff.
42. Ref. 6, §2.13ff.
43. Anderson, Antony. *Los Angeles Times,* February 20, 1921.
44. *Peoria Journal,* March 26, 1916.
45. *Chicago Evening Post,* April, 1916.
46. Brown, Harold. Herron Art Institute, ltr. May 12, 1917.
47. Ref. 6, §10.1ff.
48. Buff, Conrad. Transcript under the auspices of the Oral History Program, 1968. Ref. No. 300/53, p. 88-89. Department of Special Collections, University Library, UCLA.
49. Ref. 2, §15.1.
50. Ref. 2, §15.5ff.
51. *Santa Ana Daily Tribune,* December 3, 1920.
52. *South Coast News,* July 9, 1943.
53. The painting of *The Old Post Office* (which was also the general store) by Joseph Kleitsch is a view from the early gallery. See the reproduction in Janet Dominick, *Early Artists in Laguna Beach,* Laguna Art Museum, 1986, p. 53.
54. Hills, Anna A. "The Laguna Beach Art Association", *The American Magazine of Art,* 10:459, October 1919.
55. For a good discussion of the Laguna Beach art colony see Thomas Kenneth Enman and Ruth Westphal, "Earliest Days of the Laguna Beach Art Colony" in Ref. 88, pp. 122-126.
56. *South Coast News,* February 15, 1929.
57. Ref. 2, §15.4.
58. Personal communications, George Wilson and John Schober.
59. Telegram, Eggers, Art Institute of Chicago, to Edgar Payne, November 3, 1920.
60. Pennsylvania Academy exhibition record.
61. Moure, Nancy. *Publications in Southern California Art,* 1984, p. B83.
62. Payne, Edgar. *Composition of Outdoor Painting,* Payne Studios Inc., 1985 p. 66.

63. *Ibid.* p. 58.
64. *Ibid.* p. 52.
65. William H. Gerdts, who coined the phrase "glare esthetic," describes it in *American Impressionism,* Henry Art Gallery, University of Washington, Seattle, 1980. pp. 17-18.
66. Brown, Vandyke. Los Angeles Letter in *Life and Art,* June 2, 1922.
67. Ref. 6, §7.1.
68. Payne, Edgar. Ltr. quoted in *Los Angeles Times,* November 12, 1922, §3, p. 20.
69. Ref. 2, §17.1.
70. *Ibid.* §17.3.
71. *Edgar Alwin Payne and His Work,* Stendahl Art Galleries, Los Angeles, 1926.
72. Anderson, Antony. *Los Angeles Times,* April 22 and 29, 1923.
73. Payne, Edgar. Ltr, quoted in *Laguna Life,* v. 19, May 18, 1923.
74. Ref. 6, §2.10ff.
75. *Ibid.* §3.5ff.
76. *Ibid.* §11.7.
77. *Laguna Life,* August 10, 1923.
78. Catalogue, Stendahl Galleries, April 1923.
79. Catalogue, American Art Association Exhibition, Paris, January 27th to February 10, 1924.
80. Catalogue, Galeries Jacque Seligmann, 15 March to 1 April, 1924.
81. *La Revue Moderne,* v. 24, no. 9, May 15, 1924, p. 5-7.
82. *New York Herald,* Paris, March 16, 1924.
83. *Chicago Daily News,* 1924.
84. *Gaulois,* April 3, 1924.
85. Menu, dated March 31, 1924.
86. *Chicago Evening Post,* December 16, 1924.
87. Clipping, Column, *The Latin Quarter,* ns nd.
88. Westphal, Ruth Lily. *Plein Air Painters of California: The Southland,* Westphal Publishing, Irvine, 1982. p. 129.
89. Papers of the Stendahl Galleries, Archives of American Art, Reel 2721.
90. Certificat de Capacité, No. 268102, 25 August 1922.
91. Archival Records of the Art Institute of Chicago.
92. Anderson, Antony. *Los Angeles Times,* April 26, 1925, §3, p. 31.
93. *Chicago Post,* Art World Magazine, April 17, 1925.
94. *Los Angeles Times,* December 28, 1924, §3, p. 30.
95. *Laguna Beach Life,* May 14, 1926.
96. *Laguna Life,* July 2, 1925.
97. California Art Club Bulletin, 1925.
98. Clipping, ns. November 9, 1925.
99. Clipping, ns. April 1927.
100. Wolfson, Sonia. *California Graphic,* v. 4, no. 20, May 28, 1927, p. 6.
101. Anderson, Antony. *Los Angeles Times,* August 7, 1927, §3 p. 32 and Rotogravure p. 4.
102. Millier, Arthur. *Los Angeles Times,* January 22, 1928, §3, p. 8.
103. *Salt Lake Tribune,* July 29, 1928.
104. *Chicago Evening Post,* Magazine of the Art World, May 14, 1929.
105. Catalogue, *National Gallery of Art,* December 10, 1929.
106. Ltr. National Collection of Fine Arts, to Elsie Payne, April 13, 1959.
107. Ref. 62, pp. 49-50.
108. *Ibid.* p. 7.
109. *Ibid.* p. 27.
110. For the best discussion of the Impressionist in America, see William H. Gerdts, *Impressionism,* Abbeville Press, N.Y., 1984.
111. Ref. 62, p. 92.
112. *Los Angeles Times,* May 22, 1927, §2.
113. *Ibid.,* May 23, 1926 §2.
114. Santa Fe Collection of Southwestern Art, Introduction sheet, June 5, 1985.
115. We are indebted to W.D. Woodburn, Curator, Santa Fe Collection of Southwestern Art, for making available a copy of their Edgar Payne file, which provided specific details of the transactions and the trip.
116. Jewett, Eleanor. *Chicago Tribune,* May 18, 1930.
117. Clipping, ns, nd.
118. *Salt Lake Tribune,* July 13, 1930.
119. Ref. 62, pp. 96, 100.
120. Ref. 2, §19.7.
121. Ref. 6, §5.2ff.
122. *Ibid.* §18.12.
123. Clipping, ns. late 1945.
124. Payne, Elsie. Notes on teaching.
125. Ref. 6, §5.12.
126. *Los Angeles Times,* June 6, 1934.
127. *Beverly Hills Town Topics,* Feb.
128. *Los Angeles Daily News,* June 4, 1943.
129. Ref. 62, p. vii ff.
130. Ltr., agreement with Harry Altman, October 21, 1937.
131. Catalogue, *Society for Sanity in Art, Inc.,* April 1, 1940.
132. *South Coast News,* September 17, 1943.
133. The third prize the painting won was second prize for watercolor at the Wilshire Ebell Club competitive exhibition, May, 1943.
134. Clipping, ns.
135. J.W. Robinson price list, May, 1941.
136. *Laguna Beach News,* April 8, 1947.
137. *South Coast News,* Laguna Beach, August 20, 1947.
138. *Los Angeles Times,* May 2, 1948.
139. Clipping, Beverly Hills, October 21, 1948.
140. Ref. 6, §1.7.
141. Catalogue, Combined Exhibitions, November 14-28, 1948.
142. *Los Angeles Times,* April 21, 1952.

Selected Bibliography

Anderson, Antony, "Of Art and Artists", Column in *Los Angeles Times,* 1906-1926.

Arkelian, Marjorie, *The Kahn Collection of 19th Century Artists in California,* Oakland Museum, 1975.

S. Brian, *Theodore Wores and the Beginning of Internationalism in Northern California,* Joseph A. Baird, Jr., Ed., Davis Library Association, University of California, Davis, 1965.

Corn, Wanda, *Fifteen and Fifty, California Painting at the 1915 Panama Pacific International Exposition, San Francisco on Its 50th Anniversary,* University of California, Davis, 1965.

Cunningham, Elizabeth, *Masterpieces of the American West, Selections from the Anschutz Collection,* Denver, 1983.

Dominik, Janet B., "California Impressionism in Laguna Beach," *Antiques and Fine Art,* October, 1986, pp. 39-41.

Dominik, Janet B., *Early Artists in Laguna Beach, The Impressionists,* Laguna Beach, 1986.

Fine Arts Journal, "Important Exhibitions at the Art Institute," June, 1916, pp. 291-294.

Fine Arts Journal, "Palette and Chisel Club Exhibition," May 1916, pp. 235-237.

Fleischer, Morton H. Collection, *Masterworks of California Impressionism,* Franchise Finance Corporation of America, Phoenix, 1986.

Gerdts, William H., *American Impressionism,* New York, 1984.

Gerdts, William H., *Impressionism, The California View,* Oakland Museum, 1981.

Gibson, Arrel M. and Myers, Fred A., *Santa Fe Collection of Western Art,* Gilcrease Museum, Tulsa, Oklahoma, Sept. 26-Nov. 21, 1983.

Hatcher, Evelyn Payne, *Art as Culture: An Introduction to the Anthropology of Art,* University Press of America Inc., 1985.

Hinshaw, Martin E., *Painters of the West,* Santa Ana; Charles W. Bowers Memorial Museum, 1972.

Hogue, Fred S. "Payne Exhibit at Ambassador," *California Outdoors and Indoors Living,* May, 1926, p. 13.

Hughes, Edan Milton, *Artists in California, 1786-1940,* Hughes Publishing Co., San Francisco, 1986.

Jones, Harvey, *Masterpieces of the California Decorative Style,* Peregrine Smith Inc., Salt Lake City, 1980.

Los Angeles Times, selected issues from 1906.

Millier, Arthur, "Growth of Art in California," in Frank S. Taylor, *Land of Homes,* Los Angeles: Powell, 1929.

Moure, Nancy, *Los Angeles Painters of the 1920's,* Pomona College, Claremont, California, 1972.

Moure, Nancy, *Painting and Sculpture in California, 1900-1945,* Los Angeles County Museum of Art, 1980.

Moure, Nancy, *Publications in Southern California Art,* Los Angeles 1984. Includes 1. The California Watercolor Society Index to Exhibitions, 2. Artists Clubs and Exhibitions in Los Angeles Before 1930, and 3. Dictionary of Art and Artists in Southern California Before 1930.

National Museum of American Art, *Modern American Realism, The Sara Robey Foundation Collection,* Smithsonian Institution, Washington, D.C., 1987.

Orr-Cahall, Christina, *The Art of California: Selected Works from the Collection of the Oakland Museum,* Oakland, 1984.

Payne, Edgar, *The Composition of Outdoor Painting,* Seward Publishing Co., Los Angeles, 1941. 4th edition, Payne Studios Inc., 1985.

Phoenix Art Museum, *The Southwest: The Land and the People,* Selections from the First Federal Savings Collection, May 12-July 1, 1973.

Roberts Gallery, *Edgar Alwin Payne Exhibition,* April 29-June 4, 1983, Pomona, California, 1983.

Santa Fe Railroad Co., *The Santa Fe Collection of Western Art, Chicago, 1983.*

Seavey, Kent L., et al., *A Century of California Painting, 1870-1970,* Crocker-Citizens' National Bank, San Francisco, 1970.

Stendahl, Earl, *Stendahl Galleries Papers,* Archives of American Art, Smithsonian Institution, Reels 2721, 2722.

Stendahl Galleries, *Edgar Alwin Payne and His Work,* Los Angeles, 1926.

Thurston, J.S., *Laguna Beach of Early Days,* Privately Published, 1947.

Westphal, Ruth Lily, *Plein Air Painters of California, The Northland,* Westphal Publishing, Irvine, California 1986.

Westphal, Ruth Lily, *Plein Air Painters of California, The Southland,* Westphal Publishing, Irvine, California, 1982.

Chronology

(many early dates are only approximate)

	Edgar Alwin Payne (EAP)	Elsie Palmer Payne (EPP)
1883	March 1, EAP born near Washburn, Missouri.	
1884		September 9, Elsie Palmer born, San Antonio, Texas
1886		Palmer family moves to Los Angeles.
1889		Palmer family moves to Oakland.
1894	Payne family moves to Prairie Grove, Arkansas.	
1899		Palmer family moves to San Francisco.
1902	Edgar working on scenery in Lovelady, Texas, town hall.	Elsie enrolls in Best Art School, San Francisco.
1903	Itinerant painter, signs, fences, barns; with barnstorming theatrical group, general handyman.	
1904		Fashion illustrating for Rimes Advertising Co., San Francisco.
1905	In Houston, Texas, housepainting, paperhanging, scene painting.	
	Payne-Morris scene painting studio, 135 Pearl Street, Dallas.	
1907	In Chicago, enrolls in portrait class at Art Institute of Chicago (AIC); stays only two weeks.	At J. Charles Green Outdoor Advertising Co., San Francisco. Designs theater curtain, advertisements for Kellogg, Pabst, Old Dutch Cleanser, etc.
1909	First trip to California, Laguna Beach.	Meets Edgar Payne in San Francisco.
	Meets Elsie Palmer in San Francisco.	Wins prize for logo for outdoor advertising firms.
	EAP watercolor #89 at Chicago Palette and Chisel Club (PCC) Exhibition of Illustrating and Advertising Art.	
	EAP address, Tree Studio Building.	
1910	January, AIC exhibits *A Sunny Hillside.*	Goes to Chicago.
	May-June, Exhibition at PCC.	Works for Cusack Advertising Co.
1911	January, *November Woods,* and *The Golden Autumn* at AIC.	Works for Claque Advertising Co.
	In Laguna, Catalina, sketching.	Meets Edgar Payne again.
	Scene painting at Edwin Flagg Studio, Los Angeles.	
	Prize for California landscape at PCC.	
1912	March, exhibition Laguna paintings at PCC.	
	November, *Hills of El Toro* at AIC.	

1912 November 9, Elsie Palmer and Edgar Payne married.

The Paynes, EAP & EPP

1913 January 14, EAP's *Western Hills* wins first prize at the PCC "Tingel Tangel."

March 1, EAP's *A Western Valley* at AIC.

March 10, 65 EAP paintings of California and EPP's *March at Sundown* at PCC. Exhibition sold out, Paynes to California.

Hills of Marin painted.

November 4, *Hills Eternal, Mt. Lowe,* at AIC.

1914 January 12, Evelyn Payne born, Chicago.

Murals for Danville, Indiana Courthouse, and American Theater, Chicago, finished.

February, Chicago Artists Exhibitions at AIC, paintings by EAP include *Hills of Marin.*

June 15, joint exhibition of EAP and Nancy Cox McCormack at PCC.

Sketching in California.

Possibly murals for Queen's Theater, Houston, about this time.

1915 March 17, EAP paintings and several bookends by EPP at his PCC annual exhibition.

EAP has paintings at AIC's 19th annual Chicago Artists Exhibition.

Summer: EAP and EPP and Evelyn to San Francisco; several of EAP's at Panama Pacific Exposition.

To Santa Barbara, painting, sketching. Possibly local exhibition.

Visits to Santa Cruz Island.

November 1, EAP in AIC's American Artists Exhibition.

1916 January 1, Thumb Box Exhibition at PCC.

EAP, Walter Ufer, and Carl Krafft organize PCC traveling exhibition, which opens March 15th, Peoria, April 4th in St. Louis, and then to Lexington, Kentucky.

February 8th. AIC Exhibition of Chicago Artists includes EAP's paintings of Santa Barbara, other California scenes.

April 3rd, EAP in three man show at PCC with E. Martin Hennings and Maximilian Hoffman.

Summer: Santa Fe Railroad provides transportation for Paynes to Southwest, Gallup, etc.

June 25, EAP's first visit to Canyon de Chelly.

Paynes on, near, Hopi and Navajo reservations until October 15th.

1917 35 EAP paintings exhibited at Diamond Disc shop, Peoria.

July 7, EAP signs contract for Congress Hotel Murals.

Summer. Paynes in Glendale, California, working on Congress murals.

November 16, Paynes to Laguna Beach.

Possibly first Sierra trip.

1918 EAP Gold Medal, California Agricultural Society exhibition, Sacramento.

Paynes renovate studio/bungalow on Glenneyre St., Laguna.

July 27. Old Community House Pavilion in Laguna Beach opens as Gallery. Paynes driving force behind this.

August 15. Preliminary organization meeting at Payne home of Laguna Beach Art Association (LBAA). EAP first President, Anna Hill vice-president.

1919 EAP wins Silver Medal, Sacramento.

Summer, Sierra trip.

EAP paints *Rugged Slopes and Tamarack.*

1920 February 2, EAP exhibition at Cannell and Chaffin, Los Angeles.

November 3, AIC awards EAP Martin B. Cahn prize for *Rugged Slopes and Tamarack.*

1921 February 6, *Rugged Slopes and Tamarack* exhibited at Pennsylvania Academy.

February 20, EAP exhibition at Earl Stendahl Galleries, Los Angeles.

April 3, 30 EAP paintings at Orr Gallery, San Diego.

EAP awarded Southwest Museum prize.

Summer, sketching in Sierras.

1922 February 11, EAP exhibition at Stendahl Galleries.

May 29. Send-off banquet for EAP at Stendahl Galleries.

July, Paynes sail from New York; first stop Paris.

Summer, Paynes motoring through Haute Savoie to Riviera.

November, Paynes in Rome, studio on Piazza Dante.

EAP exhibits at Rome Bienniale.

1923 April 15. In Brig, Switzerland; too cold for sketching, so back to Italy, Venice.

April 23. Exhibit at Stendahl's of canvases shipped from Rome.

Spring. EAP's *Great White Peak* awarded Honorable Mention at the Paris Salon.

Summer. Paynes to Chioggia after briefly in Venice, then back to Switzerland.

October, Paynes return to Paris.

1924 Paynes at 48 Rue Varin, Paris.

January 27, EAP exhibits at American Art Association.

March 15, EAP exhibition at Seligmann Gallery.

EAP in Spring Salon? - Two canvases.

Summer: Motor through Loire Valley to Breton Coast, Concarneau and Douarenez.

Two weeks in London.

Fall, return to Chicago.

1925 February 8th, 2 EAP's at Pennsylvania Academy.

March 24, EAP exhibit at Newcomb-Macklin Gallery, Chicago.

May. Car trip to California; accident near Denver.

June, Paynes at Laguna Beach.

July, August, Sketching, Sierras.

September. EAP's *Fishermen, Concarneau* awarded prize at LBAA exhibition.

California Art Club Exhibition at Los Angeles Museum awards EAP's *Peaks and Shadows* "best landscape."

1926 Paynes living in Los Angeles, 134 Reno Street.

June 15. EAP exhibition at Stendahl Galleries.

Summer, sketching in Sierras.

Fall. Paynes moved to Westport, Connecticut, rent Bean Studio.

1927 April, EAP exhibition in Westport YMCA.

June-July, EAP exhibitions at Stendahl and Chicago Galleries.

August 7, Mural commission for St. Paul Hotel in Los Angeles.

Summer, sketching Sierras and other areas, California.

Fall, Paynes move to Spuyten Duyvil in New York, with Edgar's studio at 1931 Broadway.

October-November, EAP ill with pneumonia; paints gouaches at home.

1928 January 22, Exhibition at Wilshire Gallery, Los Angeles.

Paynes take summer trip from New York to Europe, Chioggia and Brittany.

July 29, EAP exhibition, Ogden, Utah.

Fifth Lake acquired by Henry Ward Ranger Purchase Fund of the National Academy of Design.

Fall, Paynes back in New York.

1929 May 11, EAP exhibition at Allerton House, Chicago.

Paynes to Laguna Beach.

June, EAP exhibition, Ogden, Utah.

June 23, EAP exhibition, Biltmore Galleries, Los Angeles.

July 1, EAP and EPP to Canadian Rockies to sketch, Evelyn stays in Laguna.

Fall, Paynes return to New York.

October 10, *Fifth Lake* in the Ranger Exhibition at National Gallery.

1930 June 15, EAP exhibition, University of Illinois.

Summer. Exhibition of EAP at Salt Lake Hotel, Ogden. Paynes go on to Gallup and Thoreau, New Mexico, for sketching.

1931 June 15, EAP at exhibition of Chicago Society of Artists at Midland Club, Chicago.

Summer, EAP to California, EPP joins him later.

1932 Winter, EAP and EPP in California. Evelyn stays in Fieldston School, New York.

Summer, family sketching trip in Sierras.

EAP and EPP separate.

1934 June 1. EPP opens Payne-Kahn Studio Gallery, Beverly Hills.

Summer, EAP in Sierras.

Fall, Payne-Kahn Studio now Payne-Pegler Studio Gallery.

November 3, EAP exhibition, Elsley Galleries, Ambassador Hotel, Los Angeles.

November 25, EAP one-man show of 45 small oils at Brewitt Gallery, San Francisco.

1935 January 6. EAP exhibition, Town House, Los Angeles.

1936 September 14, EPP opens her own studio at 9414 Wilshire, Beverly Hills, teaching and painting.

EAP has studio at 1142 Seward Street, Hollywood.

1939 October 4th. Los Angeles Branch, Society for Sanity in Art formed, EAP founding member.

1940 April 1. EAP in first exhibition, Society for Sanity in Art.

1941. August 20. EAP painting in Iowa Salon exhibition.

Publication of 1st edition of EAP's *Composition of Outdoor Painting* by his own Seward Publishing Co.

1942 Fall, EPP's *A Decent Burial* wins award at Women Painters of the West exhibition, Los Angeles.

November, *A Decent Burial* awarded "best watercolor" at Los Angeles Museum of Art.

1943 Spring, *A Decent Burial* wins award at California Art Club Exhibition.

May 20, *A Decent Burial* awarded 2nd prize at Ebell Club.

A Decent Burial exhibited at Bowers Museum, Santa Ana, and at Riverside Museum, New York.

1944 EPP sketches portraits of servicemen at USO and American Legion.

October, EAP at Glendale Art Association exhibition.

1945 April, EPP's *Fruit* awarded 2nd prize at Los Angeles Library exhibition.

1947 April 8, EAP dies in Los Angeles.

August 2, EAP-William Wendt joint memorial exhibition at LBAA.

1948 February 15, EAP Memorial Exhibition at Bowers Museum, Santa Ana.

April 15, EAP Memorial Exhibition at Riverside Public Library.

June 1, EAP Memorial Exhibition at Hollywood Athletic Club.

November 14, EPP's *My Mother* awarded 2nd prize at Women Painters of the West Exhibition.

EPP's *The Picnic* wins prize at Artists of the Southwest.

1949 November 3, EAP exhibition, Occidental College.

EAP exhibition, Pomona College.

EPP exhibits at California Art Club, with the Women Painters of the West at the Ebell Club, and at the Riverside Women's Club.

EPP moves into 1269 Ozeta Terrace.

1950 May, EPP receives award from Women Painters of the West at Pasadena Art Institute.

1951 EPP exhibits at Laguna Festival, wins $100 Honorable Mention.

1952 April 6th, EPP's bronze plaque of EAP dedicated at the EAP room of LBAA.

1954 September 4, EAP and EPP exhibition at Glendale Library.

1955 October 8th, EPP exhibits *Hillside Corral* with Artists of the Southwest at Greek Theater, Los Angeles.

November. EPP exhibits at LBAA with three other charter life members.

1958 May, EAP's gouaches exhibited at LBAA.

EPP exhibits with California Art Club at Greek Theater.

1960 May, EPP exhibits at Friday Morning Club; 3rd prize for *Landscape.*

June, EPP exhibits with California Art Club at Duncan Vail Gallery, Los Angeles.

1964 May 19, EPP's *Still Life* awarded first prize at Friday Morning Club Exhibition.

1967 February, American Artists Professional League Exhibition. EPP's *The Coming of the Douane,* and EAP's *The Race.*

1969 Summer, EPP moves to Minneapolis to live with Hatchers.

1970 April 4, EAP exhibition at Kennedy Galleries, New York.

1971 June 15, EPP dies in Minneapolis.

Index